In considering the role of practical music in e(
to define the art of performance in Germany (͜   ͜ baroque period.
The author examines the large number of surviving treatises and instruction manuals used in the Lutheran 'Latin' schools during the period 1530–1800 and builds up a picture of the function and status of music in both school and church. The understanding, gained through these educational texts, of music as a functional art – *musica practica* – in turn gives us insight into the thoughts of the contemporary performer and how he might have performed the sacred works of Praetorius, Schütz, Buxtehude or Bach.

For all those interested in historical performance this book provides valuable information on the growing science of performance practice and the development of a conscious awareness of style and idiom in this period.

CAMBRIDGE MUSICAL TEXTS AND MONOGRAPHS

Music education and the art of
performance in the German Baroque

CAMBRIDGE MUSICAL TEXTS AND MONOGRAPHS

The series Cambridge Musical Texts and Monographs has as its centres of interest the history of performance and the history of instruments. It includes annotated translations of important historical documents, authentic historical texts of music and monographs on various aspects of historical performance.

Published

Ian Woodfield *The early history of the viol*
Rebecca Harris-Warrick (trans. and ed.) *Principles of the harpsichord by Monsieur de Saint Lambert*
Robin Stowell *Violin technique and performance practice in the late eighteenth and early nineteenth centuries*
Vincent J. Panetta (trans. and ed.) *Treatise on harpsichord tuning by Jean Denis*
John Butt *Bach interpretation: articulation marks in primary sources of J. S. Bach*
Nicholas Thistlethwaite *The making of the Victorian organ*
Grant O'Brien *Ruckers: a harpsichord and virginal building tradition*
Christopher Page (trans. and ed.) *Summa musice: a thirteenth-century manual for singers*
Ardal Powell (trans. and ed.) *The virtuoso flute player by Johann George Tromlitz*
Keith Polk *German instrumental music of the late middle ages: players, patrons and performance practice*
Beth Bullard (trans. and ed.) *'Musica getutscht': a treatise on musical instruments by Sebastian Virdung*
David Rowland *A history of pianoforte pedalling*

Music education and the art of performance in the German Baroque

JOHN BUTT
University of California, Berkeley

CAMBRIDGE UNIVERSITY PRESS
Cambridge, New York, Melbourne, Madrid, Cape Town, Singapore, São Paulo

Cambridge University Press
The Edinburgh Building, Cambridge CB2 2RU, UK

Published in the United States of America by Cambridge University Press, New York

www.cambridge.org
Information on this title: www.cambridge.org/9780521433273

© Cambridge University Press 1994

This publication is in copyright. Subject to statutory exception
and to the provisions of relevant collective licensing agreements,
no reproduction of any part may take place without
the written permission of Cambridge University Press.

First published 1994
Reprinted 1996
This digitally printed first paperback version 2006

A catalogue record for this publication is available from the British Library

Library of Congress Cataloguing in Publication data

Butt, John
Music education and the art of performance in the German Baroque
    p. cm. – (Cambridge musical texts and monographs)
Includes bibliographical references and index.
ISBN 0 521 43327 4 (hardback)
1. Performance practice (Music) – Germany – 17th century
2. Performance practice (Music) – Germany – 18th century.   3. Music –
Instruction and study – Germany – 17th century – History.   4. Music –
Instruction and study – Germany – 18th century – History.   I. Series.
ML457.B9   1994
781.4'3' 0943 – dc20   93–17691 CIP

ISBN-13 978-0-521-43327-3 hardback
ISBN-10 0-521-43327-4 hardback

ISBN-13 978-0-521-03478-4 paperback
ISBN-10 0-521-03478-7 paperback

To the memory of Peter le Huray and Howard Mayer Brown,
editors of Cambridge Musical Texts and Monographs

Contents

List of plates   x
Preface   xi
Acknowledgements   xvii
List of abbreviations   xix

1 The establishment of Lutheran musical practice in the sixteenth century   1
2 The role of practical music in education c.1600-1750   12
3 The contents, layout and style of instruction books   52
4 The development of performance practice and the tools of expression and interpretation in the German Baroque   68
5 Ornamentation and the relation between performer and composer   121
6 The decline of the Lutheran cantorates during the eighteenth century   166

Notes   193
Bibliography   219
Index   230

Plates

1 Listenius 1533: table of notes and solmisation
   syllables   7

2 Friderici 1618/1624: example of variable tempo,
   according to the affect of the text (reproduced with
   permission of The British Library, London)   98

3 Mylius 1685: texted example showing application
   of ornaments after the manner of Bernhard (reproduced
   with permission of the Bibliothèque Nationale, Paris)   137

Preface

Modern studies of 'original' performance practices are often presented in a historical vacuum: we learn of conventions applicable to particular repertories without necessarily knowing why these conventions pertained, without imagining the original performers' thoughts and beliefs concerning performance and unaware of the extent to which the interpretative conventions matched these beliefs. The inquiry is genuinely historical only if we can learn something of the motives for the composition and performance in the first place, how the combined forces of composer and performer were assumed to affect the original listeners.

Many histories of music centre on the surviving works of a particular age, their interrelationships and influences. Some recent studies are more concerned with the social, cultural and political environments in which music was cultivated. Seldom though is a history created out of performance as a system of thought. What did it actually mean to perform, as opposed to compose? To what extent did performance presuppose the other disciplines of music, its supposed natural laws and rationale?

This study attempts to give something of the background and rationale for performance in a specific educational institution – the Lutheran school and church – over a specific period. This field is particularly fruitful, not least because of the remarkable achievements of German Baroque composers who grew on its soil, but also because practical music held such a significant place alongside the standard education of the Lutheran 'Latin' schools. Many educated men would have experienced practical music to some degree, and, given the intimate association of church and school, would have gained some notion of the function of music as a practical art. This consideration might give us a clue not only to the thoughts of the contemporary performer of a sacred work by Praetorius, Schütz or Bach, but, equally importantly, to the presuppositions of the early listeners. In gaining a sense of what music was meant to be in realised performance we can also intuit something of the relation of performance to the verbal text and the musical notation. This generates further questions: the relationship between composer and performer, the dialogue between music as a creative and rhetorical art, *musica poetica*, and music as something realised in the act of performance, *musica practica*. As I have proposed before, the rhetorical model is something which evokes a degree of continuity between these two arts.[1] Although many parts of this study directly relate to issues of performance practice, my interest here is specifically in the 'why' rather than the 'what'. The very fact that there are comments concerning performance practice and interpretation in certain primers and at certain junctures suggests the development of a conscious regard for performance and its style, something which cannot always be assumed in the history of performance.

Why confine this study to Lutheran education and practical music-making, given that the Italian tradition is at the forefront of Western musical culture throughout the period under discussion? First, the large body of published treatises on which this study is focussed forms an enclosed tradition which, at the same time, absorbs many of the innovations in performance practice from Italy. Indeed some of the German treatises codify supposedly Italian practices during years when Italian sources seem thin on the ground (such as the latter half of the seventeenth century). Secondly, the importance of music within Lutheran culture cannot be overestimated; while Catholic church music of the Baroque is hardly to be ignored, it was to some degree secondary to the newer, secular genres of opera, sonata and concerto. Lutheran music forms a separate tradition which preserved something of the Mediaeval outlook on religious music, as something metaphysically central to man's ability to understand and communicate with God. This tradition ended soon after the death of J. S. Bach and only years later was this composer to be absorbed into the 'central' tradition, which – even after the time of Mozart – was still essentially Catholic and Italian in flavour.[2]

What, in fact, does *musica practica* mean? In the traditional sense codified by Gaffurio (*Practica musicae*, Milan 1496–7), it covered all aspects of notation and composition, including just a few recommendations on

[1] See Butt 1990, especially pp. 15–19.
[2] This idea of the two traditions, one Catholic yet curiously secular, the other Lutheran and essentially sacred, was first elaborated by H. H. Eggebrecht in his essay 'Über Bachs geschichtlichen Ort', *Deutsche Vierteljahrsschrift für Literaturwissenschaft und Geistesgeschichte* 31 (1957), pp. 527–56; reprinted and enlarged, in *Johann Sebastian Bach – Wege der Forschung*, ed. W. Blankenburg (Darmstadt, 1970), pp. 247–89.

performing practice. The latter were usually very much secondary to the arts of composition; even with Zarlino 1558 (vol. III) they take up only part of a single chapter out of a total of eighty. The art of *musica practica* was practical in the sense that it contrasted with *musica theorica*, the speculative, non-practical side of music. While Italian theorists clung to this definition of *musica practica* – primarily as the art of composition – German writers from the early years of the Lutheran Reformation tended to confine it to the art of 'mere' performance, something which could be grasped quickly and easily by young boys in school. With the influence of Renaissance humanism, these theorists generally assigned composition to a third field, that of musical poetics, *musica poetica* (from the time of Listenius 1537);[3] this reflects the increasing interest in the rhetorical implications of verbal text and the art of composition as a creative act. As will emerge in the course of this study, the position of composition within the German system of *musica practica* remained ambiguous and only towards the end of the seventeenth century were the fields of composition and performance again more closely bound together.

In the tradition of the Middle Ages, *musica theorica* was one of the four components of the *quadrivium*, the higher level of the seven liberal arts, while *musica practica* (the tools of composition and performance) was essentially a worldly craft, something with which the 'true' musician would not soil his hands. But with the thinking beginning to emerge during the Renaissance era, more emphasis was placed on the human significance of sounding – as opposed to speculative – arts; there was thus a move away from the traditional Pythagorean view of music.[4] Luther, together with his reformers, gave particular attention to music as practice within elementary education. He sensed the affective significance of music in actual sound, believing it to be the supreme gift of God, standing second only to theology itself. Moreover, music was especially useful as a medium for the new vernacular texts; the concept of the chorale – potted dogma and musical mnemonic in one – was undoubtedly one of his most brilliant psychological achievements. Thus the place in education traditionally assigned to *musica theorica* could at least partly be filled by *musica practica*, that art which enabled the young pupils to acquire the basic musical competence demanded by the new liturgies (especially the chorales). The traditional respect accorded to music *per se* could well

---

[3] The tripartite division is already evident in Boethius, with his privileging of the 'true' musician (theorist) over the poet (composer) and performer; see 'Boethius', *NG* II, pp. 844–5; Moyer 1992, p. 31.

[4] For an excellent survey of these issues in Italian Renaissance theory, see Moyer 1992.

accommodate a change of emphasis in practice. On the other hand many scholarly theorists from the time of Gaffurio until the early eighteenth century saw *musica* as a whole, an art founded in eternal mathematical principles, to be defined in set rules, moving the affects in specific ways and serving to the praise of God (see Ruhnke, in *MGG* IX, pp. 949–56).

Performance of the emerging Baroque repertoire required increasing specialisation on the part of the performer, so that in the seventeenth century *musica practica* (performance, in the German sense of the term) could be a highly respected art, requiring considerable skill, insight and awareness of the rhetorically-influenced practice of composition. Performance practice thus became a 'science', a self-conscious activity which entailed some conception of the function of music as a realised, sounding art. With the onset of the eighteenth century the ancient *musica* terminology was soon to evaporate, as did – and the two are doubtless not coincidental – the solid basis of music in Lutheran education and worship. Music was becoming a more autonomous, aesthetic artefact, elevated as an attribute of culture and taste, but – as an object of bourgeois choice rather than necessity – potentially dispensable. It comes as no surprise that the Bachs (J. S. and C. P. E.) were two of the last significant composers of Lutheran church music. Truly talented composers could no longer find satisfactory employment in church and school; and reciprocally churches and schools had little incentive to attract the greatest musicians of their age.

This book is essentially the study of a literary tradition, the interconnections and influences between a large body of writings and their relation to the music of their time. As primary material I have examined a vast range of – mainly published – treatises from the period c.1530–1800, specifically the primers which seem to be addressed towards the task of training young people in the art of practical music. This art of 'practical music' was initially synonymous with singing, but it soon came to involve a certain amount of instrumental study too. My approach will obviously minimise the vast differences between establishments and areas, so the study cannot be used as a guide to the music practice of specific localities and repertories at specific junctures. Most of the information on school ordinances and curricula I have abstracted from the vast body of modern secondary literature on the musical history of specific areas, towns and schools in Germany. However, little of this has hitherto been available in English and there is no single modern survey which gives an overview of practical music instruction in Lutheran schools over the course of the Baroque period as a whole.

The bounds of this study do not permit a survey of the training which might have been offered in the more sumptuous German courts, but certain writings explored here do refer to the musical skills expected of the young court performer. Indeed some influential sources, such as the treatises of Christoph Bernhard, were doubtless written with court musicians in mind. I will also not be concerned with the place of music in the *Ritterakademien*, schools for the nobility which flourished during the seventeenth century and where music was taught as a skill considered – like fencing – essential to the pastimes of the *galant homme*.

Although this book takes the history of performance as its central issue it cannot comprehensively cover every detail of recorded performance instructions over the course of two centuries; the presentation of specific points on performance is necessarily selective.[5] While my work gravitates towards the educational environment of the Baroque era in Germany, the net will be drawn widely from the early years of Lutheranism to the last decades of the eighteenth century. This tremendous chronological breadth is necessitated by the remarkable continuity of the treatises themselves: together they portray an enclosed tradition which began in the late Renaissance and ended in the 'mid-Classical' era. At the same time, the very cohesiveness of this material also highlights the developments in educational philosophy and beliefs about music, and changes in musical style and performance practice.

While the overwhelming majority of the primary sources forming the basis of this examination are from the Lutheran provenance of German musical education, treatises addressing Catholic readers are not necessarily to be excluded. Most of these latter rely directly on Lutheran writings and thus add statistical weight to many of the developments which emerge in the course of the study. Indeed it is often difficult to distinguish Catholic writings from the Lutheran core, so ubiquitous are the traditions of music training and musical interpretation in any particular period covered by this survey. Furthermore, a major Lutheran treatise, such as Falck 1688, might contain a large number of musical examples with Latin texts – and indeed many of these were drawn from contemporary Italian publications. A consideration of some of the Italian literature is also useful in ascertaining which elements of German theory were taken directly from the Italian tradition and those which were more indigenous.

Although one of the primary aims of this book is to give a boy-in-the-desk view of practical music, it is biased toward those elements which

---

[5] The recent study of Bartels 1989 gives an exhaustive summary of the performance advice in German literature of the earlier part of the Baroque era.

are most relevant to the surviving repertories. More attention is given to *musica figuralis*, that music which requires measured notation (and is thus the category in which polyphony and concerted music were learned) than *musica choralis*, the music sung in unmeasured rhythm (i.e. chant). A further bias is made towards the education of the more musically talented pupils, those boys who sang the demanding music by the composers whose names are still familiar today.

Acknowledgements

In writing this book I have tried to tread a narrow line between providing a plethora of primary material – giving some impression of its local colour – and creating an account which is both coherent and interpretative. Many friends and colleagues have been most supportive in expressing their exasperation with various early versions of this text, encouraging and helping me to organize an enormous amount of historical information into a relatively readable whole. Any remaining failings in this regard are entirely my fault and not theirs.

Several institutions and individuals deserve special mention: the early stages of this work were sponsored by a research fellowship at Magdalene College, Cambridge; the music department at the University of California, Berkeley has latterly provided a great deal of financial and collegial support. The number of libraries to which I am indebted would be impossible to list here; those that have experienced my actual bodily presence have doubtlessly suffered the most: the British Library in London, Cambridge University Library, Glasgow University Library, the two libraries of the Staatsbibliothek zu Berlin-Preussischer Kulturbesitz and the music library of UC Berkeley.

I am most grateful to the late Peter le Huray for his encouragement of this project in its early stages and his painstaking critique of some of the first drafts; he was always a wonderful friend, teacher and colleague. His fellow editor for the series Cambridge Musical Texts and Monographs, Howard Mayer Brown, was particularly helpful and constructive in the latter stages. The very day I began printing the final copy of this manuscript I heard of his untimely death, while trying on a carnival mask in Venice. Various scholars in fields related to this survey have also been most generous with their time, both in reading the text and providing me with further ideas. Eva Linfield and Robin Leaver deserve particular mention, as do my long-suffering colleagues, Joseph Kerman and Anthony Newcomb. Finally, I should thank my wife, Sally, and baby Christopher for adhering so strictly to their view that my work on this project is least productive when it is undertaken for protracted periods.

Full details on both ancient and modern authors are available in the bibliography. Modern editions and translations of historical texts are also listed in the bibliography, where applicable. All translations, unless otherwise noted, are the author's own and the original texts are given in their idiosyncratic orthography.

Abbreviations

AcM	*Acta Musicologica*
AMw	*Archiv für Musikwissenschaft*
BJb	*Bach-Jahrbuch*
EM	*Early Music*
JAMS	*Journal of the American Musicological Society*
JRMA	*Journal of the Royal Musical Association*
MD	*Musica disciplina*
Mf	*Die Musikforschung*
MfMG	*Monatshefte für Musik-Geschichte*
MGG	*Die Musik in Geschichte und Gegenwart*, 17 vols. (Kassel/Basel, 1949–86)
ML	*Music and Letters*
MT	*The Musical Times*
MuK	*Musik und Kirche*
NG	*The New Grove Dictionary of Music and Musicians*, 20 vols. (London, 1980)
RISM	*Répertoire international des sources musicales – Écrits imprimés concernant la musique*, 2 vols. (Munich/Duisburg, 1971)
WA	*D. Martin Luthers Werke: kritische Gesamtausgabe* (Weimar, 1883–)

1

The establishment of Lutheran musical practice in the sixteenth century

Musical culture in Lutheran states was undoubtedly centred on churches and Latin schools during the sixteenth century; indeed the close bonds between these two institutions ensured the growth of musical practice for over a century to come. Music was hardly the key element in Luther's reforms, but his personal belief that it was the greatest gift of God, second only to theology itself, must have influenced many of the early reformers.[1] That he saw music as intrinsically good and not just the servant of scriptural texts is evidenced by his love of Josquin's abstract polyphony and his remark that even bad fiddlers are good, since they enable us all the better to understand that which constitutes good music (*WA* Tischreden I, no. 968, p. 490). It is important to appreciate today that Luther's belief in the reality of the Devil was as strong as his belief in God, and that music was for him one of the principal antidotes to the Devil's work. The art was not just a useful adornment of liturgy and certainly not an object for aesthetic appreciation alone; it was both a powerful rhetorical medium – capable of influencing the listener in diverse, wonderful ways – and the embodiment of the metaphysical laws of God's creation. In the words of Friedrich Kalb, 'Lutheranism is not driven to search for Biblical commands or prohibitions; for music is a spontaneous activity of life, inherent in God's creation, and needs no apology' (Kalb 1965, p. 141).

Much of the Reformation's success lay in Luther's political and social astuteness. In 1524 he wrote a pamphlet on the importance of good schools for the survival of the new reformed religion; a priesthood of all believers could, after all, hardly be founded on an ignorant populace.[2] His musical requirements were unequivocal: a schoolmaster who could not sing was not worthy of office (*WA* Tischreden V, no. 6248, p. 557). Two school ordinances prepared under Luther's direct influence set the tone for music instruction during the entire sixteenth century. Melanchthon's ordinance for Saxony and Bugenhagen's for Brunswick (both published in 1528)[3] show music defined as an essentially practical discipline, aligned with the subjects of the Mediaeval *trivium* (grammar, dialectic and rhetoric), and something to be taught to boys of all ages and abilities during the noon hour after lunch each day (Schünemann 1928, pp. 82–4).[4] The music should set both Latin and German texts and boys should be trained in both *musica choralis* (unmeasured unison singing which involved those parts of the chant repertory appropriated by the Lutheran church, and to a certain extent, the new but related genre of the chorale)[5] and *musica figuralis* (measured music, essentially polyphonic in texture).

Although such ordinances recommend daily practice in music, only certain schools followed this to the letter (Schünemann 1928, pp. 92–3). Indeed it is clear that music was not always warmly embraced by humanistic academic reformers and that its status as a fundamental of education was not always as secure as Luther himself might have wished. Many ordinances required that the theoretical component of music instruction be kept to a minimum and that not too much time be allotted to music (*ibid.*, pp. 84–5). The precise status of music varied from school to school and the situation was more complex than many modern studies have assumed; then, as now, music was ambiguously related to several conflicting elements in educational thought.

Niemöller's comprehensive study of Lutheran school music in the sixteenth century has shown that the schools were subject to many cross-currents in Renaissance culture. Foremost was the influence of Humanism, which engendered a new emphasis on classical literature, the thorough study of Latin (hence the nomenclature *Lateinische Schulen*) and the cultivation of eloquence. This, humanists believed, would revitalise spirituality and improve the quality of life. In such a context music was important only in so far as it would assist in the presentation of verbal text; indeed many scholars saw it as a waste of time and objected strongly to the daily church duties of Mediaeval practice (Niemöller 1969, pp. 611–17).[6] On the other hand, given that the Lutheran reforms abolished the hegemony of both the Latin Bible and the elite priesthood, there was less incentive to encourage boys to learn Latin and consequently the standard of education initially declined. Therefore Luther and his followers had to take great pains to restore the quality of education. Their principal move was to tighten the links between schools and churches, something which made music instruction a particularly important component of school life. It was this religious function – and not necessarily the humanistic education which Lutheranism also encouraged – which accounted for the growth in practical school music. Nevertheless, the new humanistic, philological emphasis on classics on the one side, and on the Bible on the other, were bound in the long run to affect the function of music, moving as it did towards an instrument of rhetoric.

While Luther still considered the theoretical component of music to be important, something to be learned 'with the whole of mathematics' (*An die Radherrn* 1524),[7] it is clear that he saw it primarily as a practice which, by its very magic nature, improved the moral, devotional, temperamental and intellectual disposition of the pupil (*WA* Tischreden I, no. 968, p. 490).[8] That teachers in the more academic disciplines could also see the benefits of musical practice is suggested by the foreword of Johann Reusch's psalms of 1552: all teaching is better engrained in the memory if set to music.[9] Many schools retained the Mediaeval practice of singing Latin hymns at the opening and closing of daily instruction. There was also a fashion for setting classical and humanistic odes to music (Niemöller 1969, pp. 622–3). The very placing of music in the hour after lunch points to its supposed aid to the digestion and its role as a recreation and relief from academic study. As an exercise, music was often grouped with the learning of handwriting and simple arithmetic, basic skills which were often not even mentioned on the lesson-plans and which could be taught communally rather than in individual classes. Here the boys were often divided according to ability rather than age. There are several records to show that music – at least as a theory of intervals and proportions – could be taught simultaneously with arithmetic. This doubtlessly reflects the survival of music's role as a component of the Mediaeval *quadrivium* (Schünemann 1928, p. 94). Despite its decline in academic status, practical music was, as far as religion was concerned (and religion was still the central goal of all education), the supreme tool for communicating the word of God.

The increasing emphasis on music as a practical art necessitated changes in the disposition of the teaching body. Traditionally the Schulmeister or rector was, with the help of the cantor and the other teachers, responsible for providing and training the church choirs. This remained the case in certain German states, particularly those retaining the Catholic faith and those to the west and south west, which were strongly influenced by the Swiss reformers.[10] However, in those Lutheran areas where there was a growth in figural music and a consequent need for more intense practical instruction, the cantor gradually took over the role as head of music; moreover, the various fees gave the cantor a certain degree of financial independence. At the same time the growing

4   Music education and the art of performance

humanistic orientation of education led the rector in the opposite direction, towards specialisation in academic subjects; indeed the relief from church duties must often have been welcomed. Nevertheless, the other teachers in the school were still generally involved in the music-making of church and school and the cantor was still required to teach a certain amount of academic work (Niemöller 1969, pp. 636–40). But the increasing polarity between rector and cantor (the latter now often being ranked second or third in the school hierarchy) spawned a whole series of disputes which can be traced right through to the end of the eighteenth century (see pp. 30–3 and 189–90 below).

Furthermore, with the steady expansion of the cantor's musical activity, the school authorities were increasingly concerned that music should not consume too much of the time which might more profitably be directed towards academic study. The Saxon ordinance of 1580 shows a modification of Melanchthon's original plan (Schünemann 1928, pp. 86–7): textbooks in music should be concise, teaching only the essentials to acquire skill in practical music; music practice should be confined to specific days or, if carried out every day, should not last too long. That the ordinance recommends the cultivation of music by earlier composers of Josquin's generation might evidence a reaction to the increasingly bold compositional activities of the cantors. Moreover the ordinance advises the cantors not to neglect the monophonic repertory of psalms and chorales.

Niemöller has presented the clearest account of the singing duties of the school boys at the outset of the Reformation. The terminology and division of duties are often vague and confusing: the most common categories are *Currende, Chorus symphoniacus, Chorus musicus* and *Cantorei* (Niemöller 1969, pp. 669–79). The *Currende* is the most common of several terms to describe the groups of poorer pupils who sang around the streets of the town. This tradition, which continued well into the nineteenth century, often led to an ambivalent attitude towards music on account of its association with beggary. While the term *Currende* might most appropriately – but not necessarily exclusively – be associated with unison singing (*choraliter*), the terms *Chorus symphoniacus* and *Chorus musicus* often refer to those more talented groups who sang polyphony in front of certain houses under the direction of a prefect. These two groups – the one performing monophonic and the other polyphonic music – were presumably responsible for their respective repertories in the church music; furthermore, the *Currende* usually sang for funerals while the *Symphoniaci* performed at weddings and special occasions.

The term *Cantorei* was more widely used throughout Germany, loosely to refer to the figural singing (and gradually also to the concerted instrumental playing) in church. The singers employed in this capacity were drawn primarily from the *Symphoniaci*, poor boys who earned their education and hospitality through their singing duties; but other boys who had particular talent in music could also be admitted to this group. Many schools supported a set number of *Alumni*, who were offered free lodging in the school on account of their musical abilities; in this way schools could be guaranteed a steady body of singers to form the *Cantorei* (Niemöller 1969, p. 667). Furthermore other teachers in the school, adults from the locality and the professional *Stadtpfeiffer* were recruited to furnish the lower parts of the choir and to provide accompanying instrumental parts.

The cantor normally directed the *Cantorei*, while the *Chorus symphoniacus* was traditionally organised by prefects. With the turn of the seventeenth century the cantor began to assume a wider musical responsibility as *Director Musices*, something which gave him increased independence from his traditional place in the school hierarchy (see p. 17 below). By the middle of the sixteenth century the *Stadtpfeiffer* had also become permament members of the *Cantorei* in many towns, thus giving the cantor further jurisdiction outside the school. Many new guilds of *Stadtpfeiffer* were formed in response to the new demands of the *Cantorei*, and these versatile players were often employed in the school to assist in rehearsals and general singing lessons.

In sum then, the boys in the Latin schools were musically employed on several levels. According to the first Lutheran ordinances, all boys had to attend singing lessons, join in the singing which opened and closed instruction and lead the congregational singing in the daily church services, Mass and Vespers (Schünemann 1928, p. 91). Of the poor boys, the less advanced sang around the town in the *Currende*, the more capable in the *Chorus symphoniacus*. Finally the cantor had the choice of the best singers to form the *Cantorei*, which did not usually contain more than twelve singers (Niemöller 1969, pp. 682–3). In certain places, though, due to the consolidation of several schools into one during the early Reformation years, the cantor had to provide a *Cantorei* for several churches simultaneously. As the Nordhausen ordinance of 1583 stipulated, the cantor should rehearse figural music with the boys in groups of five, so that, in an emergency, he could furnish the *Cantorei* in two places at once.[11]

This book is concerned most closely with the content of instruction in practical music, the conception the pupil might have gained of the nature and function of the art. Nevertheless it is extremely difficult to ascertain the details and sequence of instruction. We can only hope that the many surviving treatises are at least symptomatic of the ideas and methods employed. The ordinances of the first years of Lutheranism stress repeatedly that the instruction books should be as concise as possible. While most ordinances do not stipulate the specific books to be used, it is clear from those that do that Faber's *Compendiolum musicae* (1548) and Listenius's *Rudimenta musicae* (1533/1537) were the books most commonly used.[12] It is by no means certain how many of these books actually found their way into the hands of the pupils, but at the very least they would have formed the basis of the teacher's instruction.

The first significant books to be written specifically for the Lutheran lands were by Luther's close musical associate, Martin Agricola, whose *Ein kurtz deudsche musica* (1528), *Musica instrumentalis* (1529), *Musica figuralis* (1532) and *Musica choralis* (1533) seem to form a complete curriculum for the practical musician, together covering rudiments, chant, polyphony and instruments. The fact that they were written in German clearly reflects the spirit of Lutheranism, elevating the vernacular as a viable language for instruction; it might also be evidence for the initial decline of Latin instruction during the early years of the Reformation (see p. 2 above). In the first treatise of 1528 Agricola notes the need for much more concise instruction in the mother tongue;[13] nevertheless, the ensuing text (geared towards the unmeasured *musica choralis* rather than figural music) is still quite thorough and extensive, with much information on solmisation, intervals and psalm tones.

Agricola 1532 is designed to provide the remaining information on measured notation, particularly for those who might have studied the author's exhaustive treatise on instruments (1529). Despite Agricola's continued use of the German tongue, the instruction is still very extensive, including much detail on mensuration and proportions. It opens with anecdotes on the history, power and invention of music, including fifteen poems, but the remainder of the text concerns basic rules of notation rather than speculations on the essence of music.

The style of instruction – something shared with basic primers in other subjects too (Schünemann 1928, pp. 102–3) – is a basic presentation of the material in the form of tables and explanations followed by examples. In Agricola 1532 the introduction to notes and rests is followed directly by a three-part canon (but before the necessary concept of measure has been introduced). There is little direct explication of how a rule relates to the examples; presumably the pupil must infer this for himself. Agricola continues with rules for clefs and ligatures followed by exhaustive examples of mensuration. The remaining chapters cover the various signs used in music, the concept of the beat or tactus ('Schlag odder Tact'), where we learn that the singer actually learned to beat while singing,[14] and finally, proportions and their related signs. It is interesting that Agricola does not cover solmisation in detail in this treatise; this subject was covered in the *Deudsche musica* of 1528 (republished in a revised form as the *Musica choralis* of 1533).

With Listenius 1533 there is a return to Latin as the principal language of instruction; however, what made his format so popular was the incorporation of *musica choralis* and *figuralis* into the same text. With his table of all the notes and solmisation syllables he established a format which survived in German tutors well into the succeeding century (Plate 1).

Plate 1 Listenius 1533: table of notes and solmisation syllables (copied by subsequent authors for over a century to come)

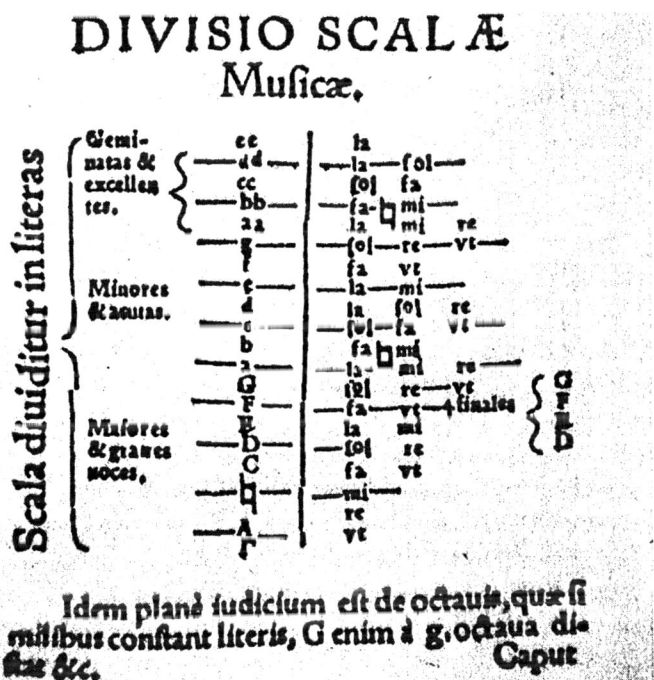

Inevitably, examples provide the means by which the pupil may assimilate and apply the rules (but again the examples are not necessarily related directly to the subject in hand). Those for the six solmisation syllables, for instance, include canons. The canon was an extremely effective means of cultivating part-singing and remained the staple of singing primers well into the Baroque era.

Listenius's text is lean in the extreme, with little speculative material. He is the first writer to define composition as the separate art of *musica poetica*, distinct from the fields of *musica theorica* and *practica*. Later theorists adopt the threefold division (e.g. Finck 1556, Oridryus 1557) or merely omit to mention composition within the context of *musica practica*. In all, then, Listenius was striving to provide the barest essentials for the performance of music, something which unashamedly neglected the fields of speculative music and composition.

Faber established the basic topics of practical music (clefs and letter names, solmisation syllables, the three hexachords, mutation and 'figures', i.e. the various notational signs) which remained standard for over a century to come (see p. 56 below). His text, first published in 1548, is even more concise than Listenius, and adopts the question-and-answer style (*erotemata*) which persisted in many subsequent publications. This presumably reflects something of the way skills such as music were taught, answers being learned by rote and tested regularly by the teacher. Indeed exactly the same attitude is evident in some of Luther's own writings on teaching: in the context of the Small Catechism (1529), for instance, he employs the question-and-answer style in the doctrinal sections and stresses that the pupil (particularly the young) should initially learn both the sacred texts and their commentaries in a single version and alter not a syllable (*WA* XXX/1, pp. 268–9).

During the latter half of the century, writers increasingly adopted German as their language; indeed treatises such as Wilflingseder 1561 and Gumpelzhaimer 1591 were basically German versions of Faber's text. Others, such as Fesser 1572, include parallel Latin and German texts. Few of these basic primers give any clue on what would today be regarded as musical interpretation, nor is there much reference to the affective nature of music. Holtheuser's description of the characteristics of the intervals between certain solmisation syllables (e.g. mi–la = *hart*, re–sol = *natürlich*, ut–fa = *weich*; Holtheuser 1586, ch. 2) is about the most explicit statement in this regard.

The simplicity and conciseness of Faber's influential text does not mean, of course, that more complex treatises disappeared from the field. Indeed Agricola himself published a Latin text, *Rudimenta musices*, in 1539 (an abridged version of the German primer of 1528), which covers all the details of notation and ends with an elaborate exposition on the monochord. Furthermore, his *Quaestiones vulgatiores* (1543) deals at length with

The establishment of Lutheran musical practice

common questions concerning the information imparted in his simpler treatises. Clearly there must have been a need for these more complex surveys of notation; some were designed for particular schools (e.g. Agricola 1543 was written for school pupils in Magdeburg), specifically for pupils who had proceeded beyond the simple rules of practical music. Schneegass seems to have had two different types of pupil in mind with his treatises of 1591 and 1592; that of 1592 is a simple question-and-answer primer written in German while that of 1591 is not only written in Latin, but also contains a detailed survey of modes, different genres of counterpoint, vocal ranges, canons, consonance and dissonance and rules for good singing. It is tempting to speculate that a series of essentially practical treatises by one author might relate to the performing divisions within the school body such as between the *Currende*, the *Chorus symphoniacus* and the *Cantorei*.

The practice of including extensive musical examples grows in the latter half of the century. Wilflingseder includes the canonic Agnus Dei of Josquin's *Missa Hercules*, directly after his exposition of solmisation syllables (Wilflingseder 1563, p. 11); Dressler includes the Sanctus of Josquin's *Missa L'Homme Armé* after presenting the mensural signs (Dressler 1571, part 3, ch. 2); he includes other examples by Josquin and also some by Lassus and Isaac. Hofmann 1572 includes Josquin's *In exitu Israel* to exemplify mensuration. All this reflects the reverence accorded to the earlier composers, particularly Josquin, something which is explicitly prescribed in the Saxon ordinance of 1580 (see p. 4 above).

While some of the most interesting treatises from the sixteenth century are those which give us information on style and performance practice, these are the exceptions rather than the norm and may thus not be typical of their age. Nevertheless, as will emerge in the course of this study, it was precisely these writings that formed the basis of many rules of musical interpretation and performance in treatises of the seventeenth century, when the interest in voice production, interpretation and ornamentation became that much more pronounced. In other words, the earlier publications must have been sufficiently known and distributed to have been influential several decades later. Most obviously influential was the *Practica musica* of Finck (1556), a comprehensive treatise which offers extensive rules on elegant singing after the basics of notation have been covered. This, and the other influential sixteenth-century treatises (C. Praetorius 1574, Schneegass 1591), will thus be relevant within the context of seventeenth-century education (see chapter 4). Here, though, we briefly examine two eccentric teatises which seem not to have influenced the later writings.

10   Music education and the art of performance

Singer's German treatise of 1531 clearly follows the prescription that primers should be concise and not include unnecessary information. However, the content and style of his short publication are unusual for the time: his intention is to teach children how to sing, how to devise counterpoint and to acquire the necessary musical background for study of lutes, violins and 'pipes'.[15] Having covered the basics of solmisation, mensuration and proportions, Singer includes five rules of concords (the vertical intervals permitted in four-part harmony). His reasons for including this elementary information on harmony are somewhat obscure:

It is further good for those youths who wish to learn instruments to know which are consonances or dissonances, that is, which notes sound well, and which not.

Noch ist den jungen die auff den instrumenten lernen wöllen güt zu wissen / welches cōcordantzen oder dissonantzen sein das ist/welche notten woll lauten / oder nicht.'   (Singer 1531, fol. 6v.)

It is not clear how such knowledge was to be used: perhaps in embellishment of melody and harmony, perhaps in the improvisation of new lines. Singer further outlines the rules concerning consecutive fifths and octaves and the avoidance of the tritone. He also gives some advice – remarkable at this time – concerning the addition of coloratura: embellishment is good when the composer so desires, but where this is not the case, the performer should rather seek edification and sweetness in the song.[16]

In all Singer prescibes an education in practical music that is far more rounded than is usual during the early Lutheran years: some pupils learn instruments and for these, in particular, a knowledge of the rules of harmony is useful. However, knowledge of harmony did not become a common component of instruction books until the end of the seventeenth century. It may be that Singer was reflecting the last traces in Germany of the old concept of *musica practica*, as an art encompassing both composition and performance.

Some twenty years later Coclico published his *Compendium*, which, like Singer's treatise, also assumes a more comprehensive approach to practical music. His work is something of a unicum in sixteenth-century German writings: he believes himself to be transmitting an art (*musica reservata*) which had hitherto been a secret withheld from the masses. Claiming to be a pupil and follower of Josquin, he insists that the arts of singing and composing should not be separated and that these basically practical arts are the essence of music. Having dealt with notation he proceeds to his favoured topic, embellishment. Counterpoint to him is essentially the art of improvising against a cantus firmus; but the pupil should be familiar with the art of notated composition too. However, Coclico's treatise can hardly be thought typical of musical education in the German cantorates and no subsequent writings show any trace of its influence.

The next chapters concentrate on the practical treatises of the seventeenth and early eighteenth centuries, turning first to the conceptions of music they offer to the incipient performer, then to considerations of performance practice and interpretation. Despite the 'advances' which this literature displays, it should be stressed that there is no definitive break with the style and format of the sixteenth-century primers and that many establishments maintained a conservative approach to performance well into the eighteenth century.

2

The role of practical music in education c.1600–1750

The Lutheran Reformation not only fostered an immediate growth of musical activity in church and school, it also nurtured the further expansion and richness of music during the seventeenth century, the seemingly delayed fulfilment of Luther's desire to place the art as second only to theology in cultural and educational life. The reasons for this delay – if the Lutheran musical achievements of the sixteenth century may provisionally be disparaged thus – perhaps lie in the dislocation of the various historical processes. First, although Luther himself believed in promoting music at both elementary and specialised levels, the emphasis initially lay with the elementary, since the chorales and their melodies were so important for the dissemination of the new confession. Secondly, despite Luther's enthusiasm for music as a practical art, schools still retained a respect for music in its ancient role as a component of the Mediaeval *quadrivium*, music as a science of proportion and number which mirrored the order of creation. Thus cantors in the newly established Lutheran foundations were primarily academics (teaching other subjects in addition to music) who were not necessarily eminent 'practical' composers and performers, and who might have considered the position of cantor as a stepping-stone towards a post as rector (head of the school), pastor, or university professor. Furthermore, other teachers on the staff at Latin schools were often musically proficient, assisting in church services and taking the lower music classes in the school. Even as late as 1723, the *Quartus* (i.e. the fourth teacher in the school hierarchy) of the Thomasschule, Leipzig was still teaching elementary music (Leipzig school ordinance 1723, p. 43).

Luther was concerned with the affective dimension of music, its power to move mankind to joy and to banish the Devil. But German musical style was itself slower to adapt to this growing conception, and not until the importation of what was frequently termed 'the new Italian style', at the turn of the seventeenth century, were musicians placing extra-musical elements (at first, the verbal text, but soon also the concomitant affects) at the forefront of their creative processes. It is not immediately obvious what writers such as Praetorius mean when they refer to the 'new Italian style': it could refer to the *Nuove musiche* of Caccini, the *seconda prattica* of Monteverdi, or even to the madrigalian idioms of the sixteenth century. If the 'newer' music that composers such as Praetorius were introducing into German repertories is anything to go by, the 'new Italian style' can refer to any of the Italian styles which were viable at the turn of the seventeenth century: expressive madrigalian gestures, polychoral and concerto textures and monody. Perhaps the greatest advance, at least to the Germans, was the growing importance of music as a form of speech and rhetoric, something which augmented (but never fully replaced) the emotionally neutral, 'unmarked' texture of traditional Renaissance polyphony.

It should immediately be noted that those writers advocating the importation of newer styles represent only one wing of the literature relating to musical education in Germany. Not only did many cantors stick doggedly to the methods of the Reformation era, but it is also clear that many were somewhat overawed by the abilities of Italian musicians.[1]

In some ways the Lutheran soil had been nurtured to support the implantation of the 'new Italian style' all along. But with this came a striking change in music's role in education: the new idiom demanded a more musically specialised cantor, one who might be expected to compose with not a little sense of the 'new' and perhaps even with some notion of the 'original'. Moreover, the new style, with its detailed notation, the demands it made on the singer as 'orator' and its inclusion of obbligato instrumental parts, took more of the cantor's time, affording him less opportunity and inclination to teach academic subjects. All in all, then, the cantor as a musical specialist was becoming something of an imposter in academic life; practical music was cultivating an agenda of its own, outside its original role in education. Inevitably, music sowed the seeds of its ultimate demise as a fundamental element of education; in the meantime, though, it enjoyed a privileged position which seemed to combine the outlook of the old with the new. The outstanding achievement of the German Baroque, not least the music of Schütz and Bach, can be viewed in the context of this glorious age of transition.

FAVOURABLE ATTITUDES TOWARDS CHURCH MUSIC

A broad spectrum of literature bears witness to the high regard in which music was held in seventeenth-century life. The city council in Hamburg acknowledged in 1615 that music was 'not a slight ornament and elegance of this city'.[2] J. Rist, in a treatise on the most noble amusements, valued music far above such practical arts as comedy and tragedy, affirming 'that music, or the art of singing, which one can simply name as a truly heavenly, even Godly gift or token, is far, far to be preferred to all tragic and comic playing'.[3] School ordinances also frequently mention music in favourable terms. The Speyer ordinance of 1654 states that 'Music is a beautiful ornament and asset in churches and schools and should thus be cultivated as a particular condiment of studies.'[4] The introduction to Büttner 1625 stresses the utility of music: the art not only contributes to the praise of God, the *Cantorei* also supports poor pupils during difficult times, enabling them to continue with their studies, developing into learned men of school and church.[5] Many of the books designed for practical musical instruction in schools include Luther's celebrated quotations about music; perhaps the most extensive in this regard is Ribovius 1638 (pp. 247f.), which includes virtually all Luther's well-known sayings regarding the beauty and use of music.

Some of the most enthusiastic supporters of music were pastors who followed the lead of their reformer in treasuring music as an element of worship. Friedrich gives a clear indication of the classic Lutheran purposes of music in an organ dedication of 1610: music celebrates divine glory foremost, secondly, it moves the human soul, affecting both teacher and listener; thirdly, it banishes the Devil and his melancholy ways and finally it gives a foretaste of heavenly joy. Friccius 1631 and Mithobius 1665 are two of the most extensive tracts supporting music during the entire century. Friccius, having presented a long justification of music in Scripture, history and nature, stresses that the schools should continue to contribute to the musical richness of the liturgy:

The school servants, together with the organists, are obliged to practise music diligently so that the service may be decorated both with organ playing and (as hitherto, so henceforth) also otherwise with music-making (as much as the opportunities of this place afford).

Die Schuldiener neben dem Organisten / denen die *Musica* zu üben obliget / daß sie Fleiß thun / damit beydes mit schlagen der Orgel / und (wie bißhero / also weiter /) auch sonstē mit Musiciren der Gottesdienst (so viel dieses Orts Gelegenheit nach geschehen kan) gezieret werde. (Friccius 1631, p. 125)

Friccius loses no opportunity in his long sermon to speak out against other denominations. While the Catholics are vaguely accused of 'superstition' and 'idolatry' ('Aberglauben', 'Abgötterey'; Friccius 1631, p. 333), the richness of Lutheran music is a particularly potent weapon with which to taunt the amusical Calvinists, well known for their destruction of organs. Their worship is not only emasculated but also contrary to the many exaltations to musical worship in the Bible. Rosinus's sermon of 1615 had likewise condemned the Calvinists' attitude to music, something which showed the influence of the Devil.[6] Anwander suggests that Lutheran music is a 'Mittel Straß' between Calvinist austerity and Catholic excess (Anwander 1606, p. 31).

Given that cantors quite often proceeded to become clerics, it is not surprising to find a pastor, Erasmus Gruber, writing a singing primer for use in schools. Gruber clearly wished to show the young student that music was essential in deepening belief and relaying the content of religious dogma:

If one sings and makes music with a beautiful learned text, psalms and Lieder, the subject and dogma themselves go far more deeply and pleasantly into the heart together with the beautiful melodies, than would surely happen through preaching

Wenn man schöne / Lehrhaffte Text / Psalmen und Lieder singt und *musiciert*, so gehen zugleich mit den lieblichen *Melodien* die *Res* und Glaubens-Lehren selber durch die Ohren viel tieffer und anmuthiger ins Herz / als wohl durchs predigen geschicht (Gruber 1673, 'Christlicher Vor-Bericht')

One element which becomes especially prominent in seventeenth-century writings about music in worship is the emphasis on instruments, these being such an integral part of the new Italianate musical style. Indeed one of the most common motivations for the longer tracts of the period (such as Friccius's) was the dedication of a new organ. Poland's *Musica instrumentalis* of 1604 links the organ celebration in the cathedral at Meissen with the use of strings in the service. He takes a verse from Psalm 69 ('Let heaven and earth praise Him, the seas and everything that moves therein') as his starting-point, since it implies so much the totality of praise; sumptuous figural music with organs and other instruments is akin to the music of heaven (this is typically coupled with a polemic against other denominations). Friedrich 1610 is based appropriately on Psalm 150, which exhorts us to worship not only with the living voice but also with all kinds of instruments.

Anwander, in another organ-dedication sermon, stresses the importance of musical instruments, the costs spent on the organ being like the costly water with which the woman anointed Christ (Anwander 1606, p. 8). He affirms that – some Old Testament objections to instruments notwithstanding – musical prosperity is good and useful in itself (pp. 16–17). Throughout his tract he is concerned to highlight music as a useful art, on account of its ability both to move and to teach the listener.[7] Friccius 1631 takes a more abstract viewpoint, likening the components and totality of the organ to the parts of the human being, of which the heart (= organist) is itself regulated by the heavenly Kapellmeister *(ibid.,* p. 252).[8] This sort of mechanistic analogy is typical of the age, reflecting the temporary integration of the new science and technology within the old theocentric order (see Dammann 1984, pp. 397–476).[9]

Rosinus argues that the musical worship of God takes place at three levels: the singing of angels; the singing of humans (the *Cantorei* thus being a vital institution which mirrors that of Heaven); and thirdly the music of dumb, unreasoning things. Instruments (with animals) fall into the third category and should be respected, albeit at the lowest level of musical worship:

When one hears the organ struck up in church, each person should strike up and cheer himself with these thoughts: Dear God, the foolish, ignorant instrument praises God in Heaven

Wann man auch Orgeln höret in Kirchen schlagen / so sol ein jeder in sich selber schlagen / und sich auffmuntern mit diesen Gedanken: Lieber Gott / lobet das tumme / unverstendige Werck GOtt im Himmel (Rosinus 1615)

THE EXPANSION OF FIGURAL MUSIC

The enthusiam of these theologians is paralleled by the great expansion of figural music during the seventeenth century. In Hamburg, figural music was sung in each church only six times per year before 1608, but after this time it was performed in each church every four weeks; the addition of galleries in several city churches is further testimony to this expansion (Krüger 1933, p. 47). In Dresden the development seems to have been even swifter with figural music every fourth Sunday in 1574, every Sunday in alternate churches by 1581 (Krickeberg 1965, pp. 59, 114). The Nordhausen ordinance of 1583 shows that cantors were beginning to furnish figural music in several churches at a time, which meant that the capable students were to be trained so that they could sing a piece with only five singers (see p. 5 above). Rosinus's *Cantorey Predigt* of 1615 shows that even in the comparatively small village church at Staucha, a motet was sung every week.

The role of practical music in education 17

According to Kuhnau, the aristocracy was frequently requesting newer, up-to-date works from the church musicians (Krickeberg 1965, p. 85). Ernest the Pious issued an ordinance for Gotha in 1642, directing that the schoolmaster should not bore the pupils with precepts and scales, but teach them which figural pieces belong to elegant and artistic singing.[10] That schoolteachers often followed this trend is suggested by the comments of a *Quintus* teacher in Flensburg during the dismissal proceedings concerning the cantor, Ewers, in 1687: the latter had performed the same pieces repeatedly without introducing anything new (Detlefsen 1961, pp. 228–9). Many city musicians tried to imitate the idioms and musical standards of court establishments: in Halle, the organist, Zahn, stated his intention in 1638 of making music in the modern fashion, just as it was done in the contemporary princely courts.[11]

Not surprisingly this expansion of figural music is reflected by changes within the school body and curriculum. First, the developing status of the cantor is immediately noticeable. Krickeberg (1965, pp. 19, 48) shows that cantors were often the leading musicians of their towns during the seventeenth century, their energies moving away from the cultivation of *musica choralis* (unmeasured monophony, for which a separate cantor was sometimes employed) to *musica figuralis*. Progressively, the cantor became the only specialist teacher in the school, with a much lighter load of academic instruction. The hardships of the Thirty Years War, which often hindered music instruction in schools, might also have encouraged the cantor to look more in the direction of the city than the school (Finkel 1973, p. 103).

One especially telling sign of this move was the seemingly silent appropriation of the title *Director Musices* by the Leipzig Thomaskantor J. H. Schein for a publication in 1618 (Krickeberg 1965, p. 104); J. S. Bach likewise claimed this title a century later. Praetorius's treatise of 1619, the first major German work to codify a complete importation of the 'new Italian style', offers the title *Director Musices* as a synonym for cantor. Many basic music primers (e.g. Demantius 1635) follow Praetorius's lead here. That there was an explicit division between two types of cantor, the academic and the Kapellmeister, is clearly evidenced by the intriguing politics surrounding Bach's Leipzig appointment in 1723; one faction of the town council desired the traditional academic cantor while the other, calling for a more purely musical candidate, won the day (see Siegele 1983, 1984, 1986). As Fuhrmann made clear in 1715, there was a distinction between the academic, but musically informed, cantor and the cantor who must understand composition so that he can harmonise a

18   Music education and the art of performance

given melody, correct mistakes, supervise the compositions of students and improve poor pieces:

> I say that a choir-leader who wants to be called not a common cantor but a *Director Musices* must understand the fundamentals of composition
>
> Ich sage, ein Choragus, der kein gemeiner *Cantor*, sondern ein *Director Musices* seyn und heissen wil, muß *Fundamentum Compositionis* verstehen
> (Fuhrmann, *Musicalische Strigel*, p. 18)

Mergerle, in his compendium of the various professions and trades, likewise implies that there are two categories of cantor: those who conduct individual choirs and those who take overall responsibility for the entire musical establishment:

> Certain cantors and singing-masters are appointed to begin the songs and their sections correctly, to lead the voices and to instruct the young. But because musical instruments are added to the vocal parts, following an ancient and praiseworthy custom, and the musicians are divided into several choirs, it was necessary not only to have various cantors, but also to have one to direct the entire *Capelle* and the main choir, whom we still nowadays call the Kapellmeister
>
> sind gewisse *Cantores* und Sing-Meister angeordnet / die Gesänge und deren Absätze richtig anzufangen / die Stimm zu führen / und die Jugend zu unterweisen. Weil aber denen Sing-Stimmen auch die Musicalische Instrumenten aus einer uralten löblichen Gewohnheit beygefüget / und die *Musici* in gewisse Chöre vertheilet worden / waren nicht allein unterschiedliche *Cantores* nöthig / sondern auch einer / so die gantze Capelle und den Haupt-Chor *dirigirte* / welchen wir noch heut zu Tage den Capell-Meister nennen
> (Mergerle 1711, p. 136)

It is interesting to find the term Kapellmeister used in connection with church music and that the reference to 'instructing the young' is conspicuously absent from this category. The authorities in Frankfurt in 1623 must have been rather progressive in relieving the school cantor altogether of the direction of the figural music and appointing a 'professional' Kapellmeister to control the music in all the churches, J. A. Herbst. Nevertheless Herbst was still required to train the eight best boys from the school.[12] Samuel Scheidt was appointed to a similar position in Halle in 1628 (see p. 30 below). These are striking instances of a general trend towards training only those boys who had special talent and neglecting the traditional singing culture in the school as a whole.

Krickeberg has shown that the musical activity and status of the cantor often varied according to area in Lutheran Germany. In the north, for instance, cantors were not traditionally composers (since there were so few composers there at the time of the Reformation), so the organists began to play more of a role, even though these were officially ranked below cantors and not necessarily associated with school music (Krickeberg 1965, pp. 124–5). As Fuhrmann so eloquently put it in 1706, the cantor should be well-informed in *musica theorica, practica* and *poetica*, since it would be a bad thing if the organist were cleverer than the cantor.[13] On the other hand, Buxtehude, as organist of the Marienkirche, Lübeck, became so important in the town's musical life that he was often addressed in the manner of a Kapellmeister (Krickeberg 1965, p. 149). Furthermore, while Buxtehude was still not officially responsible for the figural music in the Marienkirche, his extra-liturgical *Abendmusik* was the most famed musical event of the year, something which was, incidentally, funded by the business community (Snyder 1987, pp. 63, 66, 71–2).

In smaller towns throughout Germany the cantor was often still primarily a schoolteacher, so here again the organist sometimes could take a larger role in the direction of the church music (Krickeberg 1965, p. 133). In southern Germany too the cantor was slower to become an important musical figure since, with the proximity of Catholic states, the chorale – as the flagship of Lutheran dogma – remained the most important musical element of education and worship, to the detriment of more complex figural music (Krickeberg, p. 160).

It was in the larger cities of central Germany that the cantor was most influential, often taking up the musical directorship of several churches while still retaining some of his respected status as a schoolmaster.[14] In exceptional cases (e.g. Bach's and Telemann's) it was even possible for the cantor to hire a substitute to take the cantor's Latin lessons, but this was not greeted with universal approval.

Some of the more important cantorates were obviously very attractive to notable musicians even in the eighteenth century. As the entry on 'Cantor' in Zedler's *Grosses vollständiges universal Lexicon* (vol. V, 1733, p. 600) affirms, the name 'cantor' carries particular honour in religious institutions.[15] C. P. E. Bach tried twice to become cantor at the Thomasschule in Leipzig, but was deemed unsuitable, apparently on academic grounds (see Petzoldt 1985, pp. 7–8). Perhaps the town council was reacting against the 'exceptional' situation of his father's appointment: for over twenty years the cantorate had been controlled by a musician who did not even hold a university degree. Telemann evidently considered the Hamburg cantorate an attractive proposition in 1721, even if he was criticised for having neglected the general school singing tuition (in a document relating to his successor's (C. P. E. Bach's) appointment; see

Schulze 1977, p. 76). It may be that with the rising bourgeois interest in progressive and public music, the prospect of such a post in a free city was more promising than one in court service, where the musician was at the mercy of the aristocratic whim. In any case the traditional distinctions between church, court and theatre music were being eroded and the leading musicians were often 'complete Kapellmeisters' in the sense advocated by Mattheson's famous treatise, *Der vollkommene Kapellmeister* (1739).

The *academic* status of music seems to have declined during the seventeenth century: the 1580 Saxon ordinance (see p. 4 above) already implied that music was being regarded as a non-academic study. A century later the Leipzig rector Thomasius stated that music was no longer an essential requisite of a learned man (Krickeberg 1965, p. 49). On the other hand, some schools evidently encouraged a wide participation in musical activities. In Schleiz, for instance, all pupils were expected to sing motets in 1673, whether or not they were in the specialist choir;[16] moreover, the Brieg ordinance of 1581 stresses that only the 'amusical' may be excused from music lessons (Schünemann 1928, p. 81). In the Michaelsschule, Lüneburg the higher classes were trained to sing a certain amount of advanced figural music (Walter 1967, pp. 56–7). The average number of hours spent on general music instruction seems to have been about four per week, so the Leipzig ordinance of 1634 was probably exceptional in advocating seven hours (Schünemann 1928, p. 171, Wustman 1909, p. 110).

In most schools morning and afternoon lessons were still opened and closed with the singing of a sacred song (Schünemann 1928, p. 88); this practice is still documented in the ordinances of the Thomasschule, Leipzig in 1733.[17] Furthermore, music could still be used as a mnemonic system to learn basic facts and elements of faith, since some believed it to affect both singers and listeners alike.[18] Gruber's comment that facts and matters of belief penetrate the heart far more effectively with 'lieblich' melodies than with preaching has already been noted here (see p. 15 above). One further use of music in school is outlined by Falck 1688: music refreshes the mind exhausted by concentration, stimulating the inner senses, fantasy and memory (Falck 1688, foreword). This in turn reflects the position of music as an art somewhat apart from academic subjects.

Church records point towards a tremendous growth in instrumental performance during the seventeenth century. The case at Hamburg is particularly well documented: instruments are mentioned at the Jacobikirche for the first time in 1548, regular payments are recorded from 1563 and contracts are issued for musicians in the Catharinenkirche in 1592 and the Johanniskirche in 1609; in 1613 a general ordinance was passed to establish the apportionment of singers and instrumentalists for all churches (Krüger 1933, pp. 54–7). Similarly in Leipzig instrumentalists were established for the second choir, in addition to the first, in 1608 (Wustman 1909, p. 95). The *Stadtpfeiffer* – professional musicians who were employed (and apprenticed) by the town – were traditionally responsible for the instrumental parts, but the growth in concerted music clearly demanded that more players be available. In Freiberg, for instance, school instrumentalists were supplementing the *Stadtpfeiffer* by 1680 (Krickeberg 1965, p. 115).

School documents show a similar trend: the Weimar school ordinance of 1614 directs that instrumental music should be practised and that organists and other musicians in the town should be employed to teach instrumental music (Preussner 1924, p. 443). The introduction to Leisring 1615, a treatise specifically directed at young schoolboys, states categorically that music is industriously practised at schools and that many well-appointed churches are furnished with both vocal and instrumental music.[19] Instrumental instruction became part of the private tuition to be offered by the cantor in Freiberg in 1650 and instrumental study was mandatory by 1658 (Krickeberg 1965, pp. 83–4). Kuhnau's document of employment in Leipzig 1702 states that he was to be responsible for instrumental tuition (Schering 1926, p. 60). Several treatises also imply that singing study could be combined with instrumental tuition (see p. 61 below) and Gradenthaler 1687 even suggests that pupils who are not capable of singing – presumably at the time of the voice change – can be employed in instrumental music.[20] The extent to which instrumental music was practised and respected is demonstrated by the fact that even a Pietist rector, Vockerodt (1697), was well informed in both vocal and instrumental performance and and claimed to have greatly encouraged both activities during his time as rector at Gotha (see p. 28 below).

Another innovation of the seventeenth century, which was essentially the beginning of the concert tradition, was the *Collegium musicum*, a group of students who met regularly to perform concerts. Such *collegia* were formed in Erfurt (1608), Görlitz (1686) and Freiberg (1672 – see Preussner 1924, Schünemann 1928, p. 198) and these were often involved in the instrumental side of church music. According to Schering, a *Collegium musicum* was formed in the Leipzig Thomasschule during the latter years of the seventeenth century to cater for instrumentalists in the two highest classes and to perform in the school on special occasions (Schering 1926, p. 60). This new type of institution was not always neccessarily associated with the cantor and school music: Weckmann, organist of the Jakobikirche in Hamburg, formed a *Collegium musicum* in 1660 which became famous in its own right (Krüger 1933, pp. 97–9). In Leipzig, Kuhnau was constantly irritated by Telemann's activity at the New Church. Telemann's student *Collegium musicum* (formed in 1704) drew capable musicians away from Kuhnau's circle, and moreover, it enabled Telemann to perform music in an operatic style which offended the cantor's sense of musical decorum in church (Schering 1926, pp. 118, 192; Krickeberg 1965, p. 120).

Although it is difficult to establish how the more elaborate music was rehearsed and performed, there are a few factors which together point to how the cantor employed the pupils in his charge. First, he often had an automatic control over the pupils since many were supported in their studies through singing, whether in the streets or in the church *Cantorei*.[21] Sporadic references to private musical instruction with the cantor are found throughout the seventeenth century. Given that this practice was also well recognised in other subjects – one third of the students in Freiberg in 1688 received some form of private tuition (Krickeberg 1965, p. 47) – it was probably far more widespread than the sources suggest. The cantor Demantius at Freiberg offered private music lessons for those who had love and desire for music (*ibid.*, p. 53). The 1673 Löban school ordinance directs that the cantor should train the boys especially in figural music, both in public and in private (*ibid.*, p. 49). Mylius's treatise of 1685 is specifically designed for 'boys in schools and also in private instruction'.[22]

Given the number of instruction books, such as Mylius's, which deal with quite complex forms of ornamentation and diminution (see chapter 5, below) it is likely that some of the more talented pupils could have reached quite a high level of expertise. Certainly in Freiberg the concertists (i.e. the solo singers who were the core of the seventeenth-century chorus) were paid 4–5 Groschen more than the 'common singer' towards the end of the seventeenth century (Krickeberg 1965, p. 85). The Leipzig Thomasschule ordinances of 1634 and 1733 stipulate, at the outset of the cantor's duties, that those who are naturally gifted and inclined towards singing must be given private music instruction since it is not usually possible to achieve perfection within the cantor's ordinary singing hours.[23] The ordinance of 1723 states that those belonging to the *Cantorei* should rehearse every day at a set time.[24] Printz describes the duties of the prefects who were to direct the street-singing: rehearsal seemed to entail singing through the pieces in order to determine which could be performed without too many errors.[25]

The role of practical music in education

The rules outlined by Thomas Selle during his early years as cantor in Hamburg, 1642-8, give a useful picture of what the director of music may have expected from the school musicians. Sixteen pupils were to be given special privileges as the best singers of their part, and a further eight musicians would be financed by the churches (Krüger 1933, pp. 68-77; Krüger 1956). This accords remarkably well with the number specified for the first choir in the well-known 'Entwurff' written by J. S. Bach to the Leipzig town council in 1730 (see David and Mendel 1945/1972, p. 121; *Bach-Dokumente* I, p. 60). Selle also demanded that these concertists gave him their time on Saturdays, Sundays and festivals, that they spent an hour a day, four times a week, copying out scores and parts, and that they attended four singing lessons a week. In 1720 the cantor of Flensburg, Sternstorff, likewise referred to the time he needed to prepare scores and direct copyists; this accounted for his absence from the *Currende* singing (Detlefsen 1961, pp. 109-10). Selle even specified food for each day and various other rules of living (cf. Printz's stipulations, see p. 80 below). Furthermore, he made several demands for rehearsals with the *Ratsinstrumentisten* and requested benches in the churches to prevent the instrumentalists from going to the 'Weinhaus' during the sermon.

One further factor to consider is the employment of singers who were not currently members of the school, particularly for the lower voices which must have been difficult to furnish with younger singers. In early seventeenth-century Hamburg, the tenor and bass parts were assigned to pupils from the advanced school (*Gymnasium*) who were thus older than those from the *Lateinschule* (Krüger 1956, p. 18). Close examination of the *Cantorei* at the Leipzig Thomasschule under both Kuhnau and Bach shows that extra singers were employed on a regular basis. Indeed Kuhnau's complaint that the ex-pupils of the school were more interested in operatic and coffee-house performances than church music suggests that he expected those singers who remained in Leipzig - presumably as university students - to continue their services. In Bach's time there are records of regular payments to university students and his testimonials for private pupils frequently mention the involvement of the latter in church music (see Wagner 1986, pp. 285, 291-5). Although it must clearly have been necessary to rely on outside help for the maintenance of a high standard of church music, this practice must have weakened the connections between school and church, reflecting a move away from the fostering of general school music towards the cultivation of the more talented pupils.

DISPUTES CONCERNING MUSIC IN CHURCH AND SCHOOL

Of course the history of figural music in the seventeenth century was not without its problems, and a large body of material shows that the more enterprising musical establishments often drew adverse criticism. Friedrich, in his organ dedication of 1610, remarks that the Devil has recently inspired some to advocate the abolition of figural music altogether. The first book of Praetorius' *Syntagma musicum* (1614–15) – an exhaustive study of the use and origins of music in both Old and New Testaments – is designed as a rebuff to those Lutherans who condemned elaborate liturgy and music as inherently papist.

Such criticisms multiply during the Thirty Years War, when many must have viewed music as an irrelevant and expensive luxury. Büttner notes in the introduction to his school music primer of 1625 that many oppose the art of music and that Luther's judgement is here appropriate: 'those contemptuous of the wonderful art of music apparently hear only the grunting of the sow and the cry of the ass'.[26] Nevertheless, as Büttner affirmed, music in schools did serve the purpose of supporting some of the poorer students, particularly in times of need (see p. 14 above). But, given that many saw this as a form of beggary, they doubtless felt that the practical musician was essentially a craftsman, lacking the status of an 'educated man'. Michael's introduction to the second part of his *Musicalische Seelenlust* of 1637 states categorically that music has suffered more changes in fortune during the recent years than virtually any other art or discipline.[27] Music is constantly being denigrated as a profession:

Because enough contrary-minded people and libertines have arisen, who will begrudge both music and those who cultivate it . . . a bite of bread, not to speak of respect. On the contrary, because one can neither fill one's purse with it, nor still hunger and thirst with it, and because it is a useless and inefficient art, while not a harmful one, they take pains to get rid of it and put the money to better use.

Weil genugsam widrige Köpffe und Wüstlinge auffgestandē / welche / weder der Music noch ihren *cultoribus* . . . einigen Bissen Brodt / geschwiege dann einen *Respect* gegönnet / Ja vielmehr / weil man weder den Beutel damit füllen / noch Hunger und Durst darmit stillen könte / dieselbe / wo nicht gar als eine schädliche / doch als eine unnütze untüchtige Kunst abzuschaffen / die Kosten auff was bessers . . . zu wenden / sich bemühet.

(T. Michael, *Musicalische Seelen-Lust* II, 1637, preface to Quinta vox)

Given the high regard in which the Leipzig Thomasschule and its musical achievements were held during the Baroque period, it is likely that this downturn in Michael's fortunes was the result of the temporary pressures of war. However, it does show that music was not sufficiently grounded in society to endure well in a time of dire need. Moreover, even Schütz – writing from the relative security of the Dresden court – notes the appalling decline of music in recent years in the prefaces to the *Kleine geistliche Concerte* of 1636 and the *Symphoniae Sacrae* II of 1647.

Even in the latter part of the century Georg Falck remarks in the introduction to his *Idea boni cantoris* 1688 that the youth in school were disinclined to study music if they knew that they would not continue to make a profession of it (Falck 1688, foreword). As Pastor Sebastian Kirchmajer adds in his foreword to the same publication, 'Most people love and learn gladly only those arts which adorn and fill the purse, or which otherwise bear profit.'[20] Gradenthaller 1687 gives an enormous introduction on the historical importance of music (including relatively recent figures, the emperors Charlemagne, Ferdinand III and the contemporary Leopold I) as a rebuff to those who oppose educating the youth in music, and who shrink from allowing their children to learn it. As Furhmann wrote in the introduction of his practical treatise (1706, p. 5), people of high status often believed that music was bad for their reputations.

Some church and school officials regarded the new Italianate figural style as detrimental to the cultivation of monophony. As early as 1605 the rector of the Kreutzschule in Dresden remarked that not a single note of *Choral* had been sung in the last half year (Preussner 1924, p. 441), which implies that the cantor was spending too much time on the more elaborate figural music. Kalb has observed that orthodox Lutheran theologians of the seventeenth century never fully addressed the implications of the 'new Italian style' and judged music – on the whole favourably – on the assumption that it was still the Flemish polyphony beloved of Luther and his generation.[29] Nevertheless, there is a case for suggesting that the new styles did indeed retrospectively fulfil some of Luther's claims and desires regarding music (see p. 12 above); complaints within orthodoxy obviously centred around the secularisation that might result from the expansion of personnel and musical ambitions within the cantorate.[30]

The most vicious outbursts against elaborate music came in the last decades of the seventeenth century with the growth of the Lutheran Pietist movement: this eschewed traditional liturgy and elaborate music.[31] In Freiberg the rector complained of trumpets and drums destroying the Sabbath and the superintendent warned that figural music was driving out the German songs (Krickeberg 1965, p. 89), the simplicity and directness of which was so important to the Pietists.

26   Music education and the art of performance

The pamphlet wars of this period are testimony to the depth of the passions aroused. The most vitriolic attack on music came from J. Muscovius, first pastor and inspector of the churches and schools in Lauben, in his *Bestraffter Mißbrauch der Kirchen-Music* 1694. Immediately evident in Muscovius's tract is his desire for the simple Pietism of the early church. In the spirit of the early Enlightenment he desires to understand the New Testament texts in their true, 'original' meanings. He believes that problems of understanding are the fault of men, not of the Holy Scripture itself:

It is not the Holy Scripture in and of itself that is dark and difficult but the spoiled human understanding which is made incapable, dim and difficult through sin, which always adheres to us and makes us sluggish in our perception of that which belongs to God's spirit. . . . One should look so much more for the purpose that an author has decided on, than at the mere words, which can be forced and misinterpreted against the author's intention . . . if one wishes to understand an author correctly, one must look into what caused him to have spoken about this or that.

Nicht die Heil. Schrifft / an und vor sich selbst ist dunckel und schwer / sondern der verderbte Menschliche Verstand ist untüchtig / dunckel und schwer durch die Sünde / so uns immer anklebet / und träge macht / zu vernehmen / was des Geistes GOttes ist . . . Man so vielmehr auff den Zweck sehen / der ihn ein *Autor* hab vorgenommen / als auff die blossen Worte / selbige wieder des *Autoris* Meinung zu nöhtigen und außzudeuten . . . wenn man einen *Autorem* recht verstehen wil / so muß man auff die Ursachen sehen / umb welcher Willen er dieses oder jenes geredet hat.   (Muscovius 1694, pp. 11–12)

The matter is therefore one of accurate and historically appropriate interpretation, something which shows the Pietists to have been progressive in intellectual thought. Clearly music, which – by the very ambiguity of its exegetical properties – could cloud the 'authentic' meaning of Scripture, would be eschewed (even if, to some, it rendered the text more affectively immediate).

Predictably, Muscovius observes that instrumental music is not mentioned in the New Testament and that this doubtlessly reflects the practice of the early Christians (p. 17).[32] However, the thesis of his argument is not the total abolition of music but rather the curbing of its misuse; indeed he claims to hold vocal and instrumental music – if used correctly – in far higher regard than do the musicians themselves.[33] Clearly, he believes music to have an affective power if he affirms that music which is serious, respectable and fine makes the people likewise serious and moves them to penitence.[34]

What Muscovius detests is the florid, 'frivolous' nature of modern music which renders the text incomprehensible. His vivid commentary gives an interesting insight into the music and performance of his time. In a passage referring to Aristotle's prescription of music which leads only to virtue and good morals, he conjectures:

How would this heathen judge the church music of Christians today, if, in the gathering of the simple congregation – as often happens, especially on high feasts – he were to hear nothing more than laughing: now one of them makes a coloratura or a trill thereby shredding the text; now a small boy therein whimpers or crows like a cockerel; now the whole company cries together like hunters at the hunt; now among them there is yet fiddling, now reed-blowing, drumming and thundering, and in multifarious fashions all is therein scorned and rushed, so that one cannot perceive a word of the text and does not know what has been roared and ridiculed.

Was würde wohl dieser Heyde von der itzigen Kirchen-Music der Christen urtheilen / wenn er / wie offt / sonderlich an hohen Festen / in der gantzen Versamlung der einfältigen Gemeine / nichts mehr hörete / als ein Gelächter / da bald einer durch Zerreissung des Textes daher *coloraturiret* / oder drüllert / bald ein kleiner Knabe drein winselt / oder wie ein Hähnlein krähet / bald der gantze Hausse / wie die Jäger auff der Jagt / zusammen schreyet / darunter noch bald gefiedelt / bald geschalmeyet / bald gepaucket / bald gedrommetet / und auff mancherley Art drein gehönet und gesauset wird / daß man vom *Textu* kein Wort vernimmet / und nicht weiß / was gebrauset und ausgelachet worden.
(Muscovius 1694, p. 30)

Muscovius cites various classical precedents (notably the Spartans) to justify his puritanical bent, yet he also advocates a direct, personal approach in worship to replace the 'dead pipes' and 'artful voice-mongers'.[35] Above all, music should be used only in so far as it is understandable and in accordance with reason. His extensive complaints about the use of Latin in the liturgy also reflect his concern for comprehension and are likewise grounded in the practice of the early Christians; for instance St Paul always celebrated services in the mother tongue (p. 65). Moreover, he agrees with those who complain that they cannot join in with the music and who would dearly love to sing German songs slowly and devoutly with the organ.[36]

The Pietist position on music was also clearly outlined by the rector of the Gotha *Gymnasium*, G. Vockerodt, in his *Mißbrauch der freyen Künste* of 1697, a defence of his report on a school inspection written the previous year. This had outlined the dangers of the misuse of music, drawing on the rather disturbing examples of Nero, Claudius and Caligula. J. C. Lorber, the court poet at Weimar, responded with the obvious example of Luther's devotion to music (1697), while J. Beer of the Weissenfels court responded with a stinging attack on Vockerodt's logic, showing the absurdity of his underlying argument. For instance: 'What has harmed Caligula, Claudius and Nero must harm all leaders. Now, music, dancing and comedies harmed Caligula, Claudius and Nero; therefore music, dancing and comedies harm all leaders.'[37]

Vockerodt responded with the express intention of showing that he was not a 'Music-Feind' and that it was in the misuse of music, particularly in the theatre, that the danger lay. Indeed he claimed that the standard of music had improved in the school since he had become rector; he had been diligent in ensuring a fair division of the money earned by the choir ('Chor-Geld'), he had restored two subsidiary singing lessons per week that had formerly been dropped, he had arranged instrumental lessons, and had himself been well-practised in vocal and instrumental music since his youth (Vockerodt 1697, pp. 12–13). Vockerodt's prescription for the justified use of music is a useful summary of the Pietist position: the musician should perform from the heart, and in such a way as to inspire devotion in the listener; he should perform spiritual Lieder, psalms and songs of praise, which spread the word of Christ; he should not perform so much for the applause of men as for the fear and love of God, scorning the world and all vanity; he must use the art not for any worldly pleasure but only for the praise of God and the betterment of those who hear him; he should live a holy, goodly and God-fearing life and not misuse the tongue with which he praises God (Vockerodt 1697, pp. 22–3).

Despite his respect for music and claims that he was not starting a Pietistic inquisition (p. 17), some of Vockerodt's arguments – grounded in the simplicity of the practice of the early church – are remarkably similar to Muscovius's:

Afterwards, however, irrational worship gained the upper hand in Catholic lands, and finally in Germany too, they sing more in Latin than in German, more often colourful and curly coloratura, than understandable and edifying songs

Nachdem aber gleichwol der unvernünfftige Gottesdienst im Pabstthum überhand genommen / und endlich auch in Teutschland mehr Lateinisch als Teutsch / öffters bundte und krause *coloratu*ren / als verständliche und erbauliche Lieder gesungen worden (Vockerodt 1697, p. 24)

What angered Vockerodt in particular was the fact that various boys had played in public dances and consorted with the *Stadtpfeiffer*, wasting the time allotted to attending to God's word, lessons and the Catechism, by copying out parts to 'Quodlibeten' (pp. 14–15). Given that this sort of attitude was prevalent, Muscovius may have been justified in doubting the devotion of the specialised musicians in church, particularly since he observed that musicians frequently left the church during the sermon.[38] Significantly, Megerle (using material from Abraham à Sancta Clara – a Catholic writer) notes, in the enormous compendium of the various professions, crafts and trades, *Etwas für Alle* (vol. II, 1711), that many singers are hardly angels and sing, instead of the *Gloria Patri*:

Glory be to me, my song and my voice; you are merely men *in principio* and remain fools *in saecula saeculorum Amen*.

Ehre sey mir / meinem Gesang / und meiner Stimm; ihr seyd halt Menschen *in principio*, und bleibt Thoren *in saecula saeculorum Amen*. (Megerle 1711, p. 139)

All this suggests that it is unwise to assume that all church musicians of the Baroque period were inspired to pursue their art by an uncontrollable religious fervour. Indeed, while the florid style had flourished on the bedrock of a particular religious motivation which viewed music with favour, many of the more talented musicians probably cultivated their art as an end in itself.

It is often a matter of contention as to whether one or other writer or musician should be labelled a 'Pietist', but it is clear that many prominent musicians were inspired by the Pietistic zeal for cleansing music of its abuses. J. G. Ahle quotes Muscovius's scornful portrayal of the whining, coloratura-grinding boy in his second edition of his father's vocal primer (Ahle 1704, p. 82). While his writings in general suggest that he was not entirely averse to elaborate music and vocal diminution, it does seem that he may have been influenced by the Pietist cause, particularly since he lived in Mühlhausen, where there was a notorious pulpit war between Orthodox and Pietist pastors (see Sevier 1974, pp. 26–9). It was here that his successor, J. S. Bach, experienced opposition to elaborate church music, and was soon to resign because he was not able to compose a 'well-regulated church music' (*Bach-Dokumente* I, p. 19; David and Mendel 1945/1972, p. 60).

Kuhnau was certainly an orthodox Lutheran as a churchman, composer and writer, but he shared with the Pietists a distaste for ostentatious theatrical music (something which is elegantly stressed in his satirical novel *Der musicalische Quacksalber*, 1700). It was undoubtedly his musical conservatism and strict views on decorum in church that lost him many performers to Telemann's New Church choir during the first decade of the eighteenth century (see Schering 1926, p. 192, and p. 22 above). Significantly, the cantor in Hamburg at this time, J. Gerstenbüttel (a cantor of the traditional, academic type), experienced similar problems, since he too disapproved of the opera and modern theatrical music (Krüger 1933, p. 225). Although the disapproval of these conservative figures might have something in common with the Pietist movement, their attitude more probably derives from the distinction made in German compositional theory between music for church, chamber and theatre (most clearly articulated by Bernhard and surviving in the writings of Werckmeister and Mattheson). In other words, while the concept of differentiated musical styles was still consciously pursued by many composers and theorists, music was becoming more autonomous with an emerging aesthetic dimension that rendered the functional categorisation irrelevant. Certainly the entry on church music in Zedler's *Lexicon* suggests that some composers wrote the same type of music, whatever the purpose:

And it is very bad when those composers who, in order to show their particular skilfulness in the invention of all sorts of cultivated and agreeable singing manners, perform at the public services pieces of a kind that are better suited to the theatre or dance-place than to so holy a place and such holy matters.

Und ist es von denenjenigen Componisten sehr übel gehandelt, welche um nur ihre besondere Geschicklichkeit in Erfindung allerhand künstlicher und angenehmer Singe-Arten zu zeigen, auch bey dem öffentlichen GOttes-Dienste dergleichen Stücke aufführen, die sich entweder besser auf das Theatrum oder auf den Tantz-Platz, als an eine so heilige Stäte, und zu so heiligen Handlungen schicken. (Zedler, vol. XXII, 1739, p. 1,466)

Another area in the dispute over music concerns the authority of the cantor within the school hierarchy. It is already clear that some school rectors must have held the cantors to blame for many of the abuses, if Vockerodt's testimony is anything to go by. Furthermore, given that music no longer had such a strong academic standing in the school, many academically minded rectors felt threatened by the 'extramural' appeal of the *Cantorei*. Scheidt's experiences at the Marktkirche in Halle are especially illuminating: the city created the new office of *Director Musices* in 1628, a post independent of the *Gymnasium* but one which involved the recruiting of choirboys from the school body; Scheidt's acrimonious disputes with the school's rector led to his resignation in 1630.[39]

One particular element of the school organisation which inevitably led to conflict was the fact that many boys were financially supported in the school through their musical activities; thus some rectors were envious of the power that the cantor consequently wielded in the selection process. Even in 1614 the learned cantor of Leipzig, Seth Calvisius, found that the boys he had accepted on musical grounds were turned down by the rector (Wustman 1909, p. 91). Nevertheless, the Leipzig Thomasschule ordinance of 1634 states categorically that musical boys over the age of twelve are to be given priority in admission to the school, regardless of their other achievements.[40] Less experienced boys may be admitted, but if they do not make improvements they should be dismissed by a certain time so that they do not deny the place to a more musical boy.[41]

The most illuminating picture of the tensions between rector and cantor is given by the tract *Directorium musicum* (1706) by J. P. Bendeler, the cantor of Quedlinburg. The foreword suggests that there have recently been conflicts so intense that the entire staffs of schools have been disrupted by hate, distrust and constant disharmony; Bendeler's intention is to settle the disputes by use of reasoned argument. He begins with the affirmation that whoever is responsible for a particular matter is also the head of the same; therefore reason dictates (whether the logic is that of the Christians, Jews, Turks or heathen) that the cantor is the head of music and not the rector.[42] After all, he adds, the rector has absolutely no jurisdiction over the organists and other church musicians (over whom the cantor traditionally had precedence).

In the best of rhetorical traditions, much of Bendeler's tract comprises counter-arguments which he then proceeds to demolish. The first counter-argument affirms that the rector is the head of the pupils. Bendeler retorts that the head of the school has nothing to do with the church music or its practice; only in the conduct of the 'ordinary' singing lessons is the cantor subservient to the rector, since these belong to the school curriculum. This clearly demonstrates the break between music as an official subject in school and the cultivation of school choirs for the church liturgy. Bendeler argues that the pupils belong to the rector only when they fall within his jurisdiction. If indeed he does give music lessons, these are the only occasions for which he has musical authority.[43] Evidently some rectors were still versed in music, as in the early days of the Reformation era when the cantorate was still an academic post and many teachers taught music to a certain level; the example of Vockerodt also points to the later survival of musically informed rectors (see p. 28 above).

Another sign of the division between school and church music is the fact that in small places the director of music must take people from outside the school into the church choir: e.g. cobblers, tailors or linen-weavers. Bendeler rhetorically asks: if these people are the leaders of their professions should not the cantor be answerable to them too, just as he is answerable to the rector as head of the school profession? (Bendeler, p. 6). Surely the case is like that of the town officials and Bürgermeister, who, in the matter of hunting, must submit to the hunting-master.

32   Music education and the art of performance

The next matter for dispute is the distribution of 'Chor-geld', the money which the students earn from their church service. It appears – and the testimony of Vockerodt substantiates this (see p. 28 above) – that rectors were often responsible for dividing the money, but Bendeler retorts that it is the cantor who is responsible for church music and thus for the remuneration. Regarding the admission of boys to the choir, Bendeler outlines the practice at Quedlinburg:

When a pupil wishes to join the choir, he registers himself with the rector and with the cantor, and if they consider him capable and necessary, he is admitted; if not, he is turned away or put off until another time.

Wann ein Schüler in den Chor will / so meldet er sich bey dem Herrn *Rectore*, und bey dem *Cantore*, erachten ihn dieser tüchtig und nöthig / wird er eingenommen / wo nicht / wird er abgewiesen / oder biß auf andere Zeit vertröstet.   (Bendeler 1706, pp. 8–9)

Therefore it does seem that the rector had some authority in admitting boys to the choir in the first place, but Bendeler implies that the cantor's prerogative in dividing the money earned by the choir gives him effective control over the pupils and indeed over the intake of the school itself, particularly in the case of pupils who come from outside the town.[44] Bendeler also vehemently insists that the rector cannot appoint prefects (i.e. boys who had extra authority in the choir) since the cantor must be assured of their capacity in music, so that they can deputise for the cantor in emergencies.[45] Thus with the increasing specialisation of the cantor, the rector's 'general musicianship' could no longer be trusted. That the church singers were regarded as semi-professionals is suggested by Bendeler's use of the term *Concertisten* for those who are taken by the cantor and instructed towards the 'concert'.[46] Bendeler also shows that the furnishing of the music depends on the cantor's private instruction;[47] conversely the rector has given no special instruction to the pupils and cannot thus demand special greetings or gifts as if he were director of music.

Bendeler tries to give his document an official status by appending three short, favourable responses to his argument by lawyers from Leipzig, Halle and Helmstedt. It is interesting that his discourse is governed by cool reasoning throughout, with no resort to metaphysical or theological arguments. This shows him to be a writer of the early Enlightenment, an age which, ironically, led many to question whether complex music itself – with its rhetorical and quasi-mystical power – was an indispensable part of worship. The examples of Muscovius and Vockerodt also suggest that rationalistic thought tended to associate with a Pietistic theology, something which by its very nature eschewed 'art' music. Bendeler's tract shows the cantor on the defensive, anxious to retain his status within the school, but also concerned to establish himself outside its jurisdiction as *Director Musices* (this term appears regularly throughout his writing), answerable only to the church and its liturgical contingencies. In this light two celebrated disputes in the eighteenth century can be seen in clear perspective: Bach's dispute with the rector J. A. Ernesti of Leipzig during the 1730s (summarised in David and Mendel 1945/1972, pp. 137–49), over the appointment of prefects; the celebrated attack on music in *De vita musica* by the Freiberg rector J. G. Bidermann 1749 (see chapter 6, p. 184 below).

THE NATURE AND PURPOSE OF PRACTICAL MUSIC

The traditional respect for music in the Lutheran tradition, the cultivation of figural music during the seventeenth century, and the reservations and warnings about its misuse, together point to a network of beliefs concerning the nature and essence of music. Clearly this cannot simply be explained in the later eighteenth-century sense as a belief in the autonomous 'sublime' nature of music, since the study and practice of music was still tethered to specific extra-musical functions. In the case of educational establishments, the principal purpose of music was to accompany and disseminate religion; indeed the art might even be described as a mode of religious discourse, one which many considered essential to the quality and integrity of Lutheranism. Thus the beliefs about music and religion itself doubtless shared many metaphysical premises.

The recent writings of Ruhnke, Dammann and Rivera show that seventeenth-century German music theory could be deeply speculative, drawing both on the Pythagorean, mathematical view of music and on more modern elements of rationalist philosophy. Certainly the traditional Mediaeval distinction between the great musician-philosopher and the mere 'practical' musician still pertained (in some minds, at least) during the eighteenth century, if the Bach–Scheibe controversy is representative. Bach's champion, Birnbaum, was particularly critical of Scheibe's use of the word 'Musicant' to describe Bach (David and Mendel 1945/1972, pp. 237–52). On the other hand, Bach's obituary suggests that the composer kept clear of theoretical abstractions *(Bach-Dokumente* III, p. 89; David and Mendel 1945/1972, p. 224), so perhaps Scheibe was indeed applying the correct term. A writer such as the cantor Fokkerodt 1698 insists that the true *Musicus* must be familiar with all aspects of music: its history and origins, the mathematical basis, how to move the affects in the listener, how to sing, play and understand the instruments and how to compose. In all, then, we need to retain a clear distinction between what we generally today describe as musical quality and depth of musical insight (i.e. the aesthetic and structural perspectives by which we often judge the existing repertories) and the concerns of many Baroque theorists. Furthermore, the concepts lying beneath 'practical' music and the act of music-making may only tenuously have been linked with speculative musical thought, even if some writers wrote in both fields; and if those writers did assume a connection – as indeed we may do today – this might disintegrate on closer inspection.

The aim here is to construct some sort of spectrum of musical awareness for performance of the German Baroque: did the more advanced musician steadily acquire a more advanced insight into the nature of music as part of his advancing studies? Were there any changes in the perspective of the practical instruction books during the period under discussion? Obviously a study of the literature will give only a one-sided view of what actually took place in music instruction, since we can never know how the music lessons – public or private – were conducted. However, the similarities between a wide selection of surviving treatises are striking, and allow us to infer, at the very least, the common denominators governing the nature and purpose of music. One particular issue here is that most of the writers of speculative music theory were in fact also practising cantors and organists (e.g. Calvisius, Lippius, Werckmeister). Did they impart their insights to all who performed and studied with them? Or does the fact that most were cantors in the traditional academic sense – and not particularly distinguished composers – mean that their outlooks are not strictly relevant to the performance-perspective of the 'greater' composers?

The entries on 'Musica practica' and 'Musicus practicus' in Zedler's *Lexicon* suggest that, by the early eighteenth century at least, there were two types of *musica practica*: the traditional and frequently despised art of 'mere' practice and a wider, more intelligent discipline:

Music: practical . . . means either, when someone can sing or play without having learned this according to the proper principles, and therefore does not concern himself with this or with the causes of a good effect in the music, or else it is applied, in particular, when someone not only knows the rules of music, but also practises them in singing and on instruments, so that a lovely harmony is awoken and the feelings of the listeners are moved.

Musick: (Practische) . . . heisset entweder, wenn jemand singen oder spielen kan, ohne daß er solches nach ordentlichen Grundsätzen gelernet hätte, und

daher sich um selbige, oder die Ursachen des guten Effects bey der Musick nicht bekümmert; oder es wird dadurch und zwar insonderheit angedeutet, wenn jemand die Regeln der Musick nicht nur verstehet, sondern auch solche im Singen und auf den Instrumenten ausübet, dadurch eine liebliche Zusammenstimmung erwecket wird, um die Gemüther der Zuhörer zu bewegen.
(Zedler vol. XXII, 1739, p. 1,468)

This distinction might reflect the end of a process of change during the German Baroque; the emphasis of musical thought had moved from the theoretical to the practical, so the Mediaeval theoretical-practical distinction was being replaced by the distinction between 'technical' and 'informed' practical musicians. The 'informed' musician needed no longer an abstract, mathematical basis for his musical awareness, rather a 'modern' conception of the psychological implications of music, and, presumably, of the basis of affects within the conventions of harmony and figuration. Towards the end of the seventeenth century there was in German theoretical writings a tendency to place *musica poetica* (i.e. composition) within *musica practica*, something which may have reflected a trend towards more 'informed' performance. Stierlein 1691 even went as far as to unite all three concepts – *musica theorica, practica* and *poetica* – within the same performance treatise. Although his use of the three terms is eccentric in the extreme and barely relates to any other definition, the very corruption might reflect a desire to create, at all costs, the appearance of a fully-informed performer.[48] Although late seventeenth-century writers such as Werckmeister and Fokkerodt suggest that the true *Musicus* is one who is familiar with all three fields of music, their views are clearly more normative than descriptive.

THE DEFINITIONS OF MUSIC

What definition of music would have been impressed on the pupil from the very outset of his musical studies? Immediately striking is the fact that the standard Listenius/Faber definition persists well into the seventeenth century: 'Music is the art (or science) of good singing' – a very simple, if not banal, definition (ultimately derived from Augustine; see Rivera 1980, p. 30) which seems to be aimed at the merely 'technical' rather than 'informed' musician in Zedler's sense. It is to be found in early seventeenth-century primers,[49] and persists in more modern and extensive writings – e.g. Friderici 1618 (last published in 1677); Gengenbach 1626 – although sometimes amplified in a way which may reflect the increasing importance of the effect of music on the listener:

36   Music education and the art of performance

Music is an art which teaches correctly and well how to awake a sound or noise, so that it is dainty and charming to hear.

Musica ist ein Kunste / welche recht / wol / und also einen Schall oder Hall zu erwecken lehret / daß es Zierlich / unnd Lieblich zu hören seye. (Hizler 1628)

The word 'awake' ('erwecken') was also important in Zedler's definition of the 'informed' musician and perhaps reflects a sense of a universal – and humanistic – musical language, one which exists in the nature of sound and humanity (rather than in the abstract) and one which the musician in some sense 'discovers'.

The standard definition persists in primers of the mid seventeenth century,[50] through to the later years.[51] Hoffmann's elaborated definition (1693) reflects a typical attitude of the later Baroque (commonly observed in Bach's title-pages), a Janus-like synthesis of the theocentric with a more modern, humanistic orientation:

Vocal music is an art, attained through multifarious practice, so that one sings correctly and well, primarily to the glory of God and, after that also for the uplifting of the spirit and the delight of men.

Musica vocalis ist eine erlangte Kunst / durch vielfältiges üben / da man fürnemlich zu Gottes Ehren darnach auch zu Auffmunterung der Gemüther / und Ergetzligkeit der Menschen / recht und wol singet. (Hoffmann 1693, p. 1)

Falck (1688) likewise emphasises the secondary, recreational aspect of music, something which helps to refresh the mind exhausted by concentration (see p. 20 above). Speer's definition of 1697 shows similar trends but with a new sense of autonomous art and beauty:

Music is a lovely, beautiful, free art, belonging to the praise of God, in which the sound is most charmingly varied and human hearing enlivened.

Die *Music* ist eine liebliche zu Gottes Lob gehörende schöne freye Kunst / da der Thon auf das anmuthigste verändert / und das menschliche Gehör erquicket wird.   (Speer 1697, p. 1)

Similar 'updated' definitions are found in Beyer 1703; Fuhrmann 1706; Steiner 1728 (a direct copy of Fuhrmann's definition, published in Zurich); indeed relics of it persist in Schmelz 1752 and Kürzinger 1763, both of which come from the Catholic portion of Germany. Feyertag 1695 (p. 1) includes the maxim that whoever sings well, doubly prays.[52] Fuhrmann's definition is particularly interesting in giving the 'updated' definition followed by a *nota bene* to the 'old' simpler definition. His main definition is also more pointedly theological, owing something to Luther's own view of music as a foretaste of heaven:

The role of practical music in education

Music is a *Prelude* to the angelic joy in that world, which is lent from God to man in this world, so that he can daily and industriously praise Him everywhere, thereby serving himself and his neighbour well.

Die Music ist ein *Praeludium* der englischen Freuden in jener Welt / dem Menschen in dieser Welt von GOtt verliehen / ihn dadurch täglich und fleißig allhier zu loben / ihm selbst und dem Nächsten damit recht zu dienen.
(Fuhrmann 1706, p. 33)

The 'old' definition persists in Wesselius (1726), perhaps the last tutor which is strictly in the tradition of the two preceding centuries. The anonymous *Kurze Anweisung* of 1752 poses the traditional question ('What is music?') but defines it more elaborately as an art and science concerning the organisation of beautiful sounds (composition) and their presentation (performance) as a vehicle for God's praise and all virtues.[53]

It is notable that none of these definitions gives much of a sense of the speculative side of music, although affective and aesthetic elements can be inferred.[54] Only J. G. Ahle's fascinating notes (1690) to his father's Faber-influenced treatise (1673) give the beginner a taste of speculative German theory in the style of Lippius and Kircher. He tries to show that the standard definitions are really the upper level of a deeper musical reality, one which is founded on universal mathematical principles. Just as the great scientists of the seventeenth century discovered local laws which they believed would ultimately be linked into a universal theory merely with a little more time and thought, Ahle reflects the belief that music necessarily forms a unity. Science and art belong to a continuum, together with morality and the affections:

Music is a mixed mathematical discipine which concerns the origins, attributes and distinctions of sound, out of which a cultivated and lovely melody and harmony are made, so that God is honoured and praised but mankind is moved to devotion, virtue, joy and sorrow.

Die Musik ist eine vermischte Matematische Wissenschaft / welche handelt von den Ursachen / Eigenschaften / und Unterscheide des Klanges / woraus eine Künst- und liebliche Sangweise und Zusammenstimmung gemachet wird / üm dadurch Gott zu ehren und zu loben / den Menschen aber zur Andacht / zur Tugend / zur Freude / und zur Traurigkeit bewegen.
(Ahle 1690, 'Anmerkungen', p. 1)

Ahle proceeds to explain and elaborate this definition of music with a commentary owing much to Lippius (see Rivera 1980, pp. 30–3). He divides music into external and internal concepts. To the external belongs a hierarchy of causes and purposes: the *efficient cause* (*causa efficiens*) is God, who has ordered everything by mass, number and weight.[55] This phrase – from the apocryphal Book of Wisdom (11:21) – appears very frequently in German theological and musical writings of the seventeenth century. It gives a succinct view of the age, linking as it does Mediaeval theocentric thinking with the new mechanistic universe (see Dammann 1984 pp. 62–5). Ribovius 1638 even includes the familiar reference in an introductory poem: whoever cannot be joyful when the notes are in the correct mass, number and weight?[56]

For Ahle, the *particular efficient cause* (*causa efficiens particularis*) is nature, the mother of sound and the art of the composer.[57] The *intermediate purpose* (*finis intermedius*) is the moving of men towards virtue, moderate joy and 'useful' sorrow,[58] while the *ultimate purpose* (*finis ultimus*) is the honour and praise of God.

To the internal aspect belongs music as a phenomenon (that which has been caused and which, in turn, causes), divided in the classic Aristotelian manner into substance and form: the *substance* is the sound itself, which can be counted or measured ('der Zahl- und maßbare Klang') while the *form* is the song itself, the melody and the sounding together ('der Gesang selbst . . . Melodia & Symphonia').

Ahle does not show clearly how this external/internal definition (a maximal elaboration of the standard Faber/Listenius phrase) coheres with the traditional tripartite definition of music (in German theory, at least) which he discusses next: *musica theorica, poetica* and *practica*. Presumably the first, binary categorisation defines what music is, in terms of its causes, effects and phenomena, while the tripartite definition prescribes the areas of music study, or, rather, three distinct musical professions (theorist, composer and performer). Nevertheless, it is not impossible to construct parallels between the two systems: with regard to the external aspect, the *efficient cause* with its emphasis on number and measurement could be related to *musica theorica*; the *particular efficient cause* with its reference to the art of the composer forms the natural basis of *musica poetica* and the two *purposes* (the moving of the listener and the praise of God) could be related to performance (*musica practica*). Music here is both a rhetoric (also a form of teaching) and an expression of praise.

The intrinsic substance/form view of music as a phenomenon does not immediately seem to relate to one of the three *musica* categories; in some ways it is closer to the modern discipline of musical analysis. Nevertheless, it is clearly that with which composers and performers are most immediately concerned and hence which relates both to *musica poetica* and *musica practica*. Both composer and performer create and recreate the substance and form of music, following its grammar, introducing devices and figures on several levels which connote the affect and sense of the discourse (on the relationship of composer and performer see chapter 5, below).

Ahle is the only writer who overtly discusses these theoretical issues in a specifically practical treatise, but they do emerge incidentally in other writings. Furthermore, Ahle's 'Anmerkungen' were reprinted and expanded in 1704 and at least one other singing treatise recommends them.[59] The remainder of this chapter examines treatises relating to practical music instruction with the following issues in mind: music as a system reflecting cosmic unity and heavenly harmony; music as an affective medium, grounded in the nature of mankind; music as a rhetoric, designed to teach and convince the listener of various theological truths.

THE SPECULATIVE NATURE OF MUSIC

With the horrors of war and the rapid spread of the new Italianate figural style, perhaps most teachers and writers simply did not have time (or did not dare to risk boredom) to impart much of the speculative side of music. Sermons by theologians give the most information on such issues, and although these do not strictly come into the category of teaching manuals, they might reflect the general views of music to which pupils would have been exposed in church and school. Friccius's organ dedication of 1631 shows that musically minded theologians were not slow to link the newly emerging triadic system with the concept of the Trinity. This must have been tantamount to scientific proof of Luther's doctrine that music is the gift of God:

I often wonder at the fact that on the whole keyboard not more than three notes harmonise together; any more are merely octave doublings. Is that not an obvious mystery of the highly-praised Trinity?

Ich wunder mich offt / daß im gantzen *Clavir* nicht meyr als drey *claves* zusammen stimmen / die andern sind lauter *octaven*. Ist das nicht ein augenscheinlich Geheimniß der hochgelobten Dreyfaltigkeit?

(Friccius 1631, p. 35)

Together with the concept of the triad came the view of the bass as the foundation of music. Thus the bass becomes almost a metaphor for the Godly foundation of music, something which was later emphasised in the thoroughbass methods of Werckmeister, Niedt and J. S. Bach:

40   Music education and the art of performance

> The heart is set under the tongue as a majestic, deepest *Bass* which rightly decorates the song with its support; accordingly such devotion of the heart must always accompany the music, if it is to be pleasing in God's ears.
>
> Das Hertz ist der Zungen untersetzter Maiestätischer tieffester *Bass*, welcher zuforderst den Gesang recht zieret / darumb solche Andacht des Hertzens für allen Dingen bey der Music seyn muß / wenn sie in Gottes Ohren angenehm seyn sol.   (Friccius 1631, p. 257)

Throughout his text, Friccius makes allusions to consonance, as a musical unity which mirrors that of heaven and the integrity of the human.[60] As J. C. Hack wrote in a funeral sermon in 1676, the dissonance of the cross and death is restored to order by the Lord Jesus.[61] There is a moral aspect too, since the consonant basis of music is associated with a virtuous life; life should be tuned together with music (Friccius 1631, p. 265). Music is a foretaste of heavenly music which comforts us not only because of its loveliness ('unaußsprechliche Lieblichkeit') but also because of its eternity ('unauffhörliche Wärenheit' – p. 297).[62] Friccius even implies that good music is intrinsically good regardless of text.[63] This intrinsic quality of music might also explain why instrumental music was increasingly permitted in worship. Although Friccius marginally favours texted music, the basic purpose of his sermon was the dedication of an organ. He quite clearly sees music as a system and language that transcends words. Exactly the same point is made by Kuhnau in his introduction to the *Biblische Historien* (1700): instrumental music technically communicates the same affects as vocal music since the mathematical basis is the same for both (see Dammann 1984, p. 364).

Most practical treatises of the seventeenth century omit overt references to the concept of music as a mirror of heavenly unity and harmony, the traditional Pythagorean view of music, inherited from the Middle Ages. Indeed, few introduce protracted mathematical discussion after Schornburg's *Elementa Musica* of 1582 (which includes an extensive exposition of the monochord). One notable exception is Weide 1627, which introduces many speculative elements, including a chapter on the monochord (from which all harmony springs)[64] and frequent references to music as the mirror of the cosmos. Weide follows the structure of the traditional elementary tutor but introduces metaphysical elements at every turn. The seven musical notes relate to the seven days and planets, and the conjunction of Jupiter, Sun and Mercury reflects the 'liebliche *conjunctio*' of 'C.ut E.mi G.sol' (ch. 3). Moreover Weide relates each interval to equivalent numbers in nature and metaphysics. The final chapter reads like an extensive sermon demonstrating the relationship between the harmony of music and the cosmos of which God is the centre.

Erhardi 1660 must have considered the link between music and mathematics important if he included a *Rudimenta Arithmetica* (by Hirtzwigius Redivivus) at the end of his practical tutor. Although he states that music and arithmetic are foremost among the seven liberal arts, his efforts to show that the two are closely related are contrived in the extreme: the five species of arithmetic (counting, adding, subtracting, multiplication and division) correspond to the five principles of singing (the traditional sixteenth-century headings of *claves, voces, cantus, mutatio, figurae*).

MUSIC AND THE AFFECTS

Treatises concerned with musical performance are considerably more productive with regard to the natural, affective basis of music. But such information is usually only to be found in those writings which sponsor a more modern repertory, music which presupposes an expressive approach to performance. Praetorius 1619 makes the first serious effort to import the 'new Italian style' and, although his 'Instructio pro Symphoniacis' was clearly intended for the use of the teacher rather than the pupil, it is likely that pupils of this time would have sensed the need to move the affect:

Thus a musician should not only sing, but sing with particular artifice and grace; so that the heart of the listener is stirred and the affect moved, and therefore the song may attain the purpose to which it is made and to which it is directed.

Also ist eines Musicanten nicht allein singen / besondern Künstlich und anmütig singen: Damit das Hertz der Zuhörer gerühret / und die *affectus* beweget werden / und also der Gesang seine Endschafft / dazu er gemacht / und dahin er gerichtet / erreichen möge. (Praetorius 1619, p. 229)

Several points are interesting here: first, the *affectus* is described almost in mechanistic terms. It is not merely a matter of the heart being stirred but also the affect being moved. Secondly, Praetorius uses the term *Musicant* rather than the more honourable *Musicus*. This suggests that the relatively uninformed musician (i.e. the boy) can learn a system of musical expression and decoration without having to learn about the wider metaphysical basis (see also chapter 5). Thus the moving of the affects is more or less a mechanical process, requiring little more than an 'instruction book' to be set in motion.

The basic primers – their opening definitions notwithstanding – tend to concentrate more on elementary notation. Most advice on performance style is of a very rudimentary kind:

42   Music education and the art of performance

To what is one who wishes to sing correctly further required to pay attention? . . .
To match a sad voice to a sad text and a joyful voice to a joyful text.

Was ist ferner nötig von einem / der da recht singen wil / in acht zu nehmen? . . .
Daß er zu einem trawrigen Text eine trawrige / und zu einem frolichen eine
fröliche uñ liebliche Stimme bequeme.   (Demantius 1632)

It is quite interesting that one much-published primer which does contain a great deal of detailed practical advice (Friderici 1618) gives virtually no description of the affects or advice as to how to stir them. Bernhard, in an 'advanced' treatise which was widely transmitted in manuscript (c.1649), implies that there was a distinction between two types of non-ornamented singing: plain, even singing, which is the foundation of all other kinds (*cantar sodo*) and singing which took into account the affect of the words (*cantar d'affetto*). Likewise Feyertag 1695 (p. 234) suggests that singing according to the words is a specific style ('*Moderi*ren'). Certainly Schütz had a remarkably low opinion of choral institutions, if the preface of his *Historia, der Freuden- und Gnadenreichen Geburth Gottes und Marien Sohnes* 1664 is anything to go by: he did not publish the concerted choral sections, partly because they would hardly achieve the requisite effect 'outside the well-appointed royal courts'.[65] Even as late as 1647 (*Symphoniae sacrae* II) – some thirty years after Praetorius's celebrated treatise on Italianate performance – Schütz notes that many establishments still had little idea of the contemporary Italian style; indeed he even asserts that many Germans were unfamiliar with the black notation of modern Italian music. Nevertheless, given that even the most elementary primers describe the smaller note values, it may well be that Schütz actually underestimated the level of musical awareness in church and school music.

It seems then that many less advanced singers, and perhaps even many respected establishments as a whole, sang in a manner which was not influenced by the 'modern' affective view of music. As is implied by the majority of the sixteenth-century treatises, the pupil's main concern was to learn to read music and sing; the unspoken 'meaning' of the music presumably lay in its existence as a God-given harmony.

Sermons and the teaching of theologians might have been more significant in giving the young pupil some idea of the affective basis of music. Friccius's sermon is, as ever, quite productive in this regard. He relates God's order to nature, suggesting that the pleasing effect of music is both divinely and naturally based:

It is implanted in man so that an apt harmoniousness and lovely singing above all are agreeable to him.

The role of practical music in education

Es ist dem Menschen also eingepflanzet / das ihme eine *apta modulatio*, und lieblich Singen für allen dingen annemblich ist. (Friccius 1631, pp. 55–6)

To him music seems almost to be a form of natural regulation: the entire disposition is led and regulated by music.[66] In a manner far more explicit than Praetorius, Friccius suggests that there is a mechanical relation between the movements of the heart and the affect in music:

For there divine music is a Godly act: there its song and sound is a heart-bell, which penetrates every little vein of the heart and its affects (be a man a very Stoic or an immovable trunk).

Traun da ist die *Musica divinum quiddam* ein Göttliches Thun: Da ist ihr Gesang und Klang eine Hertz-glocke / welche /. . . alle Hertzenäderlein durchdringet / und desselben *Affectus* (es sey den der Mensch gar ein *Stoicus* und unbeweglicher *Truncus*) erwecket.[67] (Friccius 1631, p. 90)

The latter parts of Friccius's sermon read rather like a medicine book, the section on the 'Use' of music describing all the things that music can do, from banishing the Devil to curing illness, enlivening oneself for battle and turning away danger and misfortune (*Ibid.*, pp. 168–80). In all, this (published some twenty years before Kircher's *Musurgia Universalis*) is a vivid picture of an age when the theological, the natural and the superstitious seem to live side by side; science taught men to look for order in everything, even if this required a little imaginative invention.

The theologians' belief in the affective and moral power of music is made particularly explicit in the fears expressed by the Pietists (see p. 27 above). They see music as a gift from God which is easily abused since it has such a powerful influence over people (a parallel with sexual morality is hard to ignore here). Vockerodt makes a point of linking the strong affective categorisation of Greek modal theory to the modern musical forms: to him the Lydian mode is represented by the Sarabande, Folie d'Espagne, sonatas, toccatas, ricercars and the *stylus phantasticus* (Vockerodt 1697, p. 41).

Turning to writings of the early eighteenth century it is clear that the affective view of music was now entirely absorbed into musical culture. If some establishments still held to conservative 'pre-affective' views of performance (and the following chapters will show that this was indeed the case) they are represented only in the smaller portion of the surviving literature. Scheibel's remarks suggest that the church performers of his time were quite well aware of the affective dimension of music. In his opinion the musicians of the day were far more competent in this regard than those of some two centuries before:

At the time of the Reformation, Zwingli wanted church music in particular to be abolished; I believe though that were he to have lived in our time, now that musicians have understood the doctrine of the affects better, he would have judged differently. In his time music was still in a sorry state; small wonder that it could not have pleased everyone.

Zur Zeit der *Reformation* hat *Zwinglius* sonderlich die Kirchen-Music abgeschafft wissen wollen / ich glaub aber / wenn er zu unsrer Zeit hätte leben sollen / da die Musici besser die Lehre von den Affecten eingesehen / er würd anders geurtheilt haben. Zur selbigen Zeit war die Music noch gar schlecht bestellet / was wunder daß sie auch nicht jedem gefallen könnte. (Scheibel 1721, p. 8)

During the early eighteenth century librettists such as E. Neumeister encouraged composers to adopt wholesale the dramatic forms of modern Italian opera. Ironically the older, seventeenth-century style of composition which tended to follow directly every twist and turn of the text, might seem more immediately 'affective' than the stylised da capo forms of Italian opera. But perhaps the orthodox reformers – in direct reaction to the Pietists – considered that the modish secular forms would have more contextual appeal for the congregations; the very familiarity of the fashions would have led the listener immediately to the 'correct' affect. There might even have been Pietist support for some of Neumeister's reforms: Ahle, the organist at Mühlhausen whose opinions seem partly to have been influenced by the Pietists, asks why composers do not use the *stylus recitativus*, since this suits the words so perfectly.[68] Scheibel's prescriptions point to a larger movement which aimed to counteract the conservative style of much church music:

I always think that if our church music today were to be a little more lively and freer, *c'est à dire*, more theatrical, it would be of more use than the forced compositions that one usually uses in church.

Ich denck aber immer / weñ unsre Kirchen-Music heut zu Tage ein wenig lebhafftiger und freyer / *c'est a dire*, mehre *theatra*lisch wäre / sie würde mehr Nutzen schaffen / als die gezwungne *Composition*, der man sich in der Kirchen *ordinair* bedienet. (Scheibel 1721, p. 39)

Ruetz remarks in 1750 that the entire style of church music had changed during his age, much to its greater advantage and reception.[69] A similar observation is made by Bach in his famous 'Entwurff' of 1730: modern taste had dictated a style that was greatly different from that which was current during his youth, and this required more of the performers.[70] It is in the early eighteenth century that *taste* becomes an explicit element of musical quality, something which is often borne out by some of the performance treatises:

What are the graces in music? As it were the ornaments. But given that they are for the most part dependent on good taste, one can give no general rule about them

Was sind die Manieren in der Music? Gleichsam die Zierrathen. Da sie aber meistentheils von einem guten Geschmack abhangen, so kann man keine allgemeine Regul darüber geben (Kürzinger 1763, p. 32)

If some of these later remarks imply a more relativistic stance to musical affect – i.e. the affective nature of music is not so much absolute as conditioned by the listener's experience, era and environment – this point is made explicit in Zedler's *Lexicon*:

However, it cannot be doubted that from the differences of sound that excite someone through music, various feelings happen by means of hearing, which, according to [one's] disposition, give the opportunity for differentiated mental images, through which the mind or the will is affected in various ways, so that it experiences either a joy or a sadness.

So ist auch dieses ausser Zweiffel, daß nach dem Unterscheid des Klangs, den iemand durch die Music erreget, unterschiedene Empfindungen durch das Gehör geschehen, welche nach der Disposition des Gemüths Gelegenheit zu unterschiedenen Imaginationen geben, wodurch denn das Gemüth, oder der Wille auf verschiedene Art afficiret wird, daß es entweder eine Freude, oder Traurigkeit darüber hat. (Zedler, vol. XXII, 1739, p. 1,393)

Zedler continues to observe that each person is moved especially by a particular type of music, or a particular song, which does not affect others to such an extent. Nevertheless, some physical problems do seem to be alleviated through sound, such the bite of a tarantula which is cured with a particular type of music. Although it is probable that this somehow affects the soul, the manner and means remain hidden (an admission which could hardly have been made a few decades earlier):

Of these [manner and means], only some are documented with the names of sympathy, of magnetism; but others are ascribed to the world-spirit or also to a certain intertwining of ideas, which however are disguises for ignorance, so one does best if one regards this as a secret of nature, and freely recognises one's ignorance.

Dahero einige dieses nur mit dem Namen der Sympathie, des Magnetismi belegen; andere aber dem Welt-Geist zuschreiben, oder auch einer gewissen Verknüpffung der Ideen, welches aber Deckmäntel der Unwissenheit sind, da man am besten thut, wenn man dieses für ein natürliches Geheimniß ansiehet, und darinnen seine Unwissenheit frey bekennet. (*Ibid.*)

Even a composer as conservative as Kuhnau, writing in the introduction to his *Biblische Historien* of 1700, acknowledges that the affect of a piece of music might vary from listener to listener. While certain elements – consecutive perfect consonances, the affective difference between major and minor – relate to affective states in a manner which is apparently mathematically certain, much also depends on the humour of the hearer. Kuhnau included a verbal programme for each sonata in order to clarify affective and narrative gestures which could be interpreted in several ways. As the Leipzig poet Gottsched was later to say: 'Music alone lacks a soul and is incomprehensible if it does not hold on to words, which, as it were, must speak for it; so that one would know what it means to say.'[71]

From all this one can conclude that the seventeenth-century belief in a certain and stable connection between musical events and affective states was breaking down. Furthermore, fashion and taste seemed now to be playing a particular part in all music, church music in particular undergoing a 'modernisation'. For a time this state of affairs was a necessary condition for some of the greatest church music of all time, the cantatas, oratorios and masses of J. S. Bach, but to do this, music as a whole had forfeited its claim to represent a God-given order and a certain control over the souls of men. With music as an autonomous, aesthetically based art, it was only a matter of time before its role in church and education became a matter of luxury rather than necessity.

MUSIC AND RHETORIC

Finally we turn to considerations of the rhetorical nature of music in practical treatises. On the surface it might seem that questions of rhetoric should have been discussed within the context of the affective nature of music. After all, rhetoric is the art of persuasion, a system of devices by which the affect is moved and the text presented in a convincing and moving way. However, there are differences here: first, the performer is so much more immediately concerned with issues of rhetoric, for he must play the part of orator to bring out and embellish the affects ready-coded within the notated music. Secondly, many of the practical sources imply that the spirit of rhetoric was sometimes developed separately from a consideration of the text and its concomitant emotions. In other words, rhetoric could also be interpreted in its second traditional sense, as a system of ornament rather than persuasion.[72]

Just as with considerations of theology and affect, we cannot trust that allusions to rhetoric in vocal primers alone constituted the pupils' knowledge of the art. Indeed rhetoric was an important element of education, one of the three practical arts of the Mediaeval *trivium* and

The role of practical music in education   47

one which had received a significant boost with the rediscovery of important rhetorical treatises during the Renaissance (in particular, that of Quintilian). The German theorist who did most to make rhetoric an integral part of *musica poetica* (the birth of rhetorical and analytical thinking conveniently coinciding with the expressive revolution of the Italian Baroque) was Burmeister. As an active teacher and cantor he also wrote a book which includes issues of performance in 1601 (*Musica autoschediastike*). This contains several references to the need for the singer to portray the content of the song. Some of the terms he uses (e.g. *ornatus* and its subdivision *gestus* – how to hold the body appropriately for what is to be expressed) show a direct application of rhetorical thinking (see Ruhnke 1955). But there is nothing of the systematic musical analysis (whether prescriptive or descriptive) that is evident in Burmeister's composition treatises: clearly the singer is to perform 'as if' he were an orator rather than actually as an orator *per se*. Lippius, in his *Synopsis musicae novae* (1612) shows his desire to encompass all the branches of music by suggesting that the various ornaments used in composition can also be part of the performance practice in order to bring across the aim of the oration:

> Like an artful orator, the musician uses these ornaments to polish his harmonic oration in keeping with the nature of the text and the circumstances of persons, time, place etc., so that he may achieve his aim successfully . . . The bass may proceed slowly, while the other voices may employ apt colorations and a moderate flourish of running passages. In this style ordinary musicians often embellish a basic composition when appropriate, using pleasant elegance like an elaborate scriptural flourish.   (trans. Rivera 1977, p. 49)

> quibus Musicus ut Prudens & Artifex Orator in Oratione suâ Harmonicâ utitur expolienda juxta Textum & Circumstantias Personarum, temporum, locorum & c. adsuum ad suum foeliater obtinendum Finem . . . ut Bassus incedat tardius, reliquis interim Melodiis congruâ colorantibus & moderatè luxuriantibus celeraturâ, quâ tàm saepè in fundamentaritè componendi impingunt plebei, quam suo est loco usurpanda gratâ venustate, sicut vermiculatio scripturam condecorans.   (Lippius 1612, *De Compositione Ornatâ*)

The drawing together of the roles of composer and performer to bring across the sense and affect of the text is symptomatic of the 'new Italian style' itself and is made explicit in Caccini's famous introduction to *Le nuove musiche*, 1602. As Banchieri stated in 1614, in a summary of Cicero's first saying on oratory: 'The supreme orator is a harmonious-sounding man who, in speaking, delights the minds of his listeners and moves them'; he adds that not only does the composer take delight in this, but also singers and listeners (trans. from Cranna 1981, p. 349).[73] Evidently it

48   Music education and the art of performance

would be a mistake to suggest that the rhetorical approach to music was merely a German phenomenon. However it was the Germans who came closest to a codified system.

How do the specifically practical treatises reflect this concern for rhetoric in general music theory? The first description of practical rhetorical performance is in Praetorius's guidelines for singers (1619). Just before the quotation given on p. 41 above, Praetorius states that:

> Just as the task of an *Orator* is not only to decorate an oration with beautiful, charming and lively words, and with wonderful *Figures*, but also to *pronounce* correctly and to *move* the *affect*: in which he now lifts the voice, then lets it sink, now speaks with a powerful, now gentle, now with a full and entire voice: So is it [the task] of a musician not only to sing but to sing with art and charm. Thus is the heart of the listener stirred and the *affect* moved, so that the song may reach its purpose, for which it is made and to which it is directed.
>
> Gleich wie eines *Oratoris* Ampt ist / nicht allein eine *Oration* mit schönen anmutigen lebhafftigen Worten / unnd herrlichen *Figuris* zu zieren / sondern auch recht zu pronuncijren, und die *affectus* zu *moviren*: In dem er bald die Stimme erhebet, bald sincken lesset / bald mit mächtiger und sanffter / bald mit gantzer und voller Stimme redet: Also ist eines Musicanten nicht allein singen / besondern Künstlich und anmütig singen: Damit das Hertz der Zuhörer gerühret / und die *affectus* beweget werden / und also der Gesang seine Endschafft / dazu er gemacht / und dahin er gerichtet / erreichen möge.
>   (Praetorius 1619, p. 229)

Praetorius proceeds with a summary of what is required of a singer to achieve this quality of performance. After possessing the natural qualities of a suitable voice the performer must have a good understanding of the 'science' ('Wissenschafft') of music. This seems to comprise the various ornaments and figures of diminution rather than anything that could lead to a deeper awareness of the harmony or mathematical basis of music. He must know when these are appropriately applied and in what measure; finally he must also understand the text and the written notes. Although in the elaboration that follows there are references to the moving of the affect (e.g. the *exclamatio* – a dotted elaboration accompanied by a raising of the voice – has more *affectus* than a plain semibreve with the same dynamic effect) there is never a direct explanation of which device creates or stills which affect. The 'Doctrina' section is a careful analysis of the various figures of diminution, but there is little indication of how these are to be applied. Clearly one must learn from example rather than by rule; as Praetorius states in the context of the *trillo*: one learns this from others as a bird must learn from its fellows.[74]

The role of practical music in education 49

Praetorius intended to give more exemplification in the third section of this short treatise, the 'Exercitatio', which he never wrote. But one might expect that it would have consisted largely of practical examples similar to those afforded by his contemporaneous publication of sumptuous motets, *Polyhymnia caduceatrix* (1619), where simple and ornamented versions are printed simultaneously (see chapter 5, p. 160 below). By no stretch of the imagination could these embellishments be linked to any affective nature of the words, so it is not surprising that no treatise even attempts to show the performer how to do this. In other words the performer's role as a rhetorician requires the knowledge of a historically specific repertory of ornaments which he learns from example to apply at appropriate places in order to make the music 'more expressive'. But the rhetorical activity of the performer and the rhetorical/affective work of the composer do not necessarily coincide. While Caccini's *Le nuove musiche*, with its exhortation to closer consideration of the text, was influential in Germany (Praetorius himself acknowledges this), it is equally obvious that music was still being developed and elaborated for its own sake and with its own system of expression (related to the judicious application of dissonance). One might then speak of a musical rhetoric or a rhetorical 'flavour' without this necessarily relating to specific verbal and affective communication.

Praetorius's lead is followed by several other major writers of the seventeenth century (see chapter 5). Bernhard's two-part categorisation of singing is quite illuminating (c.1649):[75] the simpler of the two styles is further divided into two, *cantar sodo* and *cantar d'affetto*, only the latter of which takes the affect of the text into account. However he does not directly relate this affective style to his second main type of singing, *cantar passagiato*. Thus the ornamental figures constituting the diminution of *cantar passagiato* are purely musical elaborations. Bernhard's two composition treatises explain such figures in rhetorical terms as 'figures' or licenses to the *prima prattica* conventions of strict counterpoint. Again, then, they point to a form of rhetoric, but one working strictly within musical language (i.e. ornamentation rather than persuasion). Bernhard, in contradistinction to Burmeister or Kircher, does not analyse motets for their musical-verbal rhetoric. Several other writers suggest that Bernhard's distinction between plain and coloured singing was common currency: Gibel, in the foreword to his treatise of 1645, distinguishes between pure and simple singing and that with coloratura which can be learned by more advanced students.[76] Given the enormous barrage of complaints voiced specifically against coloratura during the entire seventeenth century, from clerics, rectors and musicians alike, it is quite clear that many realised that the 'new Italian style' worked as much to the detriment of the text as to its advantage.

This is not to say that Bernhard (and several other writers) never mention the text or its associated affects; but these he relates more to the style of singing and performance: the voice is loud when angry, quiet when grief-stricken; impatience requires haste; love requires bashfulness etc. These points can of course be termed a part of a scheme of rhetoric, but they might more mundanely be described as a simple mimesis common to much of the history of Western music.

Nevertheless, it may be that young singers had more idea about the rhetorical unity of their discourse than the primers would lead one to believe. After all, the conventions of rhetoric suggest that good oratory requires a sense of unity between *inventio*, the basic idea of the text, *dispositio, elaboratio, ornatus/decoratio*, the laying out and development of the idea, and *enunciatio/pronunciatio*, its delivery in performance (for an examination of this terminology, see Forchert 1985/6). This continuity is suggested by J. C. Hack's funeral sermon for the Kapellmeister M. G. L. Agricola in Gotha (1677). He affirms that the *inventio* is important ('wichtig'), the *compositio* must be correct ('richtig'), and the *capell* capable ('tüchtig'). He shows each level is dependent on the others: however good the invention, a poor composer will have little success if he sets a sad text in *b durus* and a joyous text in *b mollis*. Likewise a good composer requires good performers who are industrious ('fleissige'), quiet of heart ('die Stille wird auch bey der Music erfordert; also ist eines Christen Hertz Stille zu GOTT'), and form a capable company ('eine tüchtige Gesellschafft'); finally a quantity of instruments is required, since variety is so important to express the various texts. Given the addressee of Hack's sermon it is likely that at least one person in the musical establishment should have had a sense of the continuity from invention, through composition to performance: the Kapellmeister, Cantor or *Director Musices* himself.[77]

There were thus several views on music, its purpose and essence during the Baroque period, some old, some newer. If music was sanctioned in the church for its (old) role as a mirror of God's order and for its (newer) mechanical influence on the affects – both of which, incidentally, seem to be implied in Luther's own enthusiasm for music – this privilege brought with it various 'abuses' that, to many, upset music's very purpose of interpreting and conveying texts. In the eighteenth century, the newly developed aesthetic sensibility exploited this latent autonomy in music, something which automatically cancelled its privilege as a fundamental of worship and education. The tendency of seventeenth-century philosophy to construct unities in systems of thought and mechanics should not be allowed to detract from the fact that such unity was not necessarily there in practice.

As far as performance is concerned, there was doubtless a wide range of quality, style and insight. Certainly many performers were skilful without having a knowledge about anything outside the field of *musica practica* as a rhetorically-influenced system of musical discourse. Certainly many cantors and organists, as experts in all three fields of *musica*, might also have been skilful performers, perhaps with a 'deeper' interpretative skill. But, despite the existence of such musical polymaths as Lippius and Werckmeister, it is still unclear how the three fields related in practice, both in terms of the rationale for and the quality of performance. The next three chapters will reinforce the view that there were basically two branches of performance thought in the educational environment of the German Baroque: on the one hand, a very conservative approach which taught the basics of notation and fluent reading, but which gave little attention to the style of performance or to its function as affective oratory; on the other, an approach that attempted to assimilate and codify the latest Italian conventions (in both composition and performance). The latter approach can further be divided into two fields which do not, by necessity, interact: first, a compositional and performance style that fosters the affect of the text; secondly, that which cultivates a more autonomous system of ornamentation.

3

The contents, layout and style of instruction books

Any study relating to performance practice is based on primary sources – treatises, letters etc – which either singly or as a group give us some inkling of the context and specifics of historical performance. Problems often arise, though, for we cannot always be sure of the background of the writer concerned, his motives – benign or otherwise – or his relation to his contemporaries. Moreover, we are often equally unsure of the specific musicians to whom he addressed his remarks, or of who actually read his works. In the case of the present study there are certain factors which minimise these problems. First, the treatises concerned are, on the whole, chosen for their express relation to practical music instruction in a specific, semi-standardised education system; most writers belong to this system as practising teachers and musicians. There are sufficient similarities between the works and sufficient instances of direct plagiarism and reprinting to suggest that they offer a realistic picture of musical education and are thus not merely the speculations of a few eccentric cantors. Indeed some writers seem positively to be proud to have drawn their material from important authors; evidently adherence to tradition was often more desirable than originality.[1] On the other hand, it must continually be stressed that the body of surviving literature is no substitute for what actually happened in public and private instruction; at most it offers a trace of what successive musicians and teachers themselves must have read, and – to a lesser and vaguer extent – a summary of what each may have consciously experienced in practice.

School ordinances and records give us some account of the use of certain primers in schools. The ubiquitous Saxon ordinance of 1580, the model for Lutheran education of the time (see p. 4 above), recommends that pupils be taught music as efficiently and quickly as possible. Theoretical material should be kept to a minimum and concise books should be used, specifically Faber's *Compendiolum*, which contains the bare essentials for reading music (Schünemann 1928, p. 101). The student should not longer concern himself with elements that are more theoretical than strictly practical (e.g. church tones and mensural theory, which were rapidly becoming redundant). Finkel's study of education in the Palatinate shows that Listenius's *Rudimenta musicae* was used in several schools into the seventeenth century (Finkel 1978, pp. 179, 240–2); other books included Faber (*ibid.*, p. 331; Finkel 1973, pp. 191, 200), Lossius 1590 (Finkel 1978, p. 240) and a direct derivative of Listenius, Stenger 1635 (*ibid.*, pp. 182, 280, 331; Finkel 1973, pp. 197, 300). Salmen's study of Westphalia likewise shows that Listenius was specified on ordinances (Salmen 1963, p. 188). Library catalogues are also often of use: the library of the Thomasschule in Leipzig contained two copies of Faber, two of Calvisius and copies of treatises by Agricola and Orgosinus at some point during the seventeenth century (Schering 1926, pp. 56–7); furthermore, Kuhnau's copying of Bernhard's manuscript singing treatise (c.1649) implies that this may have influenced his teaching during the early years of the eighteenth century (*ibid.*, p. 64). Another indication of the transmission of these books is the remarkable number of reprintings that many enjoyed.[2]

While it is well known that most of the major writers were active as cantors and Kapellmeisters,[3] the title pages of primers by lesser-known authors show that many of the latter were also practising cantors who addressed their writings specifically to their local schools.[4] Sometimes tutors might be addressed to a subsidiary group of people too: Leisring 1613 is dedicated to young boys and other 'Liebhaber'; Quitschreiber 1607 is addressed to both German and Latin schools (thus distinguishing it from his earlier short treatise of 1598, which was written in Latin). Of the earlier treatises, Orgosinus 1603 is remarkable in being addressed to women as well as men.[5] In fact this seemingly enlightened approach was merely the result of Orgosinus's copying of an earlier treatise, published by Keiser (1602), which was dedicated to a female order near Steinfurt, where young women from the foundation's school sang in the services (see Niemöller 1986).

Many publications probably originated as manuscript treatises which cantors compiled (often from existing books) for their lessons. This fact is made explicit on the title page of Hizler 1623, for instance; Gibel 1645 stated that the contents of his primer were usually communicated *vivā voce* rather than on paper. Even a comparatively large treatise such as Falck 1688 survives in an earlier manuscript form (Taylor 1971, p. xv). The apparent lack of unique manuscript treatises after 1600 suggests that the use of printed books, or manuscript copies thereof, was becoming the norm.[6] Bernhard's significant manuscript vocal tutor was never published, but was widely copied (see Müller-Blattau 1926/1963, pp. 8–12) and, in any case, partly transmitted by Mylius 1685.

One further question which is particularly difficult to answer today concerns the way in which these books were used in classes. Did the pupils have access to copies or did the cantor merely relay the information? Certainly the overwhelmingly standard form of instruction, in the elementary tutors at least, is the question-and-answer format (*erotemata*), which would seem eminently suited to a teacher-pupil dialogue. The 1634 ordinance of the Thomasschule, Leipzig suggests that in most subjects the pupil was expected to read the *praecepta* without changing a word, to learn and industriously practise the questions and responses from memory.[7] The introductions of some music primers imply that the pupil actually used the copy:

I have had these present questions . . . printed for the new year, entirely and particularly for your sake, so that you can now use the time that you otherwise would have spent copying for learning from memory. Thus you are less hindered in the other lessons that you must also industriously learn besides music.

habe ich diese gegenwertige Fragen . . . umb ewren willen / semptlich und sonderlich / jetzt zum newen Jar / im Druck ausgehen lassen / auff das ihr die Zeit / die ihr sonst hettet müssen auffs abschreiben wenden / nun dieselbige auswendig zu lernen könnet anwenden / Das ihr also desto weniger an ewren andern *Lectionibus* / die ihr / neben der *Music* / auch alle fleissig Lernen müsset / verhindert werdet. (Dedekind 1589, introduction)

A similar use of the books is implied by the title page of Stenger 1635. He also shows that cantors did not necessarily always use a specific text book for music instruction:

It was found advisable to print the present music booklet anew, accordingly I have on my part gladly let this happen in consideration of the fact that in this fashion singing is learned far more quickly and with greater enjoyment; since, as in their other lessons, the boys become accustomed to a particular book in music too, out of which they are instructed and taught in an orderly and thorough manner, so that they can further research at home, and thus industriously practise for themselves, those things which are explained and shown to them in schools.

Demnach Gegenwertiges Music-Büchlein vom Newen auffzulegen rathsam befunden worden / habe ich meines Orts solches gerne geschehen lassen / in Betrachtung / daß auff diese Weise das Singen viel schleuniger / und mit besserer Lust gelernet wird / wenn die Knaben / wie sonst in andern *Lectionibus*, also auch in *Musica* an ein gewiß Buch gewehnet / aus demselben ordentlich und gründlich unterwiesen / und angeleitet werden / dem jenigen / was ihnen in der Schule erkläret und gezeiget worden / zu Hause ferner nachzuforschen / und sich also selbst fleißig zu üben.   (Stenger 1635, 1659 edn)

Crappius 1599/1608 is likewise designed for the pupils' own use with much repetition and many 'reminders' ('Erinnerungen'); the final portion is a small Latin test on the content of the primer. Petri implies that the situation had not changed much by the middle of the eighteenth century; while his treatise was primarily designed for the teacher, it could also be given directly to the pupil:[8]

If it pleases the Herren Cantors, Directors and Stadtmusici to give this book directly into the hands of their pupils, they can make it more useful by means of their learned delivery and the exercises they teach; so I have employed the utmost conciseness in all parts.

Gefällt es den Herren *Cantoribus, Directoribus,* und Stadtmusicis, dieses kleine Buch ihren Schülern in die Hände zu geben, so werden sie es durch ihren gelehrten Vortrag und beygebrachten Uebungen brauchbarer machen können, da ich mich in allen Stücken der möglichsten kürze beflissen habe.   (Petri 1767, p. 3)

THE LAYOUTS AND CONTENTS OF INSTRUCTION BOOKS

The formats of instruction books run along fairly predictable lines: foremost are the simple primers derived from (or direct copies of) Listenius and Faber. Burmeister 1601 (*Musicae Practicae*) is something of a unicum with its precise, somewhat pedantic Latin definitions; nevertheless, the material is covered quickly and concisely. The title page to Dedekind 1589 (see p. 54 above) reflects the trend towards restricting the amount of time spent on learning the rudiments of music. Many other title pages likewise stress the need for speed and efficiency in learning; indeed an anonymous primer of 1601, *Idea musicae* (issued by Keiser, see Niemöller 1986), is designed so that its contents can be learned in a single day. With the exception of sporadic references to the necessity of physically beating the *tactus* (e.g. Holtheuser 1586, ch. 9) most of the elementary primers contain no reference to the activity of performance. A typical example might be Gumpelzhaimer 1591/1600, a tabular primer based directly on Faber with parallel Latin and German texts. The author's contribution lies mainly in the enormous number of examples with which he elaborates the text. The basic topics are:

56   Music education and the art of performance

definition of music 'Was ist die Music?' (see pp. 35 above for a summary of these definitions), with examples of notation in *choralis* and *figuralis*
clefs (claves), with the standard table of letter name notes on staves with solmisation syllables (see Listenius's example, Plate 1, p. 7 above); Guidonian hand
solmisation syllables (voces/Stimmen)
hexachords (cantus/Gesang): *durus*, *naturalis* and *mollis*, with canons to demonstrate each
mutation
signs used in music (figurae): note forms and various other signs (including signs to be used for correcting poorly placed notes)
ligatures
rests and dots
mensuration signatures and proportions: all demonstrated with canonic examples
modes: each demonstrated with polyphonic examples
more examples

Some primers might offer an extra chapter on intervals (e.g. Schneegass 1591, in a second book, after the fundamentals) since the less grateful vocal lines of the newly-emerging styles required increasing mastery of these. Quitschreiber 1607 not only contains the chapter on intervals, but also an extensive section on pitch and how to set it for the choir. Descriptions of intervals can be surprisingly thorough and detailed: some, for instance, outline the difference between major and minor semitones (i.e. the interval between a letter-name note and its accidental is smaller than that between an accidental and the next letter-name note).[9]

With the increasing concern for conciseness, many primers were soon omitting the chapters on mode and proportion. As Friderici observes, the use of the surviving proportion signs, namely 3/2 and 3, is chaotically regulated; many composers observe no difference between them, so it is better to leave the matter to the discretion of the director who can alter the tempo in accordance with the text.[10] Gengenbach 1626 likewise observes that the difference between ₵ and ₵ is often not strictly followed and that tempo words such as 'Adagio' and 'Presto' are more often used (pp. 78–9). Printz 1671 employs the numerical signs in their more modern sense, in that 3/1 indicates the slowest triple metre, 3/4 the fastest (Printz 1671, ch. 4). However, proportions are still explained in the much-published *Wegweiser* (1689–1753) and in Hoffmann 1693 (pp. 6–10), although the latter states that they are no longer observed by many.[11] The remnants of the proportional system are evident in Schmiedeknecht's description of 3/2:

That one should sing three half-beat notes in one bar, two in the downbeat of the arm and one in the upbeat, whereas two such notes would otherwise be sung in one bar.

Daß man soll drey halbe Schlägs-Noten auf einen Tact singen / zwey im Niederschlagen des Arms / und eine im Aufheben / da solcher Noten sonsten zwey auf einen Tact gesungen werden.   (Schmiedeknecht 1699, p. 15)

Ligatures were also rendered redundant by the increasingly shorter note values; early prescriptions of slurs to indicate underlay are found in primers by Walliser 1611 and Gengenbach 1626 (and in Praetorius's compendium-style treatise of 1619). However, ligatures were still needed if older music was to be performed; thus they can appear in comparatively late sources (e.g. Ahle 1690).

Friderici's much-published treatise contains a long chapter on the affective nature of each mode. Explanations of mode can still be found in Falck 1688 and even in Doles's manuscript treatise of c.1760 which he doubtless used in the Thomasschule, Leipzig. Doles notes that the singer must know the 'keys of the ancients' ('die Tonarten der Alten' – Doles, in Schneiderheinze 1989, p. 30) since these are still used in many of the traditional chorale melodies. Furthermore, given that many early eighteenth-century choirs were often singing from motet collections that were over a century old, it was necessary to have a working knowledge of modes and proportions, even if these were seldom used in contemporary compositions. However, as Erhardi stated in 1660, many school teachers and church musicians were entirely ignorant of modes:

Yes indeed, I say, it has come so far that, out of ignorance of these modes, many a *Collaborator Scholae* does not know how to begin to perform a chorale – let alone a figural piece – according to the correct ambitus of the mode, either in the schools or in the churches (where no musical instrument is available).

Ja dahin / sage Ich / ist es kommen / daß mancher *Collaborator Scholae*, auß Unwissenheit dieser *Modorum*, weder in der Schulen / noch in der Kirchen (wo kein *Instrumentum Musicum* vorhanden) einen *Choral*, geschweige einen *Figural-Gesang* / nach dem rechten *Ambitu Toni* anzufangen und außzuführen weiß.
(Erhardi 1660, p. 96)

On the other hand, references to 'key' in the modern sense are relatively slow to appear. Crüger 1660 recommends that the pupil discern to which *trias harmonica* a piece belongs before beginning to sing (p. 18); presumably this is a reference to the major and minor triad. Ahle 1690 still retains a transitional nomenclature, naming sharp keys 'harder' or 'sharper' ('harter/scharfer'), flat keys 'softer' or 'milder' ('weicher/gelinder'); Hoffmann 1693 uses the old hexachordal form of *durus* and *mollis* to denote keys without signature and with the signature of one flat, respectively; however he also names signatures with more than one flat and sharp *cantus mollis totalis* and *cantus durus totalis* respectively. Stierlein 1691 introduces what we would now term key signatures as the content of his chapter on transposition: signatures with flats are transpositions of the *mollis*, sharp signatures of the *durus*. Beyer 1703 retains this transitional form in the main text (p. 8) but gives a footnote remarking that the modern sense of *durus* and *mollis* (i.e. major and minor) can also be used; so that a signature with three sharps can paradoxically be termed *mollis* if it is based on f#. Fuhrmann 1706 retains the old nomenclature (i.e. *durus* = no signature, p. 40) but states that pieces based on one of the 'seven tones' are generally distinguished by their major or minor thirds. The transitional system (where sharp keys are 'hard', flat keys 'soft') survives in Wesselius (1726) although he allows the modern sense of major and minor, if the music is to be viewed harmonically.[12]

At the outset of the seventeenth century, solmisation syllables were a vital part of singing tuition and they were evidently to be applied to the many untexted examples (especially canons) to be found in most books. However, since the music was becoming that much more complicated, exceeding the standard ranges of sixteenth-century music, developments in solmisation are demonstrated by a wide range of primers. Quitschreiber 1607, in addition to giving the clearest exposition of the ways in which a melody can be practised, implies that the solmisation system was already becoming cumbersome:

A song can also be sung or sounded in three manners:
1. That one sings with solmisation syllables or uses the letter names (which would be easier), as the beginner should do.
2. That one expresses the notes intelligibly only in sound, as instrumentalists are wont to do.
3. That one underlays the text to God's glory and to the use of one's neighbour, as singers are wont to do.

Man kan auch jeden Gesang auff dreyerley Weise singen oder klingen lassen.
1. Das man solmisirt / oder die Buchstaben braucht (welches leichter were) wie die anfahenden Schüler thun müssen.
2. Das man die Noten nur am Klange verstendlich ausdrücket / wie die Instrumentisten pflegen.
3. Das man den Text GOTt zu Ehren / und dem Nechsten zu Nutze / unterlegt / wie die Sänger pflegen.   (Quitschreiber 1607, ch. 9)

The addition of a seventh syllable (*si*) to avoid the cumbersome practice of mutation is already evident in Burmeister 1601 (*se* for B; *si* for B♭), Keiser 1601, 1602 (see Niemöller 1986), Orgosinus 1603, Kretzschmar 1605, Kraft 1607, although it was never fully to be standardised. Alternative methods of solmisation are offered in Hizler 1623/1628, who recommends reducing the syllables used to four (*la, sol, fa, mi*); he also describes a newer system of syllables, *Bebisation*. Gengenbach 1626 likewise recommends this system, together with *Bobisation*, which he states to be of Belgian origins and already employed by Calvisius and Lippius (Gengenbach 1626, p. 28). Gibel 1645 suggests that *ut* be changed to *do* and *sol* to *so*, something which reflects the increasing concern for clarity of diction and purity of vowels. This may well be symptomatic of the greater attention apparently given to performance *per se*. *Applicatio textus*, a study of underlay and pronunciation, is sometimes included as an additional basic chapter in a primer (e.g. Hase 1657).

Inevitably it was not long before writers recommended the total abolition of the solmisation system. The first of these is Profe 1641, followed by Hase 1657, who states that letter-name pitches are older, more complete (since they do not lack the seventh syllable), easier (no mutation) and more useful (since they are used in keyboard playing and composition).[13] He likens the use of the solmisation system to the experience of a drunken man who finds himself back at home but knows not how he got there.[14] J. G. Ahle significantly omits solmisation from the main text of his edition of his father J. R. Ahle's tutor in the Faber tradition; he gives a history and description of the practice (with several different systems) in the extensive 'Anmerkungen' of the appendix, stating that it had fallen from use during his own lifetime (Ahle 1690, 'Anmerkungen' pp. 25–6).

Nevertheless, some later primers such as Feyertag 1695 and Beyer 1703 describe solmisation, and since it was never abandoned in Italy, it would be a mistake to consider it totally moribund in Germany. Moreover, German treatises of Catholic provenance often introduce solmisation, as it remained a very useful method for learning Gregorian chant.[15]

It is interesting that Doles, in his manuscript treatise for the Leipzig Thomasschule of c.1760, uses the term '*solfeggiren*' to describe singing the notes to their letter-names without the text. In other words, the traditional term is still used to evoke the learning process which solmisation was originally intended to instigate. While Marpurg 1763 still recommends that solmisation and, more particularly, Graun's newer system ('Da-mi-ni-po' etc.) be used, this is not for the primary purpose of learning to sing intervals, but because such systems give the pupil practice in singing all five vowels (Marpurg 1763, pp. 39–43).

Another trend is the gradual disappearance of the non-measured *choralis* notation in the most basic primers, since the use of chant was declining and chorales, with their measured notation, could be subsumed under *musica figuralis*. As Stierlein noted in 1691:

> But because *choralis*, or equally formed music [i.e. without rhythmic differentiation] is little, indeed virtually never, used by us, we will only deal with *musica figuralis* here.
>
> ... weilen aber die *Choral* oder gleichförmige *Music* heutiges Tages bey uns wenig / ja fast gar nimmer im Gebrauch / als wollen wir von dißmal / nur allein / de *Musica Figurali* . . . handeln. (Stierlein 1691, p. 3)

Nevertheless, the two types of notation are still outlined in Quirsfeld 1675, a book which was reprinted until 1717. Anton 1743 (p. 7) preserves the term *choralis*, but redefines it as that music which requires no instruments, such as chorales.[16]

Some treatises in the 'traditional' format are expanded in certain ways. While only a handful of sixteenth-century primers contain any information relating to the specifics of performance and interpretation (e.g. posture, breathing, blend, dynamics and articulation; for a detailed survey, see chapter 4), such sections – often in the form of an appendix – become increasingly prominent in later publications.[17] These clearly show a change in perspective: performance style and elements of vocal 'technique' are presumably vital to the imported Italianate idioms. Of course it might equally point to a change in educational stance; perhaps these issues of style were hitherto communicated orally and only later written down. However, the general trend towards 'understanding' in education (see p. 66 below) probably coincides with an increased awareness of the function and nature of practical music, something of which the new affective musical styles are themselves symptomatic.

Some of the earlier seventeenth-century treatises give some information on harmonic considerations. Schneegass 1591 and the second part of Harnish 1608 contain a section on consonance and dissonance. Quitschreiber's description of the four vocal parts mentions the importance of the bass as the 'Fundament', the omission of which would sound bad since it would lead to naked fourths and sixths (Quitschreiber 1607, appendix). Magirus 1596 introduces harmony as a more detailed study, as does Beringer 1610. One of the latest elementary primers to cover the basics of harmony is Weide 1627, a book which relies heavily on the

Mediaeval conception of musical harmony as the mirror of God and His creation (see p. 40 above).

Thus in a few establishments pupils were introduced to harmonic considerations at a relatively early stage in their education; this perhaps reflects the survival of the older conception of *musica practica* in which performance and composition were combined. However, after the beginning of the seventeenth century the majority of the basic German treatises on performance (including those containing advice on improvised diminution) omit detailed references to harmony. On the other hand, such considerations become more important in some of the large 'compendium' treatises towards the end of the century, incidentally during the period when some German theorists again categorised composition and performance under the one heading (see chapter 5).

Three other factors also begin to gain prominence in the basic primers during the seventeenth century: dictionaries of the Italian words appropriate for the new music; references to instrumental performance; anecdotes on music's glorious past. Dictionaries can appear in quite small primers after the publication of Praetorius 1619, the first major German treatise specifically dedicated to the 'new' Italian style.[18] That some authors were suspicious of the new terms is suggested by Dieterich (1631), who claims that the words are confusing and awkward both for the singers and printers; he confines himself to an explanation of *forte* and *piano* alone.[19]

References to instruments are not difficult to find in the standard primers: Quitschreiber 1607 contains a survey of the ranges of various instruments; it also notes that those boys who learn the clavichord or other instrument will observe that pieces can be performed a fourth or fifth higher or lower.[20] Leisring 1615 states at the outset that both vocal and instrumental music is practised in schools; the introduction to Hizler 1623 notes that this primer is a good introduction for those students who wish subsequently to take up instrumental music. Gradenthaller 1687 states in the introduction that even if a particular boy does not have a good voice it might be worth training him in case his broken voice turns out well, or if he wishes to become an instrumentalist, since vocal and instrumental music belong together like body and soul. The fact that the first German treatise of the Baroque era to address instruments alone was not published until 1695 (Merck) shows how closely instrumental performance in schools was linked to the general purpose of providing music for church; pupils were trained in both vocal and instrumental performance as dictated by necessity. On the other hand professional instrumentalists (e.g. court musicians and the *Stadtpfeiffer*) learned by apprenticeship, so they required no specific published tutors.

Merck's *Compendium* 1695 addresses 'Die Jugend und andere Liebhaber'; it thus had the dual function of serving schools and amateur musicians. Merck notes that while many are fortunate to have a good foundation in instrumental music through the art of singing, this might have been denied to some because of a poor natural voice or because of a poor teacher (Merck 1695, 'Vorbericht'). This could point towards both an increasing specialisation on the part of cantors, ignoring the general singing instruction, and the fact that some cantors were still of the old academic type, who understood little of the practicalities of singing and playing.

It is in the larger compendium-like treatises of the late seventeenth century that the most detailed references to instruments are to be found. Speer, in his large compendium, made a wide-reaching proposal that the cities should provide subsidised instrumental tuition for all talented children, however poor ('wohlmeynender Entwurff / wie bey gemeinen Städten zur Ehre GOttes die *Vocal-* und *Instrumental-Music* in Aufnahm zu bringen und zu pflantzen wäre', Speer 1697, pp. 258–60). He himself also provides the most comprehensive information on instruments to be found in a seventeenth-century school treatise. His reasons for doing this are interesting in themselves. Clearly it was necessary not only to provide many pupils with such a background in instrumental performance, but also to show those who were contemptuous of practical music just how difficult it was:

And although envious grudgers will no doubt have nothing good to say about this, I nevertheless hope that understanding Stadt- and Kunst-Pfeiffer (because I also was once their equal) will judge reasonably; since it is not only for the good of their present apprentices and also to their own advantage, so that they thus will be spared much trouble with them; but my intention is also that other people will see from the fundamentals that this noble art of music is not only mere street musicians' stuff, as some of the scornful companions of Midas dismiss it, and that not only does the correct learning and delicate performing of such an art take considerable time, but that it also demands capable people: for just as one cannot carve a picture out of every piece of wood, so not everyone is able and skilled in music.

Und ob mir zwar von mißgünstigen Neidhammeln hievon schon nichts gutes traumet / so will ich doch hoffen / daß verständige Stätt- und Kunst-Pfeiffer / (weil ich auch weiland ihres gleichen geweßt/) vernünfftig *judici*ren werden; sintemahl es nicht allein um ihrer habenden Lehrlinge bestens / und auch derselben eigenen Vortheil / daß sie dardurch vieler Müh mit ihnen überhoben seyn werden; sondern auch mein Absehen dahin gehet / daß andere Leut auß dem Fundament sehen mögen / daß diese edle *Music*-Kunst nicht nur geringe Spielmanns-Sachen / als zum theil verächtlicher *Midas*-Gesellen davon *scoptisi*ren / und daß nicht allein solche Kunst zimliche Zeit / zum recht erlernen und zierlichen *tracti*ren gehöre / sondern auch taugliche Leut erfordere: Dann gleich wie man nicht auß jedem Holtz ein Bild schnitzeln kan; also auch nicht ein jeder zur *Music* tauglich und geschickt ist. (Speer 1697, p. 188)

Speer's emphasis on instrumental performance suggests that the need for qualified players was exceeding the resources traditionally available from schools and town musicians' guilds. It is highly likely that J. S. Bach's 'Entwurff' of 1730, which likewise outlines the shortage of musicians, was written in the light of such writings as Speer's 'wohlmeynender Entwurff' of 1697.

That instrumental tuition was becoming almost as common as vocal instruction in the early eighteenth century is suggested by Sperling in 1705:

Because a violin is almost always the first thing to be placed in the hands of a vocalist, once he is already somewhat experienced in singing and wishes to proceed to instruments, so I have, to end with, included several easy exercises for two violins.

Weil fast allzeit einem *Vocalis*ten / nachdem er im Gesang schon etwas erfahren / und zu denen *Instrument*en schreiten will / zu erst eine *Violin* in die Hand gegeben wird / als hab zum Beschluß etliche leichte *Exercitia* vor 2. *Violin*en beygefüget.
(Sperling 1705, p. 138)

However, most school vocal primers from the early eighteenth century do not cover instrumental technique. Evidently instrumental instruction was acquired privately or from the growing number of treatises dedicated specifically to instruments. That these latter were not primarily to be devised for practical music within general education, though, is suggested by the increasing concern with amateur performance, partially evident in the dedication of Merck 1695 and made explicit in Baron's treatise for lute of 1727:

Meanwhile may the reasonable reader live well and judge these pages according to what is possible and the principles of truth, and be assured that such an undertaking has been made with no other intention than to amuse the honest amateur.

Indessen lebe der vernünfftige Leser wohl, und beurtheile diese Blätter nach der Möglichkeit und denen *Principiis* der Wahrheit, und sey versichert, daß solches Unternehmen aus keiner andern Absicht als rechtschaffene Liebhaber zu vergnügen geschehen sey. (Baron 1727, introduction)

The primary purpose of references to the ancient history of music was to show that music had a long and glorious past in both Christian and pagan traditions. Moreover, given the stress laid on the affective and rhetorical power of music, it was important to have historical – and especially Biblical – anecdotes to support this. The tradition for giving extensive passages on the history and mythical power of music (*laus musicae*) stretches back into classical times. It is strongly evident in Quintilianus and Quintilian, and is characteristic of both Mediaeval and Renaissance scholarship.[21] Lutheran writers thus had a very large body of literature on which to rely; nevertheless, the uncritical nature of most of their writing, even in the later seventeenth century, suggests that they were most closely allied with the older, Pythagorean school of music theory, as exemplified in the influential writings of Gaffurio.[22]

Quitschreiber 1607 contains a short paragraph on the origin of music: it was ultimately invented by God, but within humanity it can be traced back to Genesis in the Hebrew tradition, Pythagoras within the pagan tradition. Similar introductions are found in Leisring 1615 and Weide 1627. A longer essay on the history of music is found in Sartorius 1635, after which time such material becomes quite commonplace: Herbst 1642, Zerleder 1658 etc. The Old Testament use of music is inevitably very prominent in the vocal primer by the pastor Erasmus Gruber (1673). Luther's own comments regarding music were of course especially pertinent and some treatises, particularly Ribovius 1638, contain extensive quotations from the reformer. As late as 1752, Luther's pronouncements can be found at the head of the anonymous *Kurze Anweisung zu den ersten Anfangs-Gründen der Musik*.

With the publication of Printz's *Historische Beschreibung* 1690, music history became established as a subject in its own right, the main interest being in the 'causes', 'origins' and 'invention' of music. Of the school primers, the 'Anmerkungen' of Ahle 1690 offer the most extensive speculation into the invention and origins of music. Evidently the concept of cause was becoming part of the essence of each phenomenon in the new mechanical universe.

PEDAGOGIC APPROACH

Finally, we turn to one of the most striking developments in the seventeenth-century primers: the changing attitudes towards the pedagogic process itself. The most obvious change is the move towards practical issues, something resulting from the development in musical styles which patently required more fluency from the performer. With this comes a great increase in the number of practical examples (bicinia, canons, motets and chorales). The canon (usually labelled 'Fuga') is the staple diet of practical education well into the seventeenth century; it was especially serviceable since the pupil needed only to learn one line of music in order to become acquainted with polyphony and independence of voice-parts. Even in a primer as early as Kraft 1607, it is not uncommon to find over thirty (usually untexted) canons at the end of the primer.[23] In Büttner 1625 many of the thirty-seven canonic examples are based on chorale melodies.

Some primers still include examples throughout the text which do not necessarily relate directly to the topic just discussed. Eichmann 1604 introduces four-part motets by Reddemer and Belicius after the chapters on solmisation syllables and clefs; likewise the chapter on mutation is followed by several canons (including one by Eichmann himself, and a two-part piece by Lassus). This was common in sixteenth-century treatises, where it seems that the pupil had to know considerably more than the precept just discussed (see p. 6 above). It might also give us some idea of the way lessons could have been planned, with practical examples sung at intervals to break up the teaching of new factual material.

Conciseness and the banishing of Latin are also common concerns: Büttner 1625 opens with a long complaint about the use of Latin in the common music primers, since this often turns away the most talented pupils. Presumably Büttner was reacting to the lasting influence of treatises based on the Listenius/Faber model. While these had themselves aimed to make practical music instruction as concise as possible, many writings of the early seventeenth century went even further towards presenting the material efficiently. Dieterich 1631 is a model of conciseness, dividing the basic material into two sections: 'Systema' (the clefs, staves and scales) and 'Nota' (note lengths and metre). After this he gives an explanation of coloratura, something most unusual in a short primer of this kind.

Gradenthaller 1687 (foreword) observes that in many schools the pupil is more hindered than encouraged to progress since too much worthless information is usually communicated.[24] Although it restricts the number of clefs required for singing, Gradenthaller's introduction is one of the longest appended to an elementary primer and the contents are not significantly clearer than those of other books. However, the claim that the training should be concise is typical of the seventeenth-century intention of teaching the pupil as quickly as possible and in such a manner that he understands what he is doing and why.

66   Music education and the art of performance

In response to educational developments in Europe as a whole during the early seventeenth century (especially the pansophic method of J. A. Comenius)[25] more attention was given to the learning experience and the cultivation of the pupil's understanding. The 1634 ordinance of the Thomasschule, Leipzig very clearly reflects a respect for the pupil; the teacher should encourage pleasure and joy in study and avoid unfriendliness and tyrannical gestures.[26]

Hizler 1623 and Gengenbach 1626 are among the first music books to show this tendency by suggesting at the outset that the pupil should gain the outlines of the topics first and fill in the detail only later. Treatises up to this point (and many afterwards) imply that the pupil usually had to learn an entire topic first (probably parrot-fashion if the *erotemata* style is anything to go by) before moving to the next. Thus only after having learned several chapters would the pupil have been able even to begin singing independently from notation. Hizler tries to cut this waiting-time by printing hand-signals to indicate the points a student should grasp first.[27] The remainder of the text should not be learned, but read often and understood. The various note signs and symbols should be copied so that the pupil internalises their shapes.

Gengenbach's emphasis is always on learning by experience and not merely by learning rules. Solmisation cannot be learned by reading a book: either the singing teacher must demonstrate and the pupil imitate the difference between *mi* and *fa* or (as Quitschreiber and Hizler also advise) the pupil can learn it with a tuned instrument such as a clavichord, violin or lute.

Profe 1641 and Erhardi 1660 continue this trend by covering the basic topics in a few introductory pages, after which these and additional material are studied in greater detail. Profe 1641 designs everything with the pupil's imagination and ability in mind: the scale is pictured as a ladder (p. 7), intervals are drawn from examples (p. 10) and the whole of music is succinctly summarised under *qualitas* and *quantitas*, the parameters of pitch and time. Stenger's title page (see p. 54 above) likewise shows a concern for the learning process: the pupil should practise everything he learns at home, since anything which is heard without *exercitium* is so easily forgotten.

Ribovius 1638 gives particular attention to the way in which the boy learns intervals, at the same time as he applies the text:

It is however better, when two or more boys are equally advanced, if one sings the notes [presumably to solmisation syllables] and the other, or the others, the text, and frequently alternate, so that they progress together and become confident.

welches dennoch besser ist / wenn zween oder mehr Knaben gleich weit gekommen seyn / daß einer die Noten / und der ander oder die anderen den Text singen / und offt abwechseln / damit sie also mit einander fortkommen unnd sicher werden. (Ribovius 1638, p. 195)

La Marche 1656 is very concerned with the way the pupil comprehends the material. He extends the *erotemata* technique well beyond most of his contemporaries, asking the pupil searching questions regarding his motives for singing. His short primer concludes with advice to the teacher: it is not enough that the master identifies mistakes, he should also ask the boy how he has erred and insist that he correct the mistake himself (La Marche 1656, p. 21). It is also important to rehearse the boys individually so that they do not cover up each other's mistakes; material should be introduced a little at a time and always related back to the fundamentals (*Ibid.*, pp. 21–2). Perhaps the most detailed prescription of teaching method appears at the end of Fuhrmann 1706 (pp. 94–6). Following his week-by-week course, pupils should learn to read at sight within three months. Use of the clavichord, enabling them to practise in the absence of the teacher, is vital. Fuhrmann provides a precedent for several treatises after 1750 which emphasise the learning process.

With the onset of the eighteenth century, more treatises seem to cater for the growing amateur market. While some are still designed with school music in mind this is often only one of several uses. Eisel 1738 is specifically aimed at the cultivated amateur, covering a large variety of instruments. Nevertheless he still suggests that the pursuit of music should take its place next to theology and above all the other arts and sciences.[28] Maier 1741 (first version 1732) is addressed to the *galant homme*, but, remarkably, covers both *musica practica* and *musica poetica*. Like Eisel, Maier points to the lofty God-given status of music, one that was being greatly enhanced by the growth in musical expertise among royal amateurs.[29] Thus although music was still highly regarded, it was accorded its status not necessarily within the traditional Lutheran educational system but rather within the circles of the rising bourgeoisie, taking their lead from royalty.

Having now covered the basic formats of the literature designed for elementary music instruction, I shall concentrate in the next two chapters on those elements relating specifically to the practical aspects of performance during the Baroque era: technique, interpretation and ornamentation.

4

The development of performance practice and the tools of expression and interpretation in the German Baroque

While issues of performance technique, style and expression undoubtedly come to the fore in texts from the late sixteenth century onwards, earlier musicians cannot have been entirely unconcerned with interpretation, and the lack of written documentation does not necessarily mean that it was never discussed. Nevertheless, there is obviously a striking contrast between earlier treatises dealing with the rudiments required for performance and those later ones that are equally elementary but add recommendations on technique and style. Significantly, many of the vocal rules of the early seventeenth century are drawn directly from those few sixteenth-century writings which mention vocal technique.[1] This could point either towards a codification of an existing practice or to a desire to justify rules for the present by earlier prescriptions. In any case, the noticeable expansion of treatises concerned with the actual practice of performance doubtless reflects the development of *musica practica* in Germany as the science of performance, something with its own rules and defining characteristics. Praetorius makes this explicit in his dedicatory foreword to *Syntagma musicum*, part 3, of 1619:

So I have now in this third, and in the following fourth, volume compiled and written the most important things that a Kapellmeister who is a *singing-master* and *musicus practicus* will need to know, particularly in the present time when music has risen so high that one can hardly believe that it can come any higher.

So hab ich nun in diesem *Tertio* und folgendem *Quarto Tomo*, das fürnembste so einem Capellmeister *Phonasco* und *Musico Practico*, Sonderlich jetziger zeit / da die *Music* so hoch gestiegen / das fast nicht zu gleuben / dieselbe numehr höher werde kommen können / zu wissen von nöhten sein wird / begriffen und verfasset.

As chapter 2 suggests, the elevation of performance was not only a factor of the 'new Italian style' but also something inherent in the spirit of

68

The development of performance practice 69

Lutheranism: practical music as an affective theological discourse. It should, however, be remembered that this chapter concentrates on only a portion of the treatises written between c.1600 and 1750; the remainder preserve the pattern of Listenius and Faber, something which suggests that the more conservative attitude to performance survived side-by-side with that of the 'modernists'.

This is the survey of a *textual* tradition and not a fully documented record of actual performance style. As will quickly emerge, the texts rely strongly on each other, forming a body of performance theories reflecting the contemporary awareness of performance practice and its role in musical and educational life.

SINGING TECHNIQUE

The first half of the seventeenth century

The variety of practice in the first half of the seventeenth century is well demonstrated in Bernhard's manuscript vocal treatise, c.1649: according to him there were two basic styles of singing, that preserving the notes and that changing them (*cantar sodo/d'affetto* and *cantar passagiato*; see p. 49 above). The survival of the basic sixteenth-century format in seventeenth-century treatises suggests that many cantorates still promoted a relatively 'inexpressive' performance style which did not even necessarily relate to the textual affect (Bernhard's *cantar d'affetto* – in which the affective implications of the text are regarded – is a subcategory and not a prerequisite of plain singing). That many choirs were still unfamiliar with differentiated dynamics is suggested by a direction Tobias Michael added to the last piece in his *Musicalische Seelenlust* part I (1634): whoever has no taste for the indicated piano–forte contrasts may simply omit them.[2] The relatively extensive treatises of Gengenbach 1626 and Hizler 1623 are representative of a large number of primers that – like most from the sixteenth century – barely mention matters of vocal style, not to speak of ornamentation. This is particularly interesting in view of the fact that these two adopt a progressive pedagogical stance (see p. 66 above).

The most elaborated form of singing was clearly reserved for the more sumptuous establishments (e.g. Bernhard's own at the Dresden court). On the other hand, Bernhard lists some devices which he regards as indispensable for the plain style. Only one of these comes into the category of vocal technique proper, the concept of *fermo*, a steady voice without the defect of *tremulo* (Müller-Blattau 1926/1963 pp. 31–2). That

Bernhard calls for vibrato as part of the the ornament *ardire*, suggests it was an element of ornamentation rather than a constant in 'plain singing'. The remaining devices are the one-note graces which, in Bernhard's view, are essential to the fundamentals of 'plain singing'. Indeed, according to Printz 1671, the pupil should start learning the figures of diminution when he first learns to apply the text (see p. 132 below). The lack of fundamental physiological information, which is common to all German sources on the Italian style, implies that singing 'technique' was still the by-product of a concern for musical style and ornamentation rather than an art in its own right.[3]

Bernhard's categorisation is useful in showing not only that a variety of performance styles was permissible in the early seventeenth century but also that there was a certain amount of interplay between the categories. The sources suggest that, while many authors (e.g. Gengenbach) taught nothing but 'plain' singing, there is a large middleground of writers who recommend a certain amount of expressive interpretation without necessarily outlining details of improvised ornamentation. It is perhaps these writers who – as the 'mean', so to speak – best reflect the basic German tradition of performance during the Baroque era as a whole, something on to which the more progressive advocates of the 'new Italian style' grafted their own developments. Furthermore, it should not be discounted that these 'middleground' writers codified conventions which many of the writers in the Listenius/Faber traditions took for granted.

Several factors might account for the increasing interest in and awareness of vocal technique at the outset of the Baroque era. First, there is the proliferation of the 'new Italian style' which, with its renewed emphasis on textual expression, engendered an interest in certain aspects of vocal delivery. Secondly, the increasingly close links between music and rhetoric in German theory – part of the elevation of practical music as an element of the *trivium* – inspired closer study of classical rhetorical texts and their advice on the cultivation of the orator's voice.

The writings drawn from the sixteenth century do not generally present a theory of performance as such, rather a loosely connected list of rules, empirically derived, which publication had hardened into a tradition. Much of the German tradition stretches back to the writings of Conrad von Zabern (1474) and Hermann Finck (1556; see Ruhnke 1955, p. 98): clear and correct expression of vowels; the forming of the notes in the lungs and throat and not with the lips or tongue; the avoidance of singing through the nose; the clear and distinct performance of fast notes in passages (but without aspiration); correct pitching; gentle performance of high notes; steady tempo; clear vocal entries in fugal passages; correct underlay; correct posture. These rules reappear, almost literally, in the writings of C. Praetorius (1574) and Schneegass (1591), who also stress that the singers must establish a balanced sound between the parts and that the mouth should not be opened so wide as to preclude a sweet vocal style. Praetorius insists that the style of singing conform to the words so that it can express a joyous affect with joyful words, a sorrowful one with sorrowful words.[4] Quitschreiber further suggests that some form of vibrato should be cultivated, 'Tremula voce optime canitur' (Quitschreiber 1598, 'De canendi elegantia').

With Calvisius 1602 comes the most thorough summary and amplification of these traditional German rules. He also introduces detailed advice on breathing; the first rules emphasise sweetness of tone, the virtues of a long breath with steady tone on sustained notes and the dangers of ruining the tone by giving too much strength to the high notes.[5] The rule that the singer should sing more gently the higher he goes, stronger the deeper he goes, derives from Finck and remained an element of German vocal technique for more than a century after Calvisius.[6] The next rules emphasise the need for sustaining the tone and breath on a long note over several beats and on divisions, giving particular attention to the higher notes. In contradistinction to most of the other writers of his age, Calvisius recommends a somewhat smooth performance of crotchets and quavers, perhaps to guard against the aspiration of vowels:

Crotchets or quavers that ascend or descend by step must be formed in the throat, not with the lips, and the sounds must be joined together in such a way that the steps are not greatly perceived.

Semiminime vel Fusae quae gradatim ascendunt vel descendunt, gutture, non labijs, formandae sunt, & sono ita coniungandae, ne gradus magnopere exaudiantur. (Calvisius 1602, rule 7)

He may have taken some of his advice from sixteenth-century Italian writers, since he repeats Zarlino's direction that the voices should be louder in churches and public places than in smaller, private chambers.[7]

Burmeister 1601 (*Musica autoschediastike*) stands apart in giving a more theoretical underpinning of these conventions; it introduces material from the classical rhetorical tradition, namely the chapter 'De pronunciatione' from Quintilian's *Institutiones oratoriae* (see Ruhnke 1955, pp. 94–8). The effectiveness of the oratory/song is achieved with the firm, elegant and affective voice. All aspects of vocal technique depend on achieving moderation between all extremes: between light and dark, strong and weak, delicate and raw; breath which is neither too long nor too short; a performance which is neither to fast nor too slow. This moderation in style accords well with the traditional German rules summarised in Calvisius 1602, so Burmeister probably found the ancient rules of rhetoric a useful way of justifying the *status quo*. The rhetorical tradition also recommends that each singer cultivate what Nature has given him, something which would refreshingly discount a single dogma of vocal technique. Most important is the level-headed, abstinent, and hardened lifestyle, combined with daily singing and faith in portraying the content of the song. The second part of Burmeister's rules (appropriated as they are from Quintilian) concerns the *pronunciatio affectuosa*, achieved primarily through the decoration of the oratory/song (see chapter 5, below).

Gesture is an essential element of rhetorical delivery, one that is often ignored in considerations of historical performance. Burmeister cites the example of the deaf-mute who must express all his feelings through his gestures. According to Quintilian's advice on *gestus*, it is important that the content and style of the singing is not contradicted by inappropriate gestures. Furthermore, the most potent performance is achieved when both aspects are united; thus the eyes, the head and every limb should adopt the gestures directly implied by the text.

While Burmeister is suspicious of the wholesale application of modern Italian mannerisms, Praetorius strikes a remarkable balance both by outlining the practice of the ancients and by establishing the modern Italian style in German performance theory. In the first part of his *Syntagma musicum* (1614–15, book 2, pp. 188–98), he gives perhaps the most thorough compilation of classical writings on voice production. Only a few years later, he wrote the most influential German essay on 'modern' Italian practices, in the third part of *Syntagma musicum* (1619). Although the volume as a whole is too cumbersome to have been used as a regular school primer (it is designed more for the teacher than the pupil), it contains prescriptions that were a tremendous influence on later pedagogical writings. As he states in the introduction, the Italians have so changed the art of music that a good survey is required for 'Capellmeisters / Directores / Cantores / Organisten / Lautenisten'. In his rules on Italianate ornamentation and diminution he mentions two specific Italian authors – Caccini and Bovicelli – both of whom emphasise the need for matching ornaments with the appropriate affects.

His prescription of the *natura* required of the incipient singer is a useful summary of the vocal presuppositions of the age: the singer must

The development of performance practice 73

have a natural, beautiful voice with a smooth, round neck for fast passages, a steady long breath and finally a voice which fits one of the four vocal ranges, which can be used with a full sound, brightly and without falsetto (Praetorius 1619, p. 231). His distaste of the falsetto register may derive directly from Caccini 1601; at least one German contemporary does not share this prejudice.[8] The list of *vitia*, the common deficiencies in singing, is also a useful summary of many previous German and Italian writings: the singer should not take too many breaths (see Caccini 1601) and should avoid singing through the nose, holding the voice in the neck with the teeth biting together (see Bovicelli 1594).

What is particularly striking about a treatise as thorough and comprehensive as Praetorius's is the comparative lack of a theory of vocal production (in the modern sense, at least). The emphasis is on the free and 'natural' working of the vocal organs, supported by long, deep breathing. Praetorius interestingly regards vibrato as a fundamental of singing, given by God and nature (something of which Quitschreiber 1598 also approves, see p. 71 above):

Whereas those who are endowed by God and nature with a particularly lovely shaking, wavering or trembling voice and also with a round neck and throat for diminution, but who do not heed the rules of music, are not to be praised

Sintemal die jenigen gar nicht zu loben / welche von Gott und der Natur / mit einer sonderbahren lieblichen zitterten und schwebenden oder bebenden Stimm / auch einem runden Halß unnd Gurgel zum diminuiren begabet / sich an den *Musicorum Leges* nicht binden lassen (Praetorius 1619, pp. 229–30)

Another detail that Praetorius requires as part of the *natura* of the incipient singer is the *exclamatio*, apparently a dynamic increase to be applied to certain notes. This is something quite new in German vocal treatises (which up to, and often beyond, Praetorius still recommended a steady tone and, presumably, dynamic). The *exclamatio* and the apparent *messa di voce* that Praetorius specifies for semibreves are dynamic devices he took from Caccini 1601, essentially to express the sense and affect of the words. Praetorius evidently considered such dynamic shading to be a fundamental of singing rather than merely an optional expressive device:

Exclamatio is the true means to move the affects, which must be achieved by increasing the voice. And it can be employed with all descending dotted minims and crotchets. And the following note especially, which thus moves somewhat quickly, is more affective, and also has better grace, than the semibreve, which takes place more often with a raising and lowering of the voice, without *exclamatio*.

74   Music education and the art of performance

Exclamatio ist das rechte Mittel die *affectus* zu *moviren*, so mit erhebung der Stimm geschehen muß: Und kan in allen *Minimis* und *Semiminimis* mit dem Punct / *Descendendo* angebracht unnd gebraucht werden. Unnd *moviret* sonderlich die folgende *Nota*, so etwas geschwinde fortgehet / mehr *affectus*, als die *Semibrevis*, welche in erhebung und verringerung der Stimm ohn *Exclamation* mehr stadt findet / auch bessere *gratiam* hat.   (Praetorius 1619, p. 231)

This somewhat ambiguous explanation seems to suggest that semibreves are commonly made more expressive with dynamic nuancing, while the *exclamatio* refers specifically to the crescendo applied to dotted rhythms (or perhaps even an improvised elaboration of the semibreve into a dotted rhythm for 'more affect'?).[9] Beyond this it is clear that elements of vocal technique are directly connected to the various 'manners'; in other words, techniques are directly connected to musical interpretation, expression and ornamentation. Never do these form an abstract, normative voice-culture. It is the selection and interpretation of 'Manners' which Praetorius and his followers most closely related to the singer's role as orator. The concept of music as a rhetoric was a central impetus – and alternatively a justification – for developments of vocal style in Germany during the seventeenth century (see pp. 46–50 above, and chapter 5). The 'new Italian style' was also particularly well represented by Herbst 1642/1653 in what was essentially an expansion of Praetorius's pioneering work of 1619.

While Praetorius 1619 established a German textual tradition that purported to outline the Italian style (i.e. the most advanced of Bernhard's categories), many treatises showed this influence but were more modest in their ambitions. Particularly influential was Friderici's, *Musica Figuralis*, first published in 1618, but republished numerous times until 1677.[10] The penultimate chapter (chapter 7, enlarged with four more rules in the 1624 edition),[11] on the numerous rules for singing, provides one of the most useful and comprehensive summaries of vocal style of the time. This gives a good impression of the 'middleground' as it stood at the time of Praetorius. The latter's influence is strongly evident in the sections added in 1624: Praetorius's prescriptions of the suitable voice and the moderation of physical gestures appear almost word for word and Friderici's advice on the placement of singers is doubtlessly influenced by Praetorius's exhaustive discussion.

Many of Friderici's rules can be traced back to the earlier German treatises up to Calvisius 1602: e.g. correct pronunciation of vowels; attention to the other voices. Of foremost concern is the suitability of the boy, who must have pleasure and love of singing ('Lust und Liebe'), something which may suggest that the era when all school boys were expected to attend communal singing lessons was passing. Suitable boys should have a natural control of breath, particularly when they sing high, and should not screech and shout.[12] His emphasis on singing which is joyful ('freudig') and fresh ('frisch') and not to be confused with shouting, gives us a figurative idea of the vocal style to be cultivated, something which conjures up the sense of a free, natural technique.

Most impressive are the closing exercises on vocal agility (added in 1624) which give a good account of how vocal training could be conducted:

Here follow various exercises, in which a teacher can rehearse and instruct his pupils who are beginning to learn singing by singing to them one *clausula* after the other, finely expressing himself, after which each can sing individually or all together, so that they can learn from him the correct voice and tone and thus each day become more skilful at other music.

Folgen etliche *Exercitia*, darinnen ein *Praeceptor* seine *Discipulos*, so da anfangen / singen zu lernen / üben und unterweisen / ihnen eine *Clausulam* nach der andern vorsingen / und sich fein *articulatè*, entweder von jedem insonderheit / oder von allen zugleich ins gemein nach singen lassen kan / damit sie ihm die Stimme und den Thon recht lernen abnehmen / und also täglich geschickter zu anderer Musick gemacht werden.

(Friderici 1618/1624, introduction to exercises)

The first example involves singing a succession of notes in progressively decreasing note values; if the capacity of the boys allows, they may even try semiquavers (Example 1). The subsequent example provides variations

Example 1   Friderici 1618/1624

1. *Exemplum* die Noten in *unisono* auff einen Schlag recht zu theilen u. *pronuncire* zu lernen.

Wofern es der *captus puerorum* ertragen kan
so kan man den Knaben auch wol Noten mit zwey Schwänzen vorschreiben.

on each of the six solmisation syllables (Example 2), followed by exercises on successive intervals and dotted rhythms (Example 3). The remaining examples are patently diminution exercises which cultivate both vocal agility and a sense of how to embellish simple note-patterns. Several other writers share this 'middleground' interest in the fluency cultivated by diminution exercises, even if they did not advocate the wholesale

76 Music education and the art of performance

improvisation of ornamental figures.[13] Friderici states in his 'Conclusio' (1624, and thus after Praetorius) that he has omitted numerous Italian manners (he specifies here exactly those given by Praetorius), since they are too difficult for young boys and are used only in the most distinguished establishments. Furthermore, coloratura can lead to great misuse,

Example 2 Friderici 1618/1624

2. *Exempl.* darin Man lernet
ut, re, mi, fa, sol, la, verändern.

3. Ein anders auff dem selbigen Schlag.

Example 3   Friderici 1618/1624

10. *Exempl.* die *Puncta* in die Noten zu versetzen

ruining the music; and many such devices are more appropriate for instrumentalists; there is, in any case, already easily enough for boys to learn in singing. Nevertheless, the strong emphasis that Friderici has already given diminution suggests that he is referring to a more extreme practice here (as Bernhard's categories of vocal style suggest, some ornaments are required even in the 'plainest' style, p. 69 above).[14]

The growth in the consciousness of singing technique and style during the early seventeenth century is reflected in the comparison of the 1607 and the 1632 editions of Demantius's *Isagoge Artis Musicae*. While the first contained some general singing exercises similar to the patterns found in Italian diminution manuals (typically arrayed with the simplest forms moving to the most complex), the later edition introduces rules of singing clearly influenced by Friderici's publication. There is also a tremendous increase in the number of exercises in vocal agility and one hundred canons in two to seven parts.

The latter half of the seventeenth century

After 1650 we can observe many continuities with the earlier part of the century; conservative writings still appear side by side with those giving attention to details of performance, for instance. The 'middleground' material (i.e. that which addresses issues of performance but does not necessarily advocate the most elaborate forms of improvised ornamentation) is greatly expanded and many texts, at all levels, show the influence of educational reforms (see p. 66 above). On the whole the understanding and responsibility of the pupil are more noticeably enouraged.

By far the most informative writer on German singing in the entire seventeenth century is Wolfgang Caspar Printz, *Director Musices* and cantor at Sorau. His most extensive practical treatise is *Musica modulatoria vocalis* of 1678, a work, like Praetorius's, that represents the 'high ground' of the German tradition.[15] Not only does he sum up much of the

German literature on singing, but he also consults Herr Gottfried Giganti, court doctor in Sorau, on a suitable diet for the singer. His demanding list of the requirements of the good singer includes natural inclination and ability, a clear and beautiful voice, a complete knowledge of musical signs, a clear forming of all intervals and knowledge of all rhythmic notation, clear pronunciation of the text and knowledge of all ornamental figures (Printz 1678, pp. 10–11). In sum, the natural abilities can be reduced to good memory (for pitching intervals); delicate ear (to perceive the good and bad in singing); judgement and understanding (particularly for matters of interpretation and ornamentation; Printz 1678, p. 14). Clearly Printz was advocating singing as a vocational choice within education, a position reflecting the increasing specialisation of the singers selected to perform the figural church music of the age.

Printz's attitude to dynamics seems to combine the traditional German teaching with the more 'modern' concern for text and affect. While he stresses that the singer should not sing too loudly and should cultivate a pleasing sound, and that all the voices should be balanced etc. (p. 21) – rules that are common in earlier writings – he also proscribes singing which is too quiet and that can barely be heard ten steps away:

The notes should be sung at a consistent strength, so that they do not sound weak and strong by turns; it should rather be the text or the affect that requires either stronger or more soothing singing

Die Noten sollen mit einerley Stärcke gesungen werden / daß nicht eine Schwach / die andere Starck laute / es sey denn / daß der Text, oder der *Adfectus* erfordere entweder stärcker oder linder zu singen   (Printz 1678, p. 21)

Like many writers before him, Printz gives close attention to the correct pronunciation of vowels, together with the correct mouth-shape. Furthermore he also remarks on the importance of consonants, particularly since they must be more sharply pronounced in a large building (p. 41).

What seems particularly new in Printz's approach is the responsibility he places on the pupil himself to guarantee his own progress. From the start he is to act intelligently, cultivating his own judgement and establishing a routine of personal practice. This undoubtedly reflects the growing stress laid on the pupil's understanding in seventeenth-century education (see p. 66 above). But it must also relate to a change in musical approach, namely the need for the performer to recognise the affect and sense of the musical setting and to have some view of his role as an orator. The latter responsibility is fulfilled most directly in the singer's addition and control of ornamental figures (see chapter 5).

The boy should first practise singing German Lieder – learning not to sing like a gross peasant – and introducing sweet *trilletti* or the sharp *trillo* from the start (Printz evidently expects the singer to add a variety of ornaments from the earliest stage of his singing *career*).[16] In this way he can practise while all are singing so that his mistakes are not heard. Only with practice does the singer develop a soft, moderate and full voice with a long breath. Thus he will learn to sing with twice as long a breath as someone who does not practise, something which will also enable him to sing passages and trills with more facility (Printz 1678, pp. 15–16). A particularly interesting point of advice is Printz's view that a building with a resonant acoustic will enable the singer to hear and correct his mistakes. Printz may have acquired this advice from an Italian source, since it can be found in Maffei 1562.[17]

A boy can also use a well-responding echo to practise his voice, and in particular he can try to form each and every figure correctly, and so notice if it does not sound well

Ein Knab sol auch seine Stimme ausüben bey einer wol *respondiren*den *Echo*, und da sol er sonderlich versuchen alle und jede *Figur*en recht zu *formir*en / und so er mercket / daß es nicht wol klinge (Printz 1678, p. 16)

Printz stresses that the singer must practise all the intervals. First he can learn these from the teacher, but since the latter usually does not have enough time, the pupil should also practise alone for half an hour a day with a tuned instrument and, for the best training, with a monochord (pp. 23–4).

It is significant that Printz lists many general faults in singing under the heading of common errors in diminution practice, something which shows the fundamental importance of improvised ornamentation to the very basis of singing technique. The faults in 'figured' singing are mainly concerned with articulation, specifically the use of the wrong sort of attack with particular figures. To the general faults of singing (which, reciprocally, also contain points relating to coloratura), belong sharp and flat singing, incorrect intervals, distasteful tone, incorrect rhythm, poor enunciation of text, sloppy intonation and inconsistent tone, no attention to the Fundament and adjacent parts (which can lead to compositional abuses when figures are added), too many dissonances in added figures, breathing in the middle of a figure, and the stringing together of figures like a peasant or 'beer-fiddler'. As ever, imitation of good singers provides the best learning experience (Printz 1678, pp. 74–9).

Printz's general concern for lifestyle doubtless owes something to the classical rhetorical tradition, where the care of the orator's voice and health were just as important as his expertise in rhetorical delivery (see Burmeister, p. 71 above). Certainly Italian authors such as Cerone, Doni and Rossetti wrote much on the lifestyle of the incipient singer, in direct emulation of the discipline of the ancients (see Ulrich 1973, pp. 26–33). Printz laments that general advice on the care of the voice is not generally available in German and that many young *Discantisten* are not well experienced in Latin. His recommendations are most explicit:

But we must first remember that the vocalist should protect himself from impure, foggy, very cold or hot air, north winds, smoke and dust (particularly that from flax and lime), and that he looks after his chest well all the time and keeps it warm.

Wir erinnern aber erstlich / daß sich ein *Voca*list hüte für unreiner / neblichter / sehr kalter oder hitziger Lufft / Nordwinden / Rauch und Staub / sonderlich von Flachs und Kalck / und daß er darneben die Brust allezeit wol verwahre und warm halte. (Printz 1678, p. 17)

He recommends only temperate foods which are to be consumed in moderation, providing an extensive list of prohibited food and drink which includes lentils, white cabbage, sauerkraut, mustard, raw onions, garlic, and radish, sour wine, sour beer and very cold water (p. 18). He even provides an extensive recipe for a drink which lengthens the breath (p. 20). The singer should avoid too much sleep, particularly during the day (p. 18). Moderate bodily exercise is to be recommended before meals, but not so much that it becomes an art and thus leads to a wasting of valuable time. The singer should avoid anger and sadness, too much singing or loud shouting. Perhaps the most alarming recommendation relates to the singer's behaviour:

Fifthly it is to be remembered that vocalists, particularly discantists and altos, should live chastely and modestly, and generally should stay away from women, nor converse with them; for nothing is more harmful to the high voice than the conversation of womenfolk.

Fürs fünfte ist zu erinnern / daß ein *Voca*list / sonderlich *Discant*ist und *Alt*ist / keusch und züchtig lebe / und den Frauenzimmer durchaus nicht zu nahe komme / noch mit ihnen *conversire*: Weil der hohen Stimme nichts schädlichers / als die *Conversation* des Frauenvolckes. (Printz 1678, p. 19)

Printz's misogyny probably derives from the conception that the voice breaks more quickly if the boy becomes sexually aware. Indeed he later explains that the best means of preserving the beautiful high voice is castration, but that this is as little used as justified 'by us Germans' (p. 19).[18]

Printz's writings on vocal training in the cantorates – especially *Musica modulatoria* of 1678 – mark a watershed in the history of German texts on performance: many subsequent treatises are similarly comprehensive, offering instruction from the rudiments through to relatively complex details of ornamentation. Furthermore, some consideration of the rules of singing becomes common in even the most modest of primers; the 'middleground' has thus been greatly extended. For instance, Quirsfeld's *Breviarium Musicum* first appeared in 1675, but singing rules were not included until the 1688 reprint (which continued to be published until 1717). These show the persistence of the traditional German rules codified by Calvisius and Friderici: a lighter voice for high notes, the mouth to be opened only moderately for the greatest beauty of tone, the avoidance of singing through the teeth and nose, correct pronunciation of vowels.

Contrary to Calvisius's advice of 1602, but in agreement with most other sources, Quirsfeld recommends an articulation of runs; he is more precise about how the articulation is to be achieved, showing considerably more knowledge of the physiology involved:[19]

> If there are fast runs, he should not only touch on the notes, but attack each and every one with its own sound. Not with the chest however, which is highly damaging to the lungs, but between the pharynx and the neck, so that the palate is used somewhat.
>
> Wenn geschwinde Läuffer kommen / soll er nicht die Noten nur heraus hauchen / sondern eine jede mit ihrem Tone ausschlagen. Doch nicht mit der Brust / welches der Lungen höchst schädlich ist / sondern zwischen dem Schlunde und der Kehlen / darzu der Gaumen etwas gebraucht wird.
>
> (Quirsfeld 1675/1688, p. 28)

Quirsfeld's requirement that the song begin quietly, gradually increase in dynamics and remain loud to the end, modifies the traditional German stipulation of a steady voice throughout.[20] This advice is duplicated almost word for word in Sperling 1705 (p. 86). It might imply the more widespread acceptance of dynamic flexibility, as recommended by Germans importing the 'new Italian style'. However, it hardly accords with Praetorius's *exclamatio*, which concerned the performance of individual patterns of dotted notes (see p. 73 above).

Mylius 1685, Falck 1688 and Stierlein 1691 are compendia much on the same scale as Printz's, likewise containing extensive surveys of ornamentation. The fact that they are drawn largely from several earlier sources (without apparently copying Printz's work) is striking; it suggests that the need to codify and prescribe vocal practices was very much part of the spirit of the age. Mylius takes much of his information on

82   Music education and the art of performance

mannered singing directly from the manuscript treatise by his teacher Christoph Bernhard; Falck relies on the Praetorius/Herbst tradition; Stierlein's rules on ornamentation seem to derive from Bernhard's manuscript treatise without the intermediate influence of Mylius (he also clearly had access to Bernhard's treatises on composition, which contain much more detailed definitions of the various ornamental devices).

Stierlein 1691 and Hoffmann 1693 (a much more modest tutor) introduce some of the requirements for a suitable singer and the traditional singing rules at the outset, before describing notation. At the beginning of the century such comments would have been added only after the traditional chapters of the Faber/Listenius tradition had been covered. Clearly the suitability of the boy concerned and physiological factors were now important issues in an age when even school musicians were becoming more specialised. Both writers also give dietary advice at this stage, similar to Printz's, prohibiting foods such as raw fruit and nuts (Stierlein 1691, p. 3; Hoffmann 1693, p. 3). The introduction to another large compendium, Feyertag 1695, gives clear testimony that the fundamentals of singing involve interpretative and physiological factors together with a concern for correct posture:

This book, I say, is aimed not only at the use and moderation of one's art or one's voice, but also at how to preserve the outer demeanour of the body while singing and to maintain the limbs in seemly order

Es zielet dieses Buch nicht nur allein auf die Kunst oder Stim̃e zugebrauchẽ u. zu *moderiren*, sage ich / sondern auch die äusserliche Minen des Leibs und der Glieder in geziemender Sittlichkeit unter dem Singen zu halten
(Feyertag 1695, introduction)

Beyer 1703 likewise introduces questions of posture at the outset of his description of the *vitia*: the head should not be hung low so that it inhibits the freedom of the neck (Beyer 1703, p. 65).

It is quite significant that Feyertag describes *moderiren* as a style of singing which is concerned with the sense of the words (Feyertag 1695, p. 234), as if it were a special case to be distinguished from singing without concern for word or affect (see also Bernhard's categorisation, p. 49 above). He states at the outset that he draws most of his material from other sources, so it may be that he is unwittingly preserving an anachronistic distinction. Nevertheless, Falck 1688 similarly sees expressive performance, with dynamics varied according to the text, as part of the special category of ornamented singing, *musica figuralis ornata*.[21] Likewise, Beyer 1703 implies that singing according to the affect of the

The development of performance practice

text is a special type of singing – *musica ornata seu colorata* – in which the concept of ornamentation is vaguely fused with that of dynamic and affective textual expression:

When the notes in a song are not sung simply but decorated with beautiful coloraturas and figures in accordance with the text beneath, so that the singer's voice is heard now strong, now weak, now joyful, now sad.

Wenn in einem Gesang die Noten nicht schlecht hin gesungen / sondern mit schönen *Coloratu*ren und Figuren / nach Anleitung des unterlegten Textes / ausgezieret werden / also; daß der Sänger seine Stimme bald starck / bald schwach / bald freudig / bald traurig hören lässet. (Beyer 1703, p. 53)

Clearly, then, expressive singing was still not to be taken for granted, even at the close of the seventeenth century (certainly Schütz condemned the German ignorance of the style during the middle of the seventeenth century; see p. 42 above).

Furthermore, the advances in vocal technique evident in Printz 1678 did not necessarily infiltrate even the larger treatises. The most comprehensive German school primer at the end of the century is Speer 1697 (a more systematic version of an earlier treatise of 1687). Nowhere else is the student introduced to so many skills in one publication: singing, keyboard and thoroughbass, instruments and composition. Nevertheless, Speer's rules on singing (including some dietary proscriptions) break little new ground, merely repeating the same rules on pronunciation, articulation and breathing that were listed in treatises over a century before (Speer 1697, pp. 19–30). Likewise, the singing rules and *vitia* of Beyer 1703, Fuhrmann 1705 and Sperling 1705 are written firmly in the German tradition and contribute little that is new. Beyer's repeated reference to 'free and unforced singing' ('frey und ungezwungen singen' – pp. 53, 65), and Fuhrmann's prescription of moderate singing so that the voices blend and balance (Furhmann 1705, p. 74), show an approach to choral singing that had not changed for over a century.

The late Baroque era – Tosi, Agricola, Mattheson and the science of singing

The most influential treatise of the late Italian Baroque is Tosi 1723, a text which transmits the details of a practice stretching right back to the time of Caccini. In the decades after its publication it enjoyed a wide reception and was eventually translated into several other languages, including English (1743) and German (1757). No other singing treatise

84 Music education and the art of performance

gives such detail on the interpretation of specific musical genres, or on the type of ornamentation appropriate to each. Although the work is not directly relevant to the German school milieu – since Tosi's main concern is the international, secular world of Italian opera – its basic rules of vocal production accord remarkably closely with German ones; clearly even the traditional German rules on voice production reflected Italian theory and practice. Tosi cautions against singing through the nose and choking the voice in the throat, stresses the importance of intonation (including the difference between major and minor semitones), and advocates careful attention to accurate vowels, good posture and appearance. A long breath should be cultivated and high notes expressed softly. The practice of subtle dynamic changes from the softest *piano* to the loudest *forte* can be traced in Italian literature back to Caccini; dynamic variety is a particular element of the German writers who claimed to transmit the Italian style, in the tradition of Praetorius. Tosi's comments on uniting and blending the two registers, *di petto* and *di testa*, show that the Italians had a greater grasp of this aspect of singing than the Germans. All further detail on singing technique is the direct result of specific ornamental patterns, just as is the case in the German tradition.

The early eighteenth century was a time of marked advances in physiological awareness of the vocal organs. Although little of this filtered through into the standard school manuals (which, if Wesselius 1726 is anything to go by, could still be astonishingly conservative), some of it is evident in Mattheson's *Der vollkommene Kapellmeister* of 1739. The second part of this book opens with a chapter on the 'Examination and the care of the human voice', a subject which Mattheson describes as phonology. His first study is of the *mutation* of the male voice:

with [boys], the strongly increasing ardours and humours generally enlarge and distend all of the ducts and canals of the body. This does not have such a good effect as is manifest with the female sex about the same time.[!] As is easily seen, the natural accretion and release of the ardours and humours, hence also the enlargement of the passages and ducts in the throat whence undeniably derives the lowering of pitch, is impeded in castrati by the early removal of those organs from which all of the fertile humours come, and indeed before the power of enlargement of this last appears.   (trans. from Harriss 1981, p. 240)

bey den letztgenannten die starck-zunehmende Wärme und Feuchtigkeiten überhaupt alle Gänge und Röhren des Leibes erweitern und auftreiben, denen jedoch kein solcher heilsamer Abgang bestimmt ist, als sich bey dem weiblichen Geschlechte um dieselbe Zeit äussert. Bey Verschnittenen wird, wie leicht zu crachten, der natürlichen Wärme und Säffte Anwachs und Ausbruch, einfolglich auch die Erweiterung der Röhren und Gänge in der Kehle, als wovon die Erniedrigung des Tones unwiedersprechlich herrühret, durch frühzeitige Beraubung derjenigen Gliedmaassen verhindert, denen alle fruchtbare Feuchtigkeiten hauptsächlich bestimmet sind: und zwar, ehe die ausdehnende Krafft dieser letzten sich meldet. (Mattheson 1739, p. 95)

It appears that Mattheson expected boys to sing alto and had little experience of mature male falsettists, since he notes that the soprano voice usually breaks to a tenor and the alto to bass. Nevertheless, several earlier German writers imply that broken voices could provide the alto part, Praetorius's distaste for the falsetto register notwithstanding (see p. 73 above).

Mattheson affirms that the knowledge of how to aid and preserve the voice was common in 'olden times' when one could make an actual profession of voice culture, but that modern singers have forgotten it, with the exception of some Italians.[22] He is not slow to note that the great classical orators and actors were constantly advised by skilled teachers off the stage. Nonetheless, the general tone of his writing, and particularly the fact that he believes he is communicating some information for the first time in his own age, may well imply that the vocal training in schools was quite backward during the early eighteenth century. Certainly there are far fewer surviving school primers from this period than from the 'golden years' of the seventeenth century.

Mattheson's description of the vocal organs is the first detailed account of its kind in German literature, relating certain components to specific vocal techniques:

It is indubitably true that such an epiglottis contributes to the delicacy and tenderness of sound, especially as far as trills, mordents, etc., are concerned. It also contributes much, perhaps more than the uvula in the mouth, to everyday pronunciation . . . Thus neither the lung nor the tongue, neither the throat nor the palate, is the true cause of the tone. Even less are the teeth and lips, which have no part in this except that the first yields the air, while the second, after the sound has been produced by means of thirteen muscles through the cleft of the glottis above the windpipe, emits it quite sonorously, clearly, properly, and unrestrictedly.

Thus the unique human glottis is the most sonorous, pleasant, perfect, and accurate instrument. Or, to put it better, it is the single and only true instrument among the great number of instruments of sound, be they produced through art or through nature; for all these wind or string instruments, excluding only the violins, are altogether imprecise compared with the human voice, even if they are perfectly tuned. These words of a very scholarly mathematician . . . confirm my throughts . . . that the human voice is the most beautiful instrument.

(trans. Harriss 1981, p. 243)

Daß nun auch sothanes Oberzünglein zur feinern Bildung und zärtlichern Einrichtung des Klanges, absonderlich was die Triller, Mordanten &c. betrifft, ein grosses und vieleicht mehr, als der Zapffen im Munde zur gemeinen Aussprache, beitrage, solches ist wol ausser Zweifel wahr; dennoch aber thut die Glottis selbst gantz gewiß das meiste und vornehmste dabey: und ist also weder die Lunge, noch die Zunge, weder die Gurgel, noch der Gaumen die rechte Ursache des Tones; vielweniger sind es die Zähne und Lefzen, welche alle keinen weitern Antheil daran haben, als daß die erste den Wind hergibt, die andern aber, nachdem der Schall durch die Spalte des Züngleins oben an der Lufftröhre, mittelst dreizehn Musceln gezeuget worden, fein hohl, vernehmlich, richtig, und ungehindert heraus lassen.

Es ist also die eintzige menschliche Glottis das klangreicheste, angenehmste, vollenkommenste und richtigste Instrument, oder besser zu sagen, sie ist das eintzige und allein richtige Instrument unter der grossen Menge klingender Werckzeuge, sie mögen durch Kunst verfertiget, oder von der Natur hervorgebracht werden; denn alle diese vom Winde getriebene oder mit Saiten bezogene Instrumente, nur die Geigen ausgenommen, sind mit einander falsch, gegen die menschliche Stimme zu rechnen, und wenn sie auch auf das beste gestimmet wären. Diese Worte eines grundgelehrten Mathematici bestätigen zugleich meine anderswo geführte Gedancken, daß nehmlich die Menschen-Stimme das schönste Instrument sey.   (Mattheson 1739, p. 96)

Mattheson draws this latter opinion from Dodart's *Memoir de l'Acad. Roy. des Sciences. l'An 1700,* something which shows the respect that the French sciences enjoyed in the early part of the eighteenth century. It also demonstrates the tendency to seek a scientific explanation and justification for all matters of art and taste.

But Mattheson is rather a Janus-like figure in music literature, seemingly equally open to the ancient and modern trends of his age, a quality which makes him a particularly useful historian. He is clearly conversant with some of the writings of Printz, since he mentions the use of communal chorale singing as a good opportunity for individual vocal practice (see p. 79 above); and he mentions Printz by name at one point, as the only writer to distinguish between vocal and instrumental ornamentation (Mattheson 1739, p. 109). His directions on how to develop the voice are really an amplification of the rules in the more informative German treatises: first the singer should practise sustained notes with as long a breath as possible, without straining the voice; then he should cultivate a wide range of dynamic control (since the innumerable degrees of softness and loudness 'will also move the emotions of his listeners'; Harriss 1981, p. 244).[23] It is striking that Mattheson claims to have encountered no singing master locally 'who had the desire or knowledge to train his charges in this practice', something which may further reflect a certain stagnation in German singing practice at this time. His next advice is a scientific explanation of a familiar rule:

> just as little concern is taken in our singing schools for not forming the sound midway in the rasping throat, by means of the tongue, or between the cheeks and lips . . . Yet if at first sufficient and full breath were drawn and amassed deeply from the chest and lungs to the windpipe and then the tone were given its correct form through a well-calculated division of it by the glottis and its delicate cleft, then, if it has been well-formed to this point, the hollow of the mouth together with the adequate opening of it merely permits a favourable passage. (trans. Harriss 1981, p. 244)

> Eben so wenig bekümmert man sich in unsern Sing-Schulen . . . daß der Klang nicht mitten in der schnarrenden Gurgel, mittelst der Zunge, oder zwischen den Backen und Lippen seine Form bekommen möge . . . sondern wenn erstlich gnugsamer und völliger Athem von unten herauf aus der Brust und Lunge in die Lufftröhre geholet und gesammlet worden, alsdenn mit wolabgemessener Austheilung desselben, durch die Glottis selbst und ihre zarte Spalte, dem Ton seine rechte Gestalt gegeben werde, welchem hernach, wenn er bereits wolgebildet worden, die Höle des Mundes, samt dessen gnugsamer Oefnung, nur einen vortheilhafften Durchgang verstattet. (Mattheson 1739, p. 97)

Mattheson continues with some advice on voice-care which shows more of his reliance on the German tradition, particularly the writings of Printz: certain wines and beers are better for different voices, over-rich foods are to be avoided, and he is sceptical of certain medicines employed by 'so-called virtuosos'.

Mattheson's debt to Printz is also made explicit in his chapter 'On the art of singing and playing with graces' (Mattheson 1739, pp. 109–20). Here he adds more voice rules which correspond closely with the *natura* and *vitia* specified in German treatises on ornamentation: e.g. breaths must never taken be too frequently; pitch and vowels should correctly be observed; one should avoid singing through the nose, with clenched teeth or with the mouth open too far (Mattheson credits Finck with this rule). Another ancient rule of Finck's – that the voice should become lighter the higher it goes, stronger the lower it goes – Mattheson considers to be largely ignored in 'the present wanton world'.

Although Mattheson gives detailed explanations of the various ornaments he deems necessary for the singer of his age, he repeats another maxim of Finck's which must sum up the reality of 'mannered' performance practice over the previous two centuries: 'the matter is not merely determined by rules but more so by usage, long practice, and experience'.[24]

Mattheson's information on phonology is greatly expanded with Agricola's annotated translation of Tosi 1723, the *Anleitung zur Singkunst* of 1757. This was not directly intended for use in schools, although it is difficult to envisage that its influence was not felt in certain establishments. Rather, it belongs to the genre of literature on performance practice most characteristic of the eighteenth century: that which addressed the growing market of cultivated amateurs and the professional secular musicians who were active in the rapidly expanding worlds of the concert hall and opera house. This situation is symptomatic of the decline of music as an indispensable adjunct of education, worship and municipal life, and its rise as an autonomous 'fine' art.

Agricola confirms Mattheson's view that the Germans have not perfected the art of singing to the extent of the Italians (Agricola 1757, p. vii). He similarly takes much of his information on the physiology of the voice from the recent research of the Paris Académie (p. 38), and gives particularly detailed advice on the vocal registers. Many comments amplifying Tosi's original advice might point to specific tastes in the performance of Agricola's own day, a period when the whole concept of 'taste' was of particular importance. Thus the issue of performance practice and style was necessarily a self-conscious activity:

Mezza di voce; the practice of strengthening and then weakening sustained longer notes can be applied to every kind of singing. For here is a fundamental rule of good taste, that each note, no matter how short its duration, must be given with increasing and decreasing strength; this can be compared exceedingly well with the so-called beauty-line in bodies and paintings (see Hogarth's Anatomy of Beauty).

Mezza di voce Die Uebung in dem verstärcken und wieder abnehmenden Aushalten langer Noten, verbreitet ihren Nutzen in das ganze Singen überhaupt. Denn da es eine Grundregel des guten Geschmackes ist, daß jeder Note, wenn sie nur irgend von einige Dauer ist, ihr zu- und abnehmende Stärcke gegeben werden müsse; welches sich mit der sogennanten Schönheitslinie in der Körpern und Gemälden, (siehe Hogarths Zergliederung der Schönheit) überaus wohl vergleichen läßt. (Agricola 1757, p. 48)

This may be distinguished from the seventeenth-century Baroque mentality in which vocal expression was tied (officially at least) to the rhetorical implications of the text and a natural, quasi-mechanical system of affects; style was then the result rather than the aim of performance (see, in particular, Praetorius's similar *exclamatio*, p. 73 above).

Most of the Agricola/Tosi text concerns the performance of specific ornamental figures, those which are improvised by the performer now being termed the 'willkührliche Veränderungen' (free variations). Evidently the ability to ornament remained an essential element of singing well into the eighteenth century. Indeed it was still within this realm that the bulk of what we might call 'singing technique' was learned.

School primers of the mid eighteenth century: Marpurg, Doles, Petri and Kürzinger

Fortunately, there are several tutors designed specifically for schools which give a good picture of the extent to which the developments reflected in Mattheson and Agricola filtered through to the practice of at least some of the cantorates. Marpurg 1763 makes explicit its debt to Tosi at several points and shows a 'modern' approach to the education of the singer and the responsibilities of the teacher. Another manuscript primer from this period is the *Anfangsgründe zum Singen* by Johann Friedrich Doles, cantor at the Thomasschule, Leipzig from 1756.[25] It is difficult to know exactly when Doles wrote this; a date of origin before the end of the 1760s has been suggested, since this was the time E. L. Gerber (the copyist of the surviving manuscript) left Leipzig (Schneiderheinze 1989, p. 6). However, so exactly do various sections and indeed specific expressions correspond with Petri's *Anleitung zur practischen Musik* of 1767 (chapter 9 of which is entitled 'Die ersten Anfangsgründe vor einen Sänger') that it is highly likely that Doles was influenced by this publication.

General singing rules and lifestyle

Doles and Petri follow the traditional format of the German vocal primers of the Faber/Listenius tradition remarkably closely, beginning with the basics of music, the notes, vocal ranges, staves, clefs, intervals and keys etc. Kürzinger 1763, writing in Catholic Germany, follows a similar scheme. Doles's first requirement is a good open and broad chest that allows the singer to perform long notes both strongly and quietly (Doles, in Schneiderheinze 1989, p. 40); although German tutors had traditionally recommended a long breath, control of a variety of dynamics assumes first place here.

Doles and Marpurg mention various rules of life style and diet, much on the lines of Printz;[26] Doles's comments on good hearing, correct pronunciation of vowels, the avoidance of singing through the nose or teeth, of grimaces or shaking, the requirement of a mouth that is not too widely or narrowly opened, and of a voice suited to one of the four standard ranges also show him still to be adhering to the long tradition of vocal rules. Marpurg shows that many schools still maintained the traditional hour after lunch for their singing lessons:

Since it is bad to sing on a full stomach, it would be good if school singing lessons were not held from 1 till 2 in the afternoon, but at a more comfortable hour. The best time for singing practice is in the morning.

Da es nicht gut ist, mit vollgefülltem Magen zu singen, so wäre es gut, daß in manchen Schulen die Singstunden nicht von 1 bis 2 Nachmittags gehalten, sondern in eine bequemere Stunde verleget würden. Die bequemsten Stunden zur Uebung im Singen sind die Morgenstunden. (Marpurg 1763, p. 34)

This reflects both changes in the role of music in education and the developments in musical style. While practical music was less demanding in the sixteenth century when the most influential Lutheran school ordinances were written, music was a good, semi-recreational activity to aid digestion before the afternoon classes. However, since the musical demands made on the more talented pupils had considerably increased, more attention was given to the fundamentals of singing and the care of the voice.

Marpurg, like Doles, repeats much traditional advice, including the ancient rules that one should sing higher notes softer, the lower ones louder, and that one should maintain an even dynamic unless dynamics are otherwise marked (Marpurg 1763, pp. 23–8). The latter rule is particularly interesting: Marpurg takes a convention which stretches back to sixteenth-century tutors, and which (although modified by some seventeenth-century writers advocating a closer attention to the affective content of the text) could still be applied in the mid eighteenth century when the necessary dynamic changes were more likely to be included in the notation. Nevertheless, Marpurg, like Doles and Petri, still advocates the spontaneous application of dynamic devices such as the *messa di voce* to the longer notes (Marpurg 1763, p. 29).

Articulation

While most earlier German writers on vocal style had emphasised the articulation of passages, as if it was a common fault to slur them, Agricola – in his specialist treatise – stresses at the outset that basic singing should be very smooth. Passages were of course still to be articulated, but this was secondary to the fundamental approach. This doubtless reflects a change in the musical style itself; a large amount of the basic substance of high Baroque music comprises passage-work, but

The development of performance practice 91

music of the mid eighteenth century is essentially more melodic in nature and intention. While a sustained singing style had always been implied by the prerequisite of a long breath, here with Agricola the emphasis is that much stronger:

> Here I further give to the singing teacher only the necessary reminder to take care that the notes of the pupil are properly joined and bound together. This happens when one lets the previous note sound until the following is expressed, so that no gaps may be perceived in between

> Hier gebe ich dem Sangmeister nur noch die nöthige Erinnerung daß er in Acht habe, damit die Töne, von der Schüler, gehörig mit einander verbunden und zusammen gehänget werden mögen. Dieses geschieht wenn man den vorhergehenden Ton so lange klingen läßt bis der folgende ausspricht; damit nichts Leeres dazwischen vernommen werde (Agricola 1757, p. 50)

Turning to the school primers, Doles and Petri provide a precise description of articulation marks in the 'traditional' chapter on the signs used in music: slurs indicate not only underlay and ties, but also notes that are to be smoothly bound together; dots or strokes indicate short notes while dots and slurs together indicate that most *galant* of styles, 'Tragen der Töne' ('carrying of the notes'), something which is obviously not technically possible in singing, but which can be understood by analogy with string playing:

> so that one does not completely leave a note when one begins sounding the second, and so one should draw the sound of the first directly into the second.

> da man einen Ton nicht ganz verlassen soll, wenn man den Anschlag des zweyten anhebt, und also den Anschlag des ersten in den andern gleichsam hineinziehen soll.
> (Doles, in Schneiderheinze 1989, p. 39; Petri 1767, p. 26 (with minor verbal differences))

Marpurg – following closely on Agricola's advice – implies that the slurring and shortening of notes is an exception to the generally smooth (but clearly not fully 'slurred') style of singing, and that (contrary to the advice of Doles and Petri) these need not be learned until a later stage:

> and each following note is joined to the previous one in such a manner that no hiatus or space comes between the two notes. The shortening and slurring [of notes] . . . make an exception to this attack, which one does not need to know in the first singing lessons.

> und jeder folgende Ton mit dem vorhergehenden dergestalt verbunden werden, daß kein Hiatus oder keine Lücke zwischen beiden Tönen entstehe. Das

92   Music education and the art of performance

Abstossen und Schleifen . . . machen wegen dieses Anschlages eine Ausnahme,
die man in den erstern Ubungsstunden nicht zu wissen braucht.
(Marpurg 1763, pp. 22–3)

One factor which is given considerable attention by these authors is the concept of 'good' and 'bad' notes, something which had been evident in theoretical and performance writings since at least the late sixteenth century, but which gained prominence in German literature during the mid-eighteenth century. Each beat and division of the same should be divided into its strong and weak components, which are distinguished through the strengthening and weakening of the voice.[27] Marpurg gives a wider context for the concept: 'good' beats ('Tacttheile') should be aligned with long syllables and it is on them that dissonances should fall; they are furthermore the basis for the rhythmic weight of the bar (Marpurg 1763, pp. 76–7).

Doles follows his description of 'Tragen der Töne' with the sign for 'Bebung' or *tremolo*, the pulsating performance of longer notes. The inclusion of these specifically interpretative points in the notational aspect of performance reflect the development of a more normative performance style, something the pupil should assimilate at an early stage. Kürzinger likens the *tremolo* to the vibrato on the violin, and suggests that it is a particular component of the *cantabile* style:

Tremolo . . . the most gentle beating on a single note, which must at the most be an extremely gentle movement of the breath, so that, like the mere bending of the fingertips on the violin, without moving from the place, this is exactly how one succeeds in playing in a true *cantabile*.

Tremolo . . . die allergelindeste Schwebung auf einem einzigen Ton, dabey eine gar sanfte Bewegung des Athems das Meiste thun muß, so, wie auf der Violon die blosse Lenkung der Fingerspitzen, ohne von der Stelle zu weichen, eben dies ausrichtet wenn man recht *Cantabile* spielen will.   (Kürzinger 1763, p. 35)

For Kürzinger the *cantabile* must rule in all pieces that are not explicitly *staccato* in style (Kürzinger 1763, p. 46).

Registers

Another point which distinguishes these texts from most earlier German school primers is their requirement that the vocal registers be smoothly linked, something which had been well documented in Italian literature (see Foreman 1969, pp. 137–8):

The development of performance practice 93

and [he must know] how to join the natural or chest-voice with the falsetto or head-voice in the sustaining of the notes in diatonic order, rising and falling, so that one cannot perceive where the one begins or the other ends.

und die mit der natürlichen od. Bruststimme die Falset- od. Kopfstimme im Tragen der Töne nach diatonischer Ordnung, steigend und fallend, so zu verbinden weiß, daß man den Unterschied nicht wahr nimmt, wo diese od. jene anfängt und aufhört.   (Doles, in Schneiderheinze 1989, p. 42)

Marpurg gives similar advice, recommending Agricola's commentary on the uniting of registers. In his opinion this greatly elaborated translation of Tosi is so important that it should be re-translated into Italian (Marpurg 1763, pp. 19–20).

Exercises

Most impressive is Doles's insistence on thorough practice of a variety of vocal exercises, beginning with the diatonic scale, in numerous metrical and rhythmic formats. The systematic working-through of each interval, including some exercises with swift ornaments, recalls the long tradition of Italian diminution exercises which cultivated both agility and a sense of creativity. As Marpurg states, some of the most difficult intervals are found in the melodic lines of *galant* pieces, rather than those in a more traditional contrapuntal style; this might account for the particular attention given to learning and practising intervals in the performance tutors of this period (Marpurg 1763, p. 32).

Pronunciation

Doles gives very precise directions on how the mouth should be set for the singing of passages:

With these three vowels [a, e, o] he must particularly bear in mind that he should continually press the tongue downwards, make it somewhat flat, and, as far as possible, hold it straight and firmly behind the teeth, by which position of the tongue the nose and throat errors will best be avoided.

Bey diesen 3 Selbstlautern [a, e, o] . . . muß er besonders darauf bedacht seyn, daß er die Zunge stets unterwärts drücke, etwas glatt mache, und hinter den Zähnen, so viel möglich, gerade und fest halte, durch welche Lage der Zunge die Nasen- und Kehlenfehler am besten verhütet werden.

(Schneiderheinze 1989, pp. 61–2)

The attention Doles and Petri (in texts which match each other almost precisely) give to the pronunciation of vowels, final consonants, diphthongs and triphthongs shows a precision of detail that is never found in earlier German literature. Words like 'leide' should first be pronounced 'la-' with the remainder of the diphthong delayed until just before the consonant: 'la-eide' (Doles, in Schneiderheinze 1989, pp. 66–7; Petri 1767, p. 60). Marpurg gives particular attention to consonants, which for him provide the primary articulation of vocal music. Moreover, their strength must be modified according to the size of the building; large buildings and open spaces obviously require sharper performance of consonants than small places, where they must be correspondingly gentler (Marpurg 1763, pp. 38–9). Such detail in pronunciation is undoubtedly a reflection of the contemporary interest in language as the carrier of human reason, and particularly of the attention which had been given, since the time of Gottsched, to the refinement of the German tongue.

Doles introduces his final section, on ornaments, with a statement which would not have been out of place in a treatise written a century before:

It is still not enough that the pupil has achieved a skill in all that he has learned from the beginning up to this point; he must also learn to see, with the performance of each musical piece, what forms part of the beautification and ornamentation of song. And this then is done with the musical graces, which in singing and playing are introduced before, over and after the notes, now slowly, now fast, now strongly, now weakly, in order to give the song more gleaming perfection and greater pleasantness.

Noch ist es nicht genug, daß der Schüler in allem, was er vom Anfang bis hierher ist gelehret worden, eine Fertigkeit erlangt hat, er muß auch noch beym Vortrag eines jeden musicalischen Stücks darauf sehen lernen, was zur Verschönerung und Auszierung des Gesangs gehört. Und dieses thun alsdann die musicalischen Manieren, welche im Singen und Spielen, vor, über, und nach manchen Noten, bald langsam, bald geschwind, bald stark, bald schwach, angebracht werden, um dadurch dem Gesang mehrer glänzende Vollkommenheit und größere Annehmlichkeit zu geben.
(Doles, in Schneiderheinze 1989, p. 69)

Of course the ornaments that Marpurg, Doles and Petri specify belong to the mid eighteenth-century tradition and would hardly be found in a treatise of the Praetorius type (for a more detailed study of ornamentation, see chapter 5). Nevertheless, both the persistent description of ornamentation as the final expressive component of singing style and the survival of many traditional rules on singing technique (also evident in Kürzinger 1763) point to a remarkable continuity in the German pedagogic literature. Certain fundamentals – correct pronunciation, the avoidance of nasal singing, and the cultivation of a naturally balanced, flexible voice – seem to apply to the performance of three generally accepted musical epochs: the late Renaissance, Baroque and early Classical styles. Writers in the mid eighteenth century, just like those at the outset of the Baroque period, borrow from each other, reflecting – and in turn creating – several intertwined traditions of performance technique and style.

Choir direction, ensemble and organisation, and the approach to tempo

The mechanics of directing the singers and the manner in which they were distributed receive only incidental attention in the basic school primers. However, the remarks that do survive may be indicative of the various attitudes towards music in performance and how these developed during the course of the Baroque era. The question of choir direction partly hinges on considerations of the steadiness of tempo and the distribution of forces. These in turn relate to the developments in musical style and the function of music in worship and theological exegesis.

The even division and beating of the tactus is essential to late Renaissance music, and it is not surprising to discover references to this in elementary primers from the late sixteenth century. Some writers imply that the pupil himself learned to beat time as part of his study of singing:

About the tactus . . . it is a steady and measured movement of the hand of the singer, through which, as a rule directed by the signs, the equality of the voices and the notes of the song are correctly conveyed and measured. For all voices must direct themselves according to it so that the song will sound well.

Von dem Tact . . . ist ein stete und messige Bewegung der Hand deß Singers / durch welche / als ein Richtscheidt nach anweisung der zeichen / der gleichheit der Stimmen / und Noten deß Gesangs recht geleitet und gemessen wird. Denn es müssen sich alle Stimmen / so der Gsang sol wol lauten / darnach richten.

(Holtheuser 1586, ch. 9)

However, while Schneegass (1591) asserts that the measure must be even, he does allow for a modification of an even tempo if warranted by the text; Quitschreiber takes up the same statement (see Bartels 1989, p. 181). Burmeister (1601) disapproves of too great a variation of tempo, and he considers it a fault when the choir director gesticulates like an athlete. Nevertheless he does permit a measured variation of tempo on account of the character of the piece and the affective content (see Ruhnke 1955, p. 89).

While much of this information is relatively unambiguous, implying a fairly uniform metre, as directed by the notation, Burmeister reveals something of the more complex situation which prevailed at the turn of the seventeenth century. As a major prescriptive theorist who was well aware of the anomalies in the practice of his age, he was anxious to simplify and modernise the mensural system, divorcing the notated time signature from any finite concept of tempo and thus making the role of the director that much more important (Ruhnke 1955, pp. 78–84). Nevertheless, many contemporary writings still imply a metrical differentiation of tempo, at least between C and ¢.

Much of course depended on the style of the music to be performed, and the new styles proliferating at the outset of the new century provoked the most confusion. While Praetorius notes some difference between C and ¢ – in that C is appropriate for madrigals and ¢ for motets (since the former contain smaller, and thus faster note values) – he observes that a wide variety of practice prevailed:

But each can consider the matter for himself, and, from consideration of the text and harmony, observe where a slower or a faster beat should be maintained. For it is at once certain and most necessary that in concertos for the chorus an extremely slow, solemn beat must be maintained. Because in such concertos now madrigalian, now motet style are found mingled together and exchanged, one must also act according to this when beating; about which there is an extremely necessary invention, where the words of the Italians *adagio, presto* . . . are indicated in the parts from time to time; for otherwise with the two signs C and ¢, so often confused, there is and arises more confusion and hindrance.

And if I look at the Italian compositions of the present time, which in so few years have become directed in a different, singular new style, I find very great discrepancies and varieties in the use of equal and unequal tactus signs.

Es kan aber ein jeder den Sachen selbsten nachdencken / und *ex consideratione Textus & Harmoniae observiren*, wo ein langsamer oder geschwinder *Tact* gehalten werden müsse.

Dann das ist einmal gewis und hochnötig / das in *Concerten per Choros* ein gar langsamer gravitetischer *Tact* müsse gehalten werden. Weil aber in solchen *Concerten* bald Madrigalische / bald *Motetten* Art unter einander vermenget und umgewechselt befunden wird / mus man sich auch im *Tactiren* darnach richten: Darumb dann gar ein nötig *inventum*, das bißweilen . . . die *Vocabula* von den Wälschen *adagio, presto* . . . in den Stimmen darbey *notiret* und unterzeichnet werden / denn es sonsten mit den beyden *Signis* C und ¢ so offtmals umbzuwechseln / mehr *Confusiones* und verhinderungen geben und erregen möchte.

Und wenn ich jetziger zeit der *Italorum Compositiones*, so in gar wenig Jahren gantz uff eine andere sonderbahre newe Art gerichtet worden / ansehe / so befinde ich in *praefixione Signorum Tactus aequalis & Inaequalis* sehr grosse *discrepantias* und *Varieteten*. (Praetorius 1619, p. 51)

Praetorius later makes his taste for the new style particularly clear, showing that variety of tempo and dynamic is essential to the idiom, just as he also stipulated that the singer, as a good orator, must be able to apply a variety of figures (see p. 48 above):

For the motet and concerto [styles] are given a special loveliness and pleasantness and this is brought about, if at the beginning numerous extremely pathetic and slow tempi are set, after which several fast *clausulae* follow: now again slow and grave, now again with faster exchanges mixed in, so that it does not continue all the time in a single pitch and sound but with different kinds of variations, with a slow and [then with a] fast beat: and also with the most concentrated attention to singing with the voice raised and then again with an extremely quiet sound

Sintemahl es den *Motecten* und *Concerten* eine besondere lieblich: unnd anmütigkeit gibt unnd *conciliiret*, wenn im anfang etliche viel *Tempora* gar pathetisch und langsamb gesetzet seyn / hernach etliche geschwinde *Clausulen* darauff folgen: Bald widerumb langsam und gravitetisch / bald abermahl geschwindere umbwechselung mit einmischen / damit es nicht allezeit in einem *Tono* und *Sono* fortgehe / sondern solch und dergleichen verenderungen mit eim langsamen und geschwinde *Tact*: So wol auch mit erhebung der Stimmen / unnd dann bißweilen mit gar stillem Laut mit allem fleiß in acht genommen werde

(Praetorius 1619, p. 80)

Praetorius even suggests that a slower tempo can be associated with a softer dynamic, showing that more than one parameter of performance may relate to the same affect.[28]

The implications of Praetorius's general views on tempo are also evident in a text of the more traditional school-primer format, one which enjoyed wide transmission during the seventeenth century: Friderici's *Die Musica figuralis* (1618/1624). Both Friderici's proscriptions and recommendations imply a variety of practice. His example (Plate 2) shows just how varied the beat could be:

The beat should not be heard throughout in singing, but only seen, or, where it is possible, only observed and noted. (Whereas the cantors leave themselves wide open, and reveal their great folly markedly, and that they still do not know about any well-formed music, when they strike the choir-stick so that it breaks into pieces; and believe they are beating time correctly when they can only bang away in a masculine fashion, just as if they had to thresh oat-straw.)

But where the beat must be made it should not be beaten by just two or three boys alone but by the entire chorus. (Whereas those cantors who have only one or two boys standing in front of them and motion the beat to them and allow the other performers to drag behind them, just as the herdsman with his dogs, are in error.)

In singing a single beat should not be perceived throughout, but the beat should be directed towards the words of the text. (Whereas those cantors who measure out the beat so strictly in a line as the clock its minutes, and observe absolutely no decorum and accommodation towards the text and harmony, are in error. For now a faster, now a slower beat is demanded.)

Im singen sol der *Tact* durchauß nicht gehöret / sondern allein gesehen / oder wo es müglich / nur *observiret* unnd gemercket werden. (Geben demnach die *Cantores* sich zimlich bloß, und ihre grosse Thorheit mercklich zuerkennen / und daß sie noch von keiner rechtschaffenē *Musica* wissen / welche mit dē Chorstocke also zuschlagen / daß die Stücke davon fliegen; Und meinen es sey recht *tactiret*, weñ sie nur mänlich niederschlagen köñen / gleich alls weñ sie Haberstroh dreschen müsten.)

Wo aber *tactiret* werden muß / sol nicht nur zweyen oder dreyen Knaben allein / sondern dem gantzen *Choro tactiret* werden. (Irren demnach die *Cantores*, welche nur einen oder zween Knaben vor sich stehend haben / und denen den *tact* vorschlagen / und lassen die andern *Concentores*, gleich als der Hirte seine Hunde, hinter sich herziehen.)

Im singen sol durchauß nicht einerley *tact* gespüret werden: Sond'n nach dem die worte des *Textus* seyn / also muß auch der *tact* gerichtet seyn. (Irrē demnach die *Cantores*, welche den *tact* so schnurgleich abmessen / alß dz Uhrwerck seine *minuten*; uñ *observiren* gantz kein *decorum* und *convenientz* des *Textus* und der *Haarmoney*. Denn bald ein geschwinder, bald ein langsamer *tactus* erfordert wird.)

(Friderici 1618/1624, rules 17–19)

Plate 2 Friderici 1618/1624: example of variable tempo, according to the affect of the text

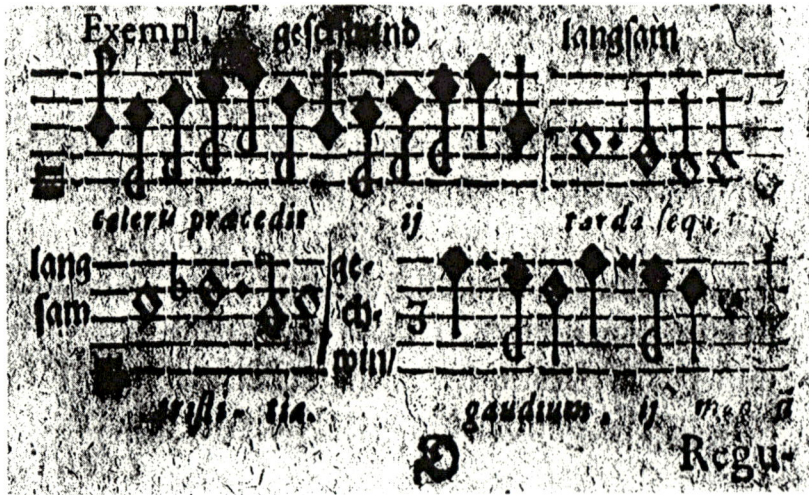

This statement reflects the older writings of Schneegass and Quitschreiber and parallels Praetorius's comments, with its reference to the parameters of text and harmony. However, it does show that many

The development of performance practice   99

cantors still adhered to the strict beating of the tactus and indeed did not confine this activity to visual gestures. Friderici, like Praetorius and most other German writers dealing with matters of tempo (see Bartels 1989, p. 179), advocates a very steady 'ground' tempo:

In singing one should not over-hurry, but sing moderately, slowly, without any fear and timidity. (While those who thus hurry in singing, as if they were hunting a hare are wrong, and, if they come across a few quavers and semiquavers and gloss over them out of fear and haste, so that they do not get half of what is correctly to be seen, even less do they sing correctly. Those who, when they hear that the song is going somewhat weakly, immediately drop their voices out of fear, are also mistaken, and often cause a distemper and confusion in the song, which they surely could have avoided.)

Im Singen sol man sich nicht übereylen / sondern messig / langsam / und ohne alle Furcht und Zagheit singen. (Irren derwegen die / welche im Singen also eylen / als wenn sie einen Hasen erjagen solten / und weñ sie bey etliche *Fusen* und *Semifusen* kommen, auß Furcht unnd Eyle überhin wischen / daß sie nicht die Helffte davon recht zu sehen bekommen / vielweniger recht singen. Auch irren die / welche wann sie hören / daß der Gesang etwan bloß gehet / alsobald ihre Stimme auß Furcht fallen lassen / und machē offt eine Verstimmelung und *Confusion*, des Gesanges, da sie es wol hetten sicher können vorbey gehen.

(Friderici 1618/1624, rule 9)

Schütz, in the preface to his *Historia Der . . . Aufferstehung unsers einigen Erlösers* (1623), similarly prescribes a well-measured, slow beat for chorus sections, something in which 'the soul and life of all music consists'.[29]

Praetorius outlines some further duties of the director, practical ones which he drew from Viadana and which were evidently necessitated by the new concerted style. Here we can see the growth in the role of the conductor in the modern sense:

And L. Viadana will have it that the Kapellmeister or choir director stands by this soloists' choir, or the concerted voices, and has the general bass or continuo part continually to hand, or that which the organist has before him, and must industriously pay attention and observe how the music proceeds; and will signal when one voice alone, when two, when three, when four or more should begin to sing; which thus must always be signified in the general bass part. But when the ripieni and chorus plenus (that is, the full-voiced choir) enter, he should turn his face to all the choirs and lift his hands up high, to show that all should enter together and proceed to make music.

Und wil der *L. Viadana* haben / daß bey diesem *Choro Vocali recitativo*, oder *Concertat-*Stimen der Capelmeister oder *Chori Director* stehen / und stetigs den *Bassum generalem seu continuum* vor sich in der Hand haben / oder aber den / welchen der Organist vor sich hat / mit fleiß in acht nemen / uñ *observiren* müsse / wie die

Music nacheinander fortgehe ; und anzeigen / weñ eine Stim̃ alleine / wenn zwo / wenn drey / wenn viere oder deren mehr / zu singen anfahen sollen; welches dann in dem *Basso Generali* allzeit darbey mus gezeichnet werden. Wenn aber die *Ripieni* und *Plenus Chorus* der vollstimmige *Chor*, angehet / so sol er sich mit dem Angesicht zu allen *Choren* wenden / unnd beyde Hände in die höhe erheben / zur anzeigung / daß sie alle zugleich miteinander einfallen und fort *Musiciren* sollen.
(Praetorius 1619, p. 126)

Friderici draws two other points on tempo from earlier German writings. The advice that the penultimate note should be held and that the bass should hold the final note slightly longer than the other voices is easily traced back to Schneegass 1591 and Quitschreiber 1607 (Bartels 1989, p. 41–2).[30] Here then are two rules of musical style which are not directly dependent on the text but show a concern and awareness of the sense of a musical cadence. While the convention of extending the penultimate chord accords with the modern sense of a ritardando at a cadence,[31] the rule that the bass should hold seems unusual today. It may indicate the importance that Friderici and his contemporaries afforded the bass as the foundation of the harmony, the guiding musical line from which all the other voices ultimately derive. As Printz 1678 adds, the bass should sustain the final note, since the last *syzygia* is always perfect and good (Printz 1678, pp. 22–3).

In the latter half of the century, it seems that the general advice of Praetorius and Friderici was still valid. With Quirsfeld 1675 there is a closer attention to the manner in which the beat is signalled, something which develops the traditional up-down tactus (which was used in both duple and triple metres). The quadruple metre is signified by a beating pattern which traces the four sides of a square or diamond and the triple metre follows a triangular pattern (Quirsfeld 1675, ch. 2). Printz – like many writers from a century before – recommends that the singer learn to beat time so that he can internalise the idea of metrical rhythm:

But because the singer must often have his eyes more on his part than on the director, it is advisable that each and every singer first learns from youth onwards to beat a correct measure himself, not so that he conducts along with the conductor, but so that he can memorise the given beat more easily once it has been seen

Weil aber ein Sänger die Augen mehr auf seiner Stimme / als den *Directorem* haben muß / so ist rathsam / daß erstlich ein jeder Sänger selbst einen richtigen *Tact* bald von Jugend auf schlagen lerne / nicht / daß er zugleich mit dem *Directore tactire* / sondern / daß er den einmal geschenen *Tact* desto leichter im Gedächtniß behalten könne
(Printz 1678, p. 38)

The development of performance practice 101

While Quirsfeld observes that there is still often a difference between C and ₵, the former indicating a very slow tempo ('gar langsam'), Mylius 1685 notes that the difficulty of pieces has increased so much that the half circle is indiscriminately used and that successful performance

> consists mostly in the discretion of an understanding director, when he performs pieces by other authors; how he will correctly understand their opinion with good judgement and industrious reflection

> bestehet meist in eines verständigen *Directoris Discretion* wenn er fremder *Autoren* Sachen machet / wie er dessen Meinung mit einem guten *judicio* und fleißigem Nachsinnen recht vorstehen will (Mylius 1685)

The role of director seems also to be more strongly emphasised in Printz 1678; the singer should always watch the director:

> which he should primarily do when he notices that the director, on account of an elegant figure, such as is made by an artistic musician, which lengthens the time of a beat, or on account of an affect or another reason, directs the measure faster or slower.

> welches er fürnehmlich Thun sol / wenn er mercket / daß der *Director* / wegen einer zierlichen *Figur* so etwan von einem künstlichen *Musico* gemacht wird / die Zeit des *Tacts* verlängert / oder eines *Affecten* oder anderer Ursach halber die *Mensur* geschwinder oder längsamer führt. (Printz 1678, pp. 37–8)

One significant divergence with Praetorius's advice here is the absence of a direct reference to the text (although the concept of affect was presumably dependent on the implications of the words). The improvisation of ornamental figures is given as the primary reason for the rhythmic freedom. This could point to a growing independence of musical performance style from its role of relaying precisely the sense and affect of the text. It is not surprising that in 1690 Ahle (– an important poet laureate influenced by the Pietist movement, who condemned excessive ornamentation and diminution –) stresses the importance of the text in influencing a fluid approach to metre. But he also shows the influence of the Cartesian outlook on the movement of human affects: just as the beating of the heart is affected by all sorts of passions:

> so, according to the disposition of the text and the emotions to be expressed, now a slower, now a faster, now a more even, now an uneven beat is used.

> also wird auch nach beschaffenheit des Textes und der auszudrükkenden Gemühtsbewegung bald ein langsamer / bald ein geschwinder / bald eine gleicher und bald ein ungleicher Takt gebrauchet. (Ahle 1690, p. 34)

The growing focus on the conductor is also evident in a very similar stipulation by Speer (Speer 1697, p. 30) and in Hoffmann's advice that the pupil should observe the director's beat and not himself beat time with the hand or foot.[32] To Feyertag the director is indispensable since all things need direction and authority to avoid chaos; he considers the director to be God's regent, someone who understands all the components of music including thoroughbass and composition (Feyertag 1695, pp. 111–12).

Tutors of the mid eighteenth century add little to our knowledge of conducting practice; however, they do suggest that the practice could still be quite conservative. While Marpurg introduces conducting patterns for each metre, similar to those specified by Quirsfeld (Marpurg 1763, pp. 79–81), Anton 1743 and Doles show that the old down–up method of beating was still applied to all metres, and that the director might even use his foot.[33] With Petri there is even the impression that the director is dispensable and quite often a nuisance. The conductor is most necessary when the singers are unpractised and the instrumentalists poor; otherwise the first violinist should lead, paying particular attention to the point at which the singers enter, where the instrumentalists should play *piano* (Petri 1767, p. 45). The director should avoid all grimaces:

For formerly one took more trouble to see him than nowadays, when one wishes that he were no longer necessary, or that he might beat only the first three bars or so of a piece. Or sometimes in emergencies a couple of bars, to bring an erring voice back to the measure.

Denn, vor diesen gab man sich mehr Mühe, ihn zu sehen, als heut zu Tage, da man wünscht, daß nirgends mehr einer nothwendig wäre, oder daß er nur etwa die drey ersten Takte eines Stücks ausschlagen möchte, und etwa. Sonst einmal in einem Nothfalle ein paar Takte einer fehlenden Stimme durch den Takt zu rechte wiese.   (Petri 1767, p. 48)

Petri also forbids noisy beating since unexpected noise puts off all musicians (*Ibid.*, p. 48). Evidently, then, the audible beat was still practised in parts of Germany at this time.

In all, it seems likely that a variety of directing practices pertained during the German Baroque. While there is an increase in the number of references to the role of the conductor towards the end of the seventeenth century, it is evident that the strict down-up beat was still common. Clearly the type of music to be performed must have been a large factor: many smaller establishments sang only pieces in the traditional motet style which required the even beating of the metre (together with such refinements as the holding of the penultimate chord and allowing the basses to sustain the last note beyond the other voices). But the flexible tempo demanded by the concerted style obviously warranted more focussed direction. There were more differences between each piece, between each composer and conductor and a concomitant centralisation of musical authority.

With the practice of the mid eighteenth century, it is interesting to note that the traditional 'neutral' style of beating seems to have come more to the fore. The 'absolute monarchy' of the director seems to have been eroded somewhat, and the performers presumably took more of a role in dictating tempo and its fluctuation. Musical style might also account for this; in the *galant* idiom the music is essentially melodic, simply textured and evenly paced. Furthermore musical notation was far more precise, composers tending to note every nuance of dynamic, tempo and articulation. As Petri recommends with respect to trumpeters who often play too loudly, the player does best when he asks the director to prescribe the appropriate dynamic for every note in his part.[34]

SETTING THE PITCH

Another duty for which the choir director was responsible was the setting of the correct pitch for the singers. Ruhnke has written a comprehensive survey of the prescriptions of three important writers at the outset of the seventeenth century, Burmeister, Calvisius and Quitschreiber (Ruhnke 1955, pp. 90–4). Burmeister (1601), writing, as ever, with classical rhetoric in mind, prescribes the middle way, a pitch which is neither too high nor too low for the singers. The organist also had much of the responsibility for transposing pieces to the most suitable pitch, using all the keys available to him and writing out transposed parts whenever necessary; the cantor should be aware of the pitch of the organ and transpose downwards if it is set too high. He may use a pipe or flute or can even use the experience of his own vocal range to work out a relative pitch suitable for the choir.

Quitschreiber also specifies how the cantor – having chosen a suitable basic pitch – should softly give to each part its first note, or teach each how to work out his notes from the discant or bass note. Alternatively one can sing a few notes of the discant part in advance so that the mode of the song can be recognised. A key ('Schlüssel' – presumably a sort of tuning fork) may also be used to establish a reference pitch (Quitschreiber 1607, 'einfeltiger Bericht / vom anstimmen der Gesenge').[35]

104   Music education and the art of performance

Both Friderici's advice and his proscription of unsuitable practices point to a wide variety of ways in which the pitch could be established:

In setting the pitch one [person] and no more should be heard. (Whereas it is wrong when as many strike up as want to sing, or when the boys are allowed to tune up together with the cantor and arouse an untimely, unworthy and impolite reciting so that the whole song to come loses its charm.)

The cantor himself should also take pains that he does not tune up all the voices individually; but, where possible, only take the principal pitch, and he should accustom his boys and fellow singers to direct themselves from that. (For it is a great impoliteness to take away the charm from a good song with much tuning-up, just as with a set of bagpipes.)

Im Anstimmen sol einer, unnd keiner mehr gehöret werden. (Wird derowegen geirret, da ihrer so viel anstimmen, als ihrer singen wollen, Oder wo den Knaben gestattet wird, daß Sie allzusammen mit dem Cantore intoniren, Und ein unzeitiges, unlöbliches und unhöffliches geplärr erwecken, Dadurch dem gantzen zukünfftigen Gesange seine Lieblichkeit genommen wird.)

Auch sol der Cantor selbst sich befleissigen, daß Er nicht alle Stimmen insonderheit anstimme: Sondern wo müglich, nur den *Principalem Clavem* nenne, und seine Knaben unnd *Concentores* gewehne, sich darnach zu richten. (Dañ es ist eine grosse Unhöffligkeit, ein guten Gesang die Lieblichkeit, mit vielem anstimmen, gleichsam als mit einer Sackpfeiffen vorher benehmen.)

(Friderici 1618/1624, rules 5–6)

Quitschreiber 1607 recommends the downward transposition of a fourth when the organ is too high, the upward transposition of a fifth when the plucked stringed instruments are too low. Quitschreiber's general prescription of possible transpositions up or down a fourth or a fifth comes directly from the pitch relationships of the three hexachords, on C, F and G:

So if the song in G with a B♭ (which with the musicians is called the first tone) is on account of an organ thus too high, I set it a fourth lower from G into D . . . But if however a song is too low on account of a lute, harp, instrument etc, I transpose it, as it suits, a fourth higher out of the hard C hexachord into the previous flat, soft hexachord, or even out of the newly invented hard hexachord on D with a B[♮], a fifth or Quint higher into the hard hexachord on A . . . Such a hard hexachord is to be counted a second higher than the first B♭, soft hexachord.

Als wenn der Gesang aus dem g b-mol (Welcher bey den *Musicis* der erste Thon genennet wird) wegen einer Orgel also zu hoch . . . so setze ich in eine Quart tieffer aus dem g in das d . . . Ist aber eine Gesang wegen einer Lauten / Harffen / Instrument &c. also zu tieff / so setze ichs nach gefallen / wie das Erste / eine Quart höher aus dem ♮-dur in voriges b-mol Gesang / oder auch wol aus jetzgedachtem d ♮-dur Gesang eine Quint oder Fünffte höher in das a ♮-dur Weise . . . Solcher ♮-dur Gesang ist nach dem ersten b-mol Gesang zu rechnen eine Secunda höher. (Quitschreiber 1607, ch. 10)

Praetorius too points to a practice of transposing certain pieces – down a fourth if there is a B♭ key signature, down a fifth into the soft hexachord with a B♭ if there is none in the signature. This should happen when the bass is notated in the high C3, C4 or F3 clefs. Clearly organists were used to a great amount of transposition, and Praetorius outlines ways of avoiding awkwardly tuned thirds which often arise with transposition; another solution, which he had learned from Calvisius, was to tune one or two 8-foot flute stops on the organ down a tone or semitone (Praetorius 1619, pp. 80–1). Praetorius also recommends transposition down a tone for pieces which have a wide range and cannot thus be taken down a fourth or fifth.[36] He later outlines the duties of the organist who must play a prelude to the concerto in such a way that the players can tune their instruments; the notes for open strings must be prominently held (Praetorius 1619, p. 151).

Erhardi 1660 and Gradenthaller 1687 show that the transposition by a fifth or fourth was still an option in the latter half of the century.[37] Although the song may also be transposed by a second or third or indeed by any interval, Erhardi notes that transposition should only be made when necessary.[38] Erhardi does not specify why this should be the case. Most probably, with the increasing use of transposed modes, musicians – and organists in particular – were developing a concept of differentiated keys which, although clearly not tied to an absolute pitch standard, must have been influenced by questions of temperament.

Nevertheless, Printz, writing a few years later, still allows for transposition of pieces which do not employ instruments; his prescription that the pitch should be chosen to suit the range of the singers recalls the advice of writers from the beginning of the century (Printz 1678, p. 7). He and Mylius both show that the convention of using an organ prelude to set the pitch still pertained in the late seventeenth century (Printz 1678, p. 21, Mylius 1685). Indeed, if Petri is to be believed, this tradition survived into the mid eighteenth century: string players should use their bows and not pluck when tuning up; organists should not play for too long and should not insert quiet passages which suddenly reveal the trumpets testing their tuning (Petri 1767, p. 47).

THE SIZE AND DISTRIBUTION OF VOCAL FORCES

Questions of balance and the number of singers to a part often relate to the changing styles and functions of church music. Schneegass 1591 and Quitschreiber 1598 both stress that points of imitation need to be clearly sung in fugal writing (Bartels 1989, p. 146). Schneegass 1591 and C. Praetorius 1574 also specify that the choral sound be homogeneous and harmonious (*ibid*., pp. 49–50). Evenness of dynamic and balance is the emphasis of Calvisius's third rule of vocal performance.[39]

Calvisius does not specify how many singers should sing to a part, but he does suggest that the pupils sometimes sing together in unison:

If one line is sung, they should begin together and end at the same time and never take breaths together other than in the rests.

Qui vnam vocem canunt, simul & concorditer incipiant & desinant, nequaquam tamen simul, nisi in pausa respirent.   (Calvisius 1602, rule 8)

Quitschreiber 1598 calls for an emphasis on the outer parts, bass and discant (Bartels 1989, p. 49), something which might reflect a new conception of the texture of music, symptomatic of the Baroque idiom *per se*. Praetorius stresses the importance of the bass as the fundament of all the voices:

And finally since the bass is thus the fundament of all voices, it must be heard at all places and distances, far more and truly than the other voices, particularly when the choirs are diversely placed far from each other in the church.

Und dieweil endlich der Baß / also / das Fundament aller Stimmen / an allen örthen unnd enden / bevorab / wenn die Chor in der Kirchen weit vor einander unterschiedlich angestellet / viel mehr und eigendlicher / als die andere Stimmen gehöret werden muß.   (Praetorius 1619, p. 92)

Even in polychoral music, Praetorius – as a composer – clearly desires the actual bass line to be doubled in certain places:

Therefore it is much better, and the song will have more harmony, if, when the choirs come together or go along with each other, all the basses are then written in unison; since they are to such a degree the voices that keep together, nourish and augment the harmony

Derowegen viel besser / und wird der Gesang vielmehr *Harmoniae* haben / daß / wenn die *Chori* zusammen kommen / oder mit einander fortgehen / alsdann die Bässe alle in *Vnisonum* gesetzt werden: Sintemaln sie dergestalt solche Stimmen seyn / welche die *Harmoniam* gleichsam erhalten / ernehren und vermehren
(Praetorius 1619, p. 94)

Friderici likewise alludes to the fundamental role of the bass when he gives a helpful diagram of how the singers are best positioned:

Also, not only the choirs – when there are diverse choirs – but also the equivalent voices of each choir should be placed and disposed with the fundamental voices standing a little further from each other, so that the resonance can come better to the listeners. Thus, in a song of eight voices:

Chori Primi	**Chori Secundi**
Cantus	Cantus
Altus	Altus
Tenor	Tenor
Bassus	Bassus

Auch sollen nicht alleine die *Chori*, wann unterschiedene *Chori* seynd, Sondern auch die gleichen Stimmen beyderseits Choren jegen einander gefüget und gestellet seyn, Doch also, daß die Fundament Stimmen ein wenig weiter von einander stehen, und die *Resonantz* besser zu den Zuhörern kommen könne. Als: in *Cantionibus 8. Voc.*[40] (Friderici 1618/1624, rule 12)

Michael, in the preface to his *Musicalische Seelenlust* II, 1637, likewise places the solo bass in a special place, at some distance from the continuo.[41]

Friderici's diagram is one of many indications of an imaginative and adaptable approach to the positioning of vocal forces during the early seventeenth century. For instance, Praetorius also provides countless suggestions in his treatise of 1619 and Schütz includes some interesting advice in the published prefaces to his music. Not only does he suggest that discrete choirs can be placed some distance from one another (e.g. *Historia Der . . . Aufferstehung unsers einigen Erlösers*, 1623; *Musicalische Exequien*, 1636), but he also advocates blending the choral sound by placing the *capella* of one choir with the *favoriti* of another (*Psalmen Davids*, 1619).[42]

The practice of vocal scoring – how many people sang each notated part – is a much more complex issue, although certain conventions emerge which might pertain for much of the Baroque period. It is not clear from Friderici's diagram whether more than one singer is to be singing each part. Nevertheless, in another context, he implies that more than one singer could sing a part in church music since he excludes this practice from 'private' (presumably chamber) music. The excepting of the bass and discant is again to be noted:

In chamber music it is not seemly that two should sing a part when the others are one to a part. (It can happen though in the bass or in the discant, with their appropriate instruments, and with a particularly pertinent disposition.)

108   Music education and the art of performance

In einer *Privat Musica* gebühret sichs nicht, daß ihrer zwene eine Stimme singen, wann die andern einfeltig besetzet. (Es möchte denn in dem *Basso*, oder in den *Discanten* mit seinen füglichen Instrumenten, und mit sonderlicher füglicher *Disposition* geschehen.)   (Friderici 1618/1624, rule 13)

While Friderici's examples and diagram imply that he is most concerned with a fairly traditional motet repertory, it is clear that Praetorius is attempting to describe the practice in 'modern' concerted music. The complexity and confusion of his instructions and terminology is testimony both to a wide variety of practices and to the fact that many of these issues were still too new to be securely categorised.[43] For example, *capella* can refer to a vocal choir that is added to the other performers when they all come together.[44] This group can contain four or more singers, or may even be omitted. The term is also applied to a choir in which all four voices are vocal (as opposed, for instance, to a choir of cornets or violins) and is therefore indispensable; thirdly, it may apply to an optional instrumental group, placed somewhat apart in the church (Praetorius 1619, pp. 133–5; for a more detailed discussion see Bartels 1989, pp. 22–4).

Praetorius also describes the two basic *types* of singers, the *voces concertatae* and the *ripieno*. The former are clearly the most expert singers who are expected to understand all the modern manners and who presumably sing one voice to a part:

I use the term concerted or rather concerting voices, for those who respond among each other, and concert and dispute as to who among them can do it best. Therefore one should select, dispose and order the best singers for such parts, those who not only are perfect and sure of themselves, but also have a good disposition to sing in the current new manner and fashion, so that the words are correctly and clearly pronounced and intelligibly recited just like an oration; because of this the Italians sometimes also call it the recitative chorus.

Ich nenne es *Voces Concertatas, vel potius Concertantes*; die gleichsam einander *Respondiren*, und untereinander *Concertiren* und streitten / wer es unter ihnen zum besten machen könne. Darumb man denn zu solchen Stimmen die besten *Cantores* und Sänger außlesen / bestellen und ordnen mus / die nicht allein *perfect* und gewiß seyn / sondern auch auff jtzige newe Manier und Weise ein gute *disposition* zu singen haben / also das die Wörter recht und deutlich *pronunciret*, und gleich als eine *Oration* vernehmlich daher *recitiret* werden; derer ursachen es die *Itali* auch bißweilen *Chorum recitativum* nennen.   (Practorius 1619, p. 126)

The solo performance of the vocal lines of concerted pieces is made explicit in Praetorius's recommendation for schools which have no instrumentalists:[45]

The development of performance practice 109

So in schools one can also – when no instrument is available – place several pupils on a part or line; and then, where *voce* is written, only one, who has the best voice, must sing; but where *instrumento*, another who also has a fine voice [should sing]; and then where *omnes* is written, there they should all join in together.

So kan man auch in Schulen / wenn kein *Instrument* vorhanden / etliche Schüler bey einen *Partem*, oder bey einer Stimme stellen; und alßdann mus / wo / *Voce*, stehet / nur einer / der die beste Stimme hat / allein singen; wo aber / *Instrumento*, ein ander der auch ein feine Stimme; und dann / wo / *Omnes*, daselbst fallen sie alle zugleich miteinander ein.   (Praetorius 1619, p. 192)

Indeed Praetorius recalls Viadana's experience of the shortage of singers in certain establishments; with only two or three singers, pieces in the traditional motet style were hardly successful. This thus necessitated the very invention of the new style as one fundamentally for soloists.[46]

With regard to the *ripieno*, Praetorius first gives a literal definition; the word implies that the full complement of musicians should join in. He then shows that this is achieved by adding doubling parts to the existing texture at important junctures:

So, when a large company of musicians is available, one can also have such ripieno parts copied out two or three times, and have them distributed and divided into different choirs placed far apart from one another; which I have then usually called *chorus pro capella* . . . And so the *ripieni* are nothing other than certain *clausulae* or small pieces out of a concerto, which are sung and sounded in the other choirs. Therefore RIPIENO actually means not the full chorus, but special reiterated full sections, the *clausulae*, which are taken from the principal voices of a concerto, and set out for other diversely separated choirs, in order to make a complete and full-voiced concerto.

So kan man auch / do eine grosse *Compagny* von *Musicis* vorhanden / solche *Ripieni* zwey: oder dreymahl abschreiben lassen / und in unterschiedene weit von einander abgesonderte *Chor distribuiren* uñ abtheilen: welches ich dañ meistentheils *Chorum pro Capella* genennet habe . . . Uñ sind also die *Ripieni* nichts anders / als gewisse *Clausulae* oder *particulae* aus einē *concert*, welche in dē andern Chore gesungē uñ geklungē wird. Heist derowegē *RIPIENO* eigentlich nicht *chorus plenus*, besondern *Reiteratae plenitudines*, die *clausulae*, welche aus den Häupt-Stimmen des *Concerts* genommen / und in andern unterschiedenen abgesonderten *Choren* auffgesetzet werden / einen völligen und vollstimmige *Concert* zumachen.
(Praetorius 1619, p. 131)

Gengenbach 1626 takes over much of Praetorius's Italianate terminology, noting the three meanings of *capella* and terming the concertising solo voices the *choro favorito*, the singers who gain much favour and praise (Gengenbach 1626, p. 145).[47] Erhardi likewise describes the *favorito* as a choir of the best singers (in one to three parts), after which the entrance of the *capella* works to the greater sounding and splendour of the music (Erhardi 1660, p. 125). Heinrich Schütz refers explicitly to the format of the vocal choirs in the preface to his *Musicalische Exequien* of 1636: the director may recopy the chorale sections from the published parts so that they can be doubled by the ripienists;[48] similarly in the preface to *Symphoniae Sacrae* III of 1650, Schütz remarks that the four parts of the *complemente* can be copied so that an alternative instrumental choir can be formed.[49] It would be a unique occurrence in music publishing today if an author recommended that copies be made of his own edition! That the *choro favorito* should comprise only four singers is suggested in the preface to Schütz's *Psalmen Davids* 1619, where the composer notes that in certain pieces the second choir can act as a *capella* (which should be strongly furnished), whereas the first choir (as the *choro favorito*), should contain only four singers.[50]

In all, then, the new German church concerto, influenced as it was by Italian monody and recitative, was essentially music for skilled soloists, doubling singers being an optional addition to the sections with fuller textures. It is thus not surprising that there were increasing problems regarding the place of music within the educational system of German schools. The cantorates had been established to foster general and competent singing in the schools, but the cantors were performing increasingly specialised music which utilised only the most talented musicians in the school. However, given that the cantorates often had to furnish music for more than one church, good solo singers were often in high demand. As Friccius observed, singers often performed on a rota system, coming together only on special occasions:

For although such singers have not all been together at one time, but have performed their office in alternation, there is no doubt however that on high feasts, where not all, but the majority, have come together, the most lovely music-making has taken place.

Denn ob wol solche *Cantores* nicht alle auff ein mal beysammen gewesen seyn / sondern wechselsweise ihr Ampt verrichtet haben / so ist doch kein Zweiffel / daß an hohen Festen / wo nicht alle / doch die meisten zusammen komen seyn / und auffs lieblichste *Musicirt* haben werden   (Friccius 1631, p. 297)

Several other forms of evidence suggest that the vocal choirs were often quite small. Thomas Selle, in a letter to the Hamburg town council, suggests that a normal Sunday required two each of basses, tenors and altos, and four discantists (Krüger 1933, p. 68). However, many of his writings suggest that he would have preferred a far larger pool of

The development of performance practice 111

performers and doubling ripienists (Krüger 1956). Snyder's study of Buxtehude's performances shows that most of his four-voice church music was performed with single singers (Snyder 1987, pp. 360–6). Furthermore, Erhardi was obviously contemplating small forces when he suggested that if the alto singer is missing the part may be sung by a discantist, falsettist or eunuch in the higher octave (Erhardi 1660, p. 103; see p. 203 below, n. 8).

Printz gives perhaps the clearest indication of vocal scoring practices for the latter part of the seventeenth century. His instructions for the prefects who direct the street and house singing (these groups often being termed the *chorus symphoniacus* – see p. 4 above) show that there were often several pupils singing from one part:

The most practised singer of each voice should carry the part himself and very promptly look up the piece which the prefect indicates

Der geübteste Sänger von jeder Stimme sol seine *Partem* selbst tragen / und das Stück / welches der *Praefectus* andeutet / fein zeitlich aufschlagen
(Printz 1678, pp. 5–6)

Furthermore, Printz notes that it is easier to bring an erring singer back to rights when the part is furnished with other singers.[51] Nevertheless, even in this repertory, which presumably comprised motet and chorale-based compositions, there were occasions when single-singer performance was preferable:

If a piece is so scored that now 1, 2, 3 or at most 4 voices are heard alone, with more later joining in, then the prefect should arrange it so that the best singers each sing a part completely alone, so long as the few parts can be heard alone. But where more voices are added to this, he should let all the choir-singers join in as a capella. For if many sing a single part in few-voiced circumstances, in general one spoils what the other has made good

Wenn ein Stück also gesetzt ist / daß bisweilen 1/2/3 oder aufs höchst 4 Stimmen alleine gehöret werden / bisweilen mehr darzu fallen / da sol der *Praefectus* anordnen / daß die besten Sänger jeder eine Stimme gantz alleine singen / so lang die wenig Stimmen sich alleine hören lassen. Wo aber mehr Stimmen darzu kommen / sol er alle Chor-Sänger gleichsam als eine Capelle mit einfallen lassen. Denn wenn in wenigstimmigen Sachen ihrer viel eine einzige Stimme singen / so verderbet gemeiniglich einer / was der ander gut machet
(Printz 1678, p. 6)

Printz also repeats the traditional advice dating back to Friderici that 'private' music should be performed with single voices, something which implies that there were public occasions on which it was feasible, if not preferable, to double parts. His clearest testimony on vocal scoring –

which complements the evidence from the earlier writings – comes with his advice on communal breathing:

When several sing one part, as tends to happen in full-voiced motets or with capella parts, they should all begin, continue and finish together, but not take breath together.

Wann ihrer etliche eine Stimme singen / wie in Vollstimmigen *Motetten* oder Capell-Stimmen zu geschehen pfleget / sollen sie zugleich anfangen / fortgehen / und aufhören / nicht aber zugleich Athem holen. (Printz 1678, p. 22)

Thus doubling voices were clearly preferred in the motet style and the *capella* sections of the 'modern' style. That these conventions pertained until at least the early eighteenth century is suggested by Fuhrmann's comments about problems of simultaneous diminution:

For if two singers sing a part simultaneously (which is often allowed in a *capella* so that the same will sound the more penetrating) . . . they will never agree on a single note

Denn wenn 2. Sänger zugleich eine Stimme singen (welches man offt in *Capella* thun läst / damit es desto durchdringender daselbst klinge) . . . so werden sie nimmermehr einerley *Noten* zusammen bringen (Fuhrmann 1706, pp. 77–8)

Scheibel gives a useful picture of the practice in the second decade of the eighteenth century. He notes that the musical practice of his time was too extravagant and that some churches maintained three or more choirs, as many organs and even Italian castrati (Scheibel 1721, p. 54). His prescription that the principal parts be sung by only one or at most two singers implies that he was countering a trend towards a fuller choral sound:

If each part or voice is furnished with one or at most two subjects, who distinguish themselves, a choir is well provided for. Especially since nowadays few arias are sung tutti but mostly solo . . . and if tuttis of such a kind occur, it is enough if the principal parts, although they comprise single persons, do their duty.

Wenn jede *Partie* oder Stimme mit einem oder auffs höchste zweyen *Subjectis* versehn / die das ihre *praestir*en / so ist ein Chor gutt bestellt. Zumahl heute zu Tage da wenig Arien *tutti*, sondern meistens *Solo* gesungen werden . . . und komen dergleichen *tutti* gleich vor / so ist es genug / wenn die Haupt-Stimmen / ob sie gleich aus eintzeln Personen bestehen / das ihrige thun.
(Scheibel 1721, pp. 54–5)

Later writers strengthen the impression that it was becoming standard practice to perform with multiple singers:

Each part must be peopled not by an even division of the number of people present but according to the respective strengths of voices, so that none stands out from another but each part is as strong as the others.

> Jede Partie muß, zwar nicht allezeit in Ansehung der Anzahl der Personen, sondern nach Beschaffenheit der Stärke ihrer Stimmen, gleich stark besetzet seyn, damit keine vor der andern hervorrage, sondern die eine so starck als die andere gehöret werde. (Marpurg 1763, p. 49)

Petri gives a more detailed version of the same advice.[52]

Of course the traditional scorings associated with the Baroque concerto style hardly pertained in the mid eighteenth century. With the importation of 'even newer' Italian styles with their sharper distinction between arias, choruses and recitatives, it may be that the vocal forces were divided more along the lines of modern practice. With neither Marpurg 1763 nor Petri 1767 is there any mention of the division of singers into concertists and ripienists, not to speak of the *favoriti*. Nevertheless in Petri's greatly extended treatise of 1782 he mentions the term *Ripienisten* within his analysis of the decline of singing in German schools.[53] But here it seems almost certain that Petri is using *Ripienisten* in a more modern sense, to describe chorus singers, those who were not trained as soloists but who presumably sang in all the pieces labelled as choruses.[54]

The testimony of Scheibel shows that some still preferred not to double tuttis with ripienists in the early eighteenth century. Indeed the rector at Osnabrück stipulated that only the best voice of each part should sing in the tuttis, in a communication of c.1750 (Bösken 1937, p. 143). Rifkin has examined Bach's practice in detail and found convincing evidence in the original sets of parts to suggest that Bach generally employed – if not indeed preferred – single voices in his choruses (Rifkin 1982). If the writings of Printz and Fuhrmann are anything to go by, it is likely that Bach would have grown up accustomed to traditional scorings: the allowance or preference for several voices to a part in motets, but solo performance of concerto pieces with the optional addition of ripienists for the tuttis. The question hinges on whether Bach consistently used the ripienists for the choruses of his 'concertos' (as he termed the cantatas) – and Rifkin suggests that Bach initially tried it at Leipzig but soon gave up. He also argues that C. P. E. Bach followed the same practice in his performance of the *Symbolum Nicenum* from the B Minor Mass in 1786 (Rifkin 1986).[55]

INSTRUMENTAL TUITION IN SCHOOL PRIMERS

The seventeenth century

It has already been shown that there was a significant growth in attention to instrumental tuition during the seventeenth century (see pp. 61–3 above). Here there is not room to give a comprehensive study of instrumental practice in the German Baroque; rather, this examination is concerned with the specific references to instruments in the 'vocal' primers, noting those factors of technique and interpretation which gain particular attention.

Independent instrumental parts were integral to the new concerto style, so it is not surprising that Praetorius, as its apologist, was the most comprehensive commentator on the instruments of his age. The standard primers do not show an immediate change of style; as Hizler states, the basic rudiments and experience in singing provide a good background for instrumental study:

But should someone also wish to go further and practise instrumental music, he would be able to have good occasion, help and encouragement towards instrumental music from this vocal music[book] and particularly through the new universal scale in the same [a diagram showing all the pitches with letter names and solmisation syllables].

Wolte aber jemand sich auch weiters und in der *Instrumental-Music* uben / der würde auß dieser *Vocal-Music*, und sonderlich durch die neure *Scalam Universalem* in der selbigen / guten Anlaß / Behelff und Fördernuß zur *Instrumental-Music* haben können. (Hizler 1623/1628, foreword)

La Marche (1656) likewise suggests that the fundamentals he has outlined can equally well be employed for instrumental performance if the pupil lacks a suitable voice; the only difference is that what the one does with the mouth the other does with the hand and fingers (La Marche 1656, p. 23).[56]

The first, very striking, description of instrumental technique and style is found in Herbst's celebrated treatise on vocal ornamentation, a greatly expanded version of Praetorius's original text of 1619. The greater emphasis given to instrumental exercises in the second edition (1653, p. 51; cadential formulae for violinists, cornettists and flautists) exemplifies the expansion of instrumental practice. The rules on bow direction are the first reference in German writings to the 'rule of the downbow'; this is the only actual information on instrumental technique, but it is significant that it relates directly to musical interpretation: strong metrical beats and divisions are played with the stronger stroke:

It is to be noticed that at the beginning of the music the bow should be drawn towards the right hand. And if whole rests appear one must [afterwards] draw the bow downwards, but where only half rests or *suspiria* are found, the same should [afterwards] be drawn upwards. It should also be known that whenever

The development of performance practice 115

the sign *T* is found one should draw the bow downwards; but when this other sign *P* occurs, it should be drawn upwards.

Es ist zu mercken / das im Anfang der *Music* der Bogen soll gegen der rechten Hand gezogen werden. Und wenn gantze Pausen vorhanden / muß mann den Bogen abwerts / da aber nur halbe Pausen oder *Suspiria* sich finden / denselben auffwarts führen. Auch ist zu wissen / daß / so offt dieses Zeichen T gefunden wird / soll man den Bogen unter sich: Wo aber dieses andere Zeichen P stehet / denselben über sich ziehen. (Herbst 1653, p. 51)

The examples are basically exercises in diminution, which, just like those for voice, are the principal didactic means for cultivating facility in performance. The bowing indications are designed to generate a down-bow on the last note of each cadence (Example 4).

Crüger 1654, on the other hand, suggests that diminution was a greatly abused practice and that the violinist should cultivate a long stroke. He repeats – almost literally – Praetorius's complaint that some performers ruin the work through excessive diminution and adds a passage concerning instrumentalists in particular:

Many instrumental musicians are also accustomed to such a bad and annoying way of playing, particularly those who play on cornetts and violins, but it would nevertheless be far more to their credit and renown and far more pleasant to the listeners, if they were to take pains to employ a steady, sustained long stroke with fine tremulants [vibrato?] on the violin.

Zu solcher bösen und verdrießlichen Art gewehnen sich auch viel Instrumentales Musici / sonderlich / auf Cornetten und Violinen / da es doch vielzierlicher / Ihnen auch rühmlicher und den Zuhörern weit angenehmer würde seyn, wenn sie sich eines steten / ausgedehnten langen Strichs mit feinen Tremulanten auf Violinen befließen und gebrauchten. (Crüger 1654, p. 190)

That the long bowstroke was not traditionally an aspect of German technique is also suggested by Schütz's remarks in the preface to *Symphoniae Sacrae* II of 1647; he observes that the modern Italian style is still largely unknown and that performers should become familiar with the correct tempo, the black notation and the steady, sustained bowstroke before attempting these pieces in public.[57]

Falck's extensive treatise of 1688 owes much to the Praetorius tradition, and, like Herbst, includes references to string playing. However, his information covers far more than bowing directions: the strings and tuning of the violin, viola and viola da gamba, purity of intervals and some quite detailed directions on holding, posture and hand position (Falck 1688, pp. 186–93). He also includes advice on how to perform

116   Music education and the art of performance

coloraturas and rapid runs, namely with strokes near the end of the bow, where it is light (*ibid.*, p. 191).[58] His comments on the rule of the downbow develop those of Herbst: sometimes two downbows or two upbows must be used in succession if the larger bowing scheme is to be satisfactory (*ibid.*, p. 192). This style of bowing, which was given particular attention in German-speaking lands with the publication of Muffat's

Example 4   Herbst 1653, pp. 57–8

Florilegium Secundum of 1698, is often regarded as the French tradition today. Nevertheless, Falck's comments suggest that the basic principles were already part of German practice, whether as the result of earlier French influence or as part of an indigenous tradition. Falck observes that players often do not agree on the correct bowing for a triple-time bar: some play it with one downbow followed by two upbow strokes, others in regular up and down strokes. The choice should not matter provided that the composition is not deformed, the intention of the composer is attained, and the players' strokes are satisfactorily coordinated (*ibid.*, p. 193).[59]

Falck's attitudes provide a useful insight into the status of performance practice of his age. Certain conventions were valid, but the *musical* result was what counted – performance conventions were a means rather than an end. And, to Falck, the end was the realisation of the composer's intentions, intentions which presumably had something to do with a composer's insight into the 'natural mechanics' of affects and the implications of the text, not necessarily the specific details of performance.

Detailed string instruction is found in the first German Baroque treatise devoted solely to the art, Merck's *Compendium musicae instrumentalis* of 1695. This is also designed to give the pupil background in the rudiments of music in case he had somehow been denied singing tuition (see p. 62 above). After describing notation, Merck gives instructions in string tuning and bowing according to the stresses of the measure; his examples and comments show that he favours the retaken downbow over successive upbows.[60] He allows an exception to this preference in triple time when the movement is fast (*ibid.*, p. 14).

While much of the information is applicable to general performance practice (trill signs, Italian terms) some of it is clearly string-specific: the sign 'm' for moving the whole hand (vibrato?), terms such as 'Spiccato' and 'Harpeggiato' which, as Merck states, are not necessary for the beginner, but are used in the publications of Biber, Walther and Westhoff (*ibid.*, pp. 14–16).

Merck's rules on holding the instrument are detailed enough to suggest that not all students could necessarily acquire the requisite private instruction. The pupil should cultivate a beautiful, long stroke (*ibid.*, p. 22), something which was also noted by Crüger in 1654 (see p. 115 above); he should not rush the upbow; the instrument should be held low, under the left part of the chest. But Merck's most telling remark is that facility can be acquired only by listening to virtuosos (*ibid.*, p. 23); clearly a publication of this nature was not an ideal replacement for first-hand experience with practising musicians.

Thoroughbass practice was another feature of performance that began to make its way into late seventeenth-century school treatises. For Stierlein, instruction in thoroughbass *was* the *musica practica* which followed the 'theory' of musical rudiments, ornamentation and diminution (see p. 35 above). He shows that the union of performance and composition was now something not only for the director of music and organist but also that which should constitute the practical education of the general performer:

> The general bass is the best and foremost fundament, according to which an entire musical piece – as much in the composition as in the performance and making of the same – must direct itself.
>
> Der *General-Bass* ist das beste und vortrefflichste *Fundament* / nach welchem sich ein gantzes *musicali*sches Stuck / so wohl in der *Composition*, als Auffführung und Machung desselben richten muß. (Stierlein 1691, p. 24)

Stierlein's *Trifolium musicale* ('Three-leafed music') of 1691 doubtless encouraged Speer to enlarge his *Grundrichtiger Unterricht der musikalischen Kunst* of 1687 ten years later, adding the alternative title *Vierfaches musikalisches Kleeblatt* ('Four-leafed musical clover'): here the pupil is led from the traditional fundamentals of singing, through keyboard and thoroughbass, the basics of all kinds of instruments to composition. With the latter three parts come some quite detailed explications of instrumental technique, something which anticipates the renowned treatises of the mid eighteenth century. His instructions for keyboard players are clear evidence of the paired fingering style as the basis of keyboard technique.[61]

Speer relates this fingering method directly to the musical result required: a light, full and short touch and a satisfactory positioning of the fingers for ornamentation.[62] The pairing of fingers and notes is a striking parallel to the elementary bowing outlined by Herbst, something which points strongly to a hierarchical view of metre and its divisions. While paired fingering had been a feature of keyboard technique throughout Europe for over a century, it was generally something noted in more specialised treatises, not in a basic school primer. Although Speer was obviously disseminating information which the more talented pupils would have learned in their private tuition throughout the seventeenth century, its summary in a single publication shows something of the greater status of instrumental performance and the cultivation of the more rounded musician.

Speer recommends that the keyboard student proceeds to learn short intonations to chorales, then the chorales themselves, since this both facilitates praise of God and forms the beginning of thoroughbass technique. Then he gives a large collection of dance-movements, preludes, toccatas and fugues, each set of which covers the keys of D, b, G, e, C, a, F, d, B♭, g, E♭ and c (Speer 1697, pp. 47–179). Having acquired considerable facility, the student can proceed to the following chapter on thoroughbass itself.

The third part or 'leaf' concerns tuition on other instruments. Speer's short descriptions of the characteristics and techniques of each instrument are not remarkable in themselves, but the number of instruments he covers is striking: violin, viola, viola da gamba, basse de violon (followed by a short description of other members of the string family), trumpet, timpani, trombones, cornetti, bassoon, fingering-schemes for flutes and flageolet. He notes that few young players manage the trumpet because it demands such bodily strength (Speer 1697, p. 218). His long list of the requirements of a good trumpeter show that this is indeed an instrument demanding professional expertise and commitment.

The eighteenth century

With the exception of Sperling 1705, few early eighteenth-century vocal primers make much reference to instruments. Presumably the rapidly expanding literature on instruments, catering mostly for the growth in amateur performance, rendered instrumental school primers redundant (see p. 63 above). Kürzinger's *Getreuer Unterricht zum Singen mit Manieren, und die Violin zu spielen* (1763) is an exception to this trend, a two-part treatise covering the fundamentals of both singing and violin performance. As virtually every significant eighteenth-century treatise in instrumental performance also affirms, Kürzinger stresses that the instrumentalist must model his performance on singing.[63]

Petri's treatise of 1767 gives the most comprehensive information on instrumental performance in church and school establishments of the mid eighteenth century. In his fundamentals for the incipient singer, it is important that the student hears much music and becomes experienced in ensemble; he should gain an insight into the whole of music by learning a 'Hauptinstrument' (i.e. one that permits chords) for thoroughbass and by studying the scores of great masters.[64] Petri's final chapters offer instruction in thoroughbass, the principal instruments and the organ (including a useful description of pedalling, mainly with alternate toes).

In all, this extensive book is a prescriptive treatise, reflecting much of Petri's experience as a cantor, with advice on how to organise church music and how to give the pupil satisfactory instruction. However, it was among the last comprehensive tutors to be addressed specifically to the cantorates. The most important achievements in vocal and instrumental performance were now being made in the fields of opera and concert life.

5

Ornamentation and the relation between performer and composer

Of all the elements of Baroque performance, ornamentation – particularly that which is not indicated by the notation – is the one which is most alien to those modern views which regard the musical text as an immutable record of the music.[1] However, it should be one of the most important considerations in any history of the music of this period, since it concerns the cross-over area between performance and composition. Indeed it may well be that much music would not have been notated in the manner in which it survives without the influence of the performer and the trends in improvised ornamentation. This point was uncannily well summarised in an observation by Christoph Bernhard (mid seventeenth century), someone who significantly combined the arts of composer, compositional theorist and performer:

> Since it has been observed that artistic singers and also instrumentalists ... have somewhat digressed from the notes here and there, and thus have given occasion to invent an agreeable kind of figure; for what can be sung with reasonable euphony might well indeed also be written down.
>
> Accordingly, composers in the last generation already began to set down one thing or another that was unknown to their predecessors, and seemed unacceptable to the unenlightened, but charming to good ears and musicians.
>
> So that by our own time music has attained such a height, that – in view of the multitude of figures, particularly in the newly discovered and ever more decorated *Stylus Recitativus* – it may indeed be compared to a rhetoric.
>
> Nachgehends hat man *observiret*, daß künstliche Sänger auch *Instrumentisten* ... von den Noten hier und dort etwas abgewichen, und also einige anmutige Art der *Figuren* zu erfinden Anlaß gegeben; denn was mit vernünfftigen Wohl-Laut kan gesungen werden, mag man auch wohl setzen.
>
> Dahero haben die *Componisten* in vorigem *Seculo* allbereits angefangen, eines und das andere zu setzen, was den vorigen unbekant, auch den Unverständigen unzuläßlich geschienen, guten Ohren aber und *Musicis* annehmlich gewesen.

Biß daß auff unsere Zeiten die *Musica* so hoch kommen, daß wegen Menge der *Figuren*, absonderlich aber in dem neu erfundenen und bisher immer mehr ausgezierten *Stylo Recitativo*, sie wohl einer *Rhetorica* zu vergleichen.
(Bernhard, *Ausführlicher Bericht vom Gebrauche der Con- und Dissonantien* (MS), in Müller-Blattau 1926/1963, p. 147)

The aim of this chapter is to give, first of all, an outline of the practice of improvised ornamentation during the Baroque era, the complex lines of the theoretical traditions and the attitudes developing during the course of the period. Then, by comparing this with the compositional theory of the time and with the stances of particular composers, I hope to produce something of a definition of *musica practica*, a concept which hinges on the fluid relationship between composer and performer.

IMPROVISED ORNAMENTATION IN THE GERMAN VOCAL TRADITION

The basis of vocal ornamentation in seventeenth- and early eighteenth-century Germany can be assessed relatively easily by surveying the large body of contemporary literature addressed to the performer, particularly the singer.[2] Most of this could be thought to represent the 'upper level' of performance practice, something which was built over the 'middleground' tradition, as outlined in the preceding two chapters. However, as has already been observed (see pp. 70, 77 above), many 'middleground' writings show at least some influence from those specifically concerned with improvised ornamentation; moreover, a handful of primers which are basic in all other respects introduce quite complex diminution techniques.

As Bernhard's reference to 'the last generation' implies, the performer's elaboration of notated musical lines was by no means new to German performance practice during the mid seventeenth century. Yet although advice and examples are to be found in some surviving German treatises of the sixteenth century, namely Coclico 1552 and Finck 1556, there is nothing as extensive or exhaustive as the methods published in Italy during the latter part of that century. Presumably performers were trained orally and the practices of ornamentation and diminution varied from one institution to another. Burmeister 1601 (*Musica autoschediastike*) sums up some basic rules derived from Finck and C. Praetorius:

The singer should not push out the faster notes or so-called coloraturas through a movement of the lips or tongue, but he should perform them with the lungs and throat so that they can be heard clearly and distinctly. One should not introduce coloraturas everywhere, but only at suitable places and not in all

Ornamentation and the performer and composer 123

voices together; on the contrary, they should be interspersed sparingly and carefully while the syllables are silent [i.e. in non-syllabic, melismatic writing]. With coloraturas one should give more consideration to sweetness than to speed. What one can no longer take in, one can no longer love.

(6). Schnellere Noten oder sog. Koloraturen soll der Sänger nicht durch eine Bewegung der Lippen oder Zunge hervorstoßen, sondern er soll sie mit der Lunge und der Kehle vortragen, so daß sie 'expresse et distincte' zu hören sind. (7). Nicht überall, sondern nur an passenden Stellen und nicht in allen Stimmen zugleich soll man Koloraturen anbringen, vielmehr sie schonend und vorsichtig einstreuen, während die Silben schweigen. (8). Bei den Koloraturn muß man mehr bedacht sein auf die 'suavitas' als auf die Schnelligkeit. Was man nicht mehr aufnehmen kann, kann man auch nicht lieben.
(Burmeister 1601, in Ruhnke 1955, p. 96)

Burmeister places coloratura and *mordantiae* (two or three fast neighbour-notes added before the beat) into the convenient rhetorical category of *practicum decorum* (*ornatus*), that which is added by the performer (as opposed to the *poeticum decorum*, the succession of consonants devised by the composer in response to the text); both of these are part of the *pronunciatio affectuosa* (Ruhnke 1955, p. 95). Although he sees these added ornaments as being part of the affective insight of the performer, he does not give any clear indication of how to acquire this discernment and facility. Nevertheless his testimony, derived as it is from C. Praetorius and Finck, points to a wide practice of improvised ornamentation in Germany, a practice which was clearly not always discreet.

Praetorius and the introduction of the 'new Italian style'

A specifically German pedagogic tradition for embellishment was founded with the publication of Praetorius's *Syntagma musicum*, part 3, in 1619, that treatise which was mainly responsible for introducing the Italian style to Germany. The final chapter, 'How boys who have particular joy and love in singing can be instructed in the current Italian manner',[3] explains how the singer's office is not unlike that of an orator, and how he must use a wide range of expressive devices in order to move the listener (see p. 48 above). Like the German writers before him, Praetorius condemns those performers who add ornamentation indiscriminately:

Whereas one should not praise those who are endowed by God and nature with a particularly lovely shaking, wavering or trembling voice and also a round neck and throat for diminution, but who do not heed the rules of music, but only go on and on with their excessive decorations, overshooting the limits prescribed

124   Music education and the art of performance

by the song, and in that manner spoil and confuse the same, so that one does not know what they are singing. Also neither the text nor the notes (as the composer has set them giving the song the best elegance and grace) can be perceived, far less understood. This bad style then (to which also numerous instrumentalists in particular are accustomed) little moves and amuses the listeners, particularly those who have some knowledge of the art, indeed it makes them far more annoyed and drowsy. Therefore, so that the song's natural life and grace, which the master has given it, is not taken away through such deformation of diminution, but so that each word and sentence will actually be understood by everyone, it is highly necessary that all cantors or singers industriously practise singing and articulated pronunciation from youth onwards, and make themselves acquainted with these things.

Sintemal die jenigen gar nicht zu loben / welche von Gott und der Natur / mit einer sonderbahren lieblichen zitterten und schwebenden oder bebenden Stimm / auch einem runden Halß unnd Gurgel zum diminuiren begabet / sich an der *Musicorum leges* nicht binden lassen / sondern nur fort unnd fort / mit ihrem allzuviel *colorirn*, die im Gesang vorgeschriebene *limites* uberschreiten / unnd denselben dermassen verderben und verdunckeln / daß man nicht weiß was sie singen / Auch weder den Text noch die Noten (so der Componist gesetzt / und dem Gesange die beste Zier und *gratiam* giebt) vernehmen / viel weniger verstehen kan.

   Welche böse Art dann / (deren sich sonderlich auch etliche Instrumentisten angewehnet) die *Auditores*, sonderlich die der Kunst etwas wissenschafft tragen / wenig *afficiret* unnd erlustiget / ja vielmehr verdrossen unnd schläfferig machet. Derowegen damit dem Gesange seine *naturalis vis* und *gratia*, die ihme der Meister gegeben / durch solche *deformitet* des *diminuirens* nit benommen / sondern von menniglichen jedes Wort und *Sententia* eigentlich verstanden werde: Ist hoch nötig / daß alle *Cantores* oder Sänger von Jugend auff *in voce & pronunciatione articulata* sich fleissig uben / und dieselbige ihnen bekat machen.
(Praetorius 1619, pp. 229–30)

Praetorius then outlines the *natura* and *doctrina* by which this facility can be achieved. To the *natura* belong the requirements of a suitable voice (see p. 72 above), including the dynamic flexibility employed particularly for dotted rhythms (*exclamatio* – see p. 73 above) and the *intonatio*, an ornamental 'scoop' to the first note of each song:

Intonatio is how a song is to be started: and there are differing opinions about it. Some desire that it be begun on the correct note, many on the second below the correct note, but so that one gradually rises with the voice and lifts the same; several on the third, some on the fourth, several with a charming and muted voice, which varied fashions are mostly conceived under the name *accentus*.

Intonatio ist / wie ein Gesang anzufangen: Und sind davon unterschiedliche Meinungen. Etliche wollen / daß er in dem rechten Thon / etliche in der

Secunda unter dem rechten Thon / doch daß man allgemach mit der Stimme steige / und dieselbe erhebe: Etliche in der *Tertia*: Etliche in der *Quarta*: etliche mit anmütiger und gedempffter Stimme anzufangen sey / welche unterschiedene Arten meistentheils unter dem Namen *Accentus* begriffen werden.

(Praetorius 1619, p. 231)[4]

Thus Praetorius outlines certain ornamental devices as components of the natural requirements of the singer, something which points to the supreme importance of matters of ornamentation to the style and very technique of singing in the Italian manner. It is in the *doctrina* that he prescribes the specific figures required in 'mannered' practice, under the general heading of *diminutiones* and *coloraturen*: *accentus, tremolo, gruppo, tirata, trillo, passaggi*; each is applied, more or less systematically, to simple note-patterns and intervals. Praetorius relies heavily on Italian sources (acknowledging the influence of Caccini and Bovicelli) and provides little that is new; however, the detail and care of categorisation render him an exceedingly useful source on the musical life of his age. It may well be this tendency to catalogue the formulae constituting diminution which distinguishes German musical thinking (and consequently style) from the 'original' practices of Italy.

The *accentus* (already partly defined as part of the *natura* of the good singer, since it is loosely synonymous with the *intonatio*) covers a variety of neighbour-note ornaments. Immediately striking is the fact that a specific style of performance (slurred) is directly connected with this: 'When the notes in the following form are drawn in the throat' (Example 5).[5] The *tremolo*, Praetorius simply defines as a shaking of the voice over a note, something organists term *mordanten* or *moderanten*. This, close to the modern main-note trill, is apparently more appropriate for organs and instruments; thus Praetorius shows a growing consideration for the idiomatic differences between various performance media. The *groppi* are trill-figures used expressly for cadences which 'must be struck more sharply than the *tremoli*' (Example 6).[6] *Tiratae* are basically runs, Praetorius's examples showing the given note approached by an octave run; the faster they are performed the clearer each note must be expressed.[7] The *trillo* is the figure of fast repeated notes on a single pitch which, according to Praetorius, is described only by Caccini in Italian sources. Its performance cannot apparently be described and must be learned by example, as a bird learns from its fellows.[8] Praetorius's description of the *passaggi* – technically the climax of the list of ornaments, since these employ the others in combination – is surprisingly lame: they are fast runs which comprise both leaps and stepwise movement.[9] Praetorius's only advice

126 Music education and the art of performance

Example 5 Praetorius 1619, p. 233, *Accentus*

Example 6 Praetorius 1619, p. 236, *Groppi*

to the singer is that he proceed from the slower, simple passages to the faster ones.

What is immediately obvious about Praetorius's practical theory of vocal (and, to a certain extent, instrumental) ornamentation, is that the performer must be familiar with a wide range of devices which, when correctly applied, show the singer to be a good musical 'orator'. He apparently sees no anomaly in the fact that these figures seem to have no semantic dimension – the text and its affects are never mentioned except in the introduction to this short manual – while together they constitute a rhetorical system that is purely musical (i.e. ornamental, rather than persuasive, rhetoric; see p. 46 above).[10] Also interesting is the fact that Praetorius makes no distinction between the art of singing *per se* and the art of ornamentation. These ornaments alone constitute correct ornamentation and diminution, presumably something which contrasts with the

Ornamentation and the performer and composer 127

excessive practices of the singers he criticises in his introduction. This tendency Praetorius probably owed to his reading of Caccini and it reflects the principal difference between the free, often excessive, diminution of the late sixteenth century and the desire for ordered and expressively-conditioned manners during the early Baroque. Perhaps the intention towards control and rationalisation is more important than the success of these in practice. Indeed Praetorius is astonishingly vague about how the figures are to be applied: the promised, but apparently never written, 'Exercitatio' would probably have consisted of examples to be experienced and emulated rather than prescriptive instruction (see p. 49 above).

Earlier in the same volume Praetorius does outline a sort of decorum to be observed by ornamenting performers (something akin to jazz practice in the twentieth century), but again no association is made with the rhetorical implications of the text or affect:

But when several people and also different instruments are present, they must watch one another to give one another room and not crash into each other at the same time, but when there are many of them, each must wait until it is his turn to demonstrate his *schertzi*, *trilli* and *accentus*; and must not twitter together like a swarm of sparrows, in which whoever can shriek the highest and loudest is cock of the walk. This then must be observed in the same way with violins and cornetti.

Wenn aber Gesellschafft und andere mehr *Instrument* verhanden seyn / müssen sie eins uffs ander sehen / ihnen untereinander raum und platz geben / nich gegen einander gleichsam stossen / sondern wenn ihrer viel seyn / ein jedes seiner zeit erwarten / biß daß die Reye / seine *Schertzi*, *Trilli* und *Accent* zu erweisen / auch an ihn komme: Und nicht / wie ein hauffen Sperlinge untereinander zwitzschern / und welches nur zum höchsten und z. stärcksten schreyen unnd krehen kan / der beste Hahn im Korbe sey. Welches dann bey *Discant* Geigen / *Cornetten*, *&c.* eben so wol zu *observiren*. (Praetorius 1619, p. 148)

Praetorius also recommends that the organist observe where a solo singer adds all kinds of ornaments, and if the latter should become tired of these, continue to add embellishment in a similar style, thus creating an echo and dialogue of embellishment between the two (*Ibid.*, p. 137).

Comprehensive treatises in the tradition of Praetorius during the later seventeenth century

Herbst reprints much of Praetorius's writing in his *Musica practica* (1642/1653), although the content is greatly expanded to match the scale of a large Italian tutor. Herbst added further ornamented examples in the second edition and included some advice and examples for instruments (see p. 114 above). He remarks in the introduction that Germans other than Praetorius, notably J. H. Schein and K. Kittel, had hoped to write similar manuals on mannered singing but never fulfilled their promises. He intends that his *Musica practica* should fulfil Praetorius's desire to write a short treatise with practical examples, something which Praetorius never achieved owing to his untimely death.

Herbst develops many of his predecessor's devices, the *accentus* examples in particular containing much more elaborate cadential figuration. Furthermore, Herbst underlays his examples with the five basic vowels so that the singer can cultivate diction at the same time as vocal facility.[11] For his extensive 'Exercitatio' Herbst takes examples from Francesco Rognoni and Adriano Banchieri and ends the practical section with a selection of ornamented solo concertos by Ignatius Donati.

Falck's treatise, some forty years later (1688), follows the Praetorius/Herbst model surprisingly closely with some modifications: the *groppo* is now shaped more like a cadential 'turn', while the *trillo* definition covers more options than the figure of fast repeated notes of a single pitch (as ever, these can only be learned directly from a teacher). Falck, like Herbst, gives extensive exercises on primary vowel sounds, each comprising sequences based on ascending notes of the scale. Some devices are specifically designed to cultivate the repeated beating of the throat (*ribattuta di gola*).[12] Particularly interesting are Falck's extensive examples of embellished monody from a recent Italian publication by G. F. Sances.

Both Crüger 1660 and Falck 1688 integrate their advice on mannered singing into larger compendia which offer a full course in the rudiments of music. Crüger, having already written two basic school primers in which he promised a thorough study of coloratura at a later date,[13] gives a full exposition of Praetorius's figures in the compositional treatise of 1654 and in the extensive vocal treatise of 1660. Although the latter is expressly addressed to the 'Jugend' he affirms that the second section, on the 'Manier', is not universally to be applied in schools. At the same time though, the simpler graces are clearly indispensable:

Now when a boy has come so far, according to this instruction, through constant and industrious practice, that he can sing a piece rather well, this is not enough: for, because the aim in music is also sweetness, he must also be guided in how to become familiar with an elegant and lovely style, in order especially to know the *accentus* . . . Now indeed with boys in schools, particularly those who do not intend to make a profession of music, it is not so greatly necessary to attain these musical standards of Italian sweetness, because this style of singing belongs far more in the well-furnished royal and princely *Capellen*: but for schoolboys it is enough that they take pains to make the *accentus* over the notes and to introduce the same as the opportunity arises, likewise with several of the easiest passages; I have nevertheless considered it prudent to include all kinds of examples with the explication of the same, so that they will have observed what constitutes the true musical Manner of singing

Wann nun ein Knabe / vorhergehender *Instruction* nach / durch stete und fleißige übungen so weit ist kommen / daß er ein Stücke zimlich fertig kan singen / ist es damit nicht genug: sonder weil *finis Musicae* auch *suavitas* ist / muß er auch angeführet werden / wie er sich zu einer zierlichen und lieblichen Manier sol gewehnen / daß er führnemlich wisse die *Accentus* . . . Ob nun zwar Knaben in Schulen / insonderheit die keine *Profession* von der *Music* zu machen in willens / nicht so groß nöthig ist / diese *modulos Musicos Italicae suavitatis* zu *exolı*ren / weil diese Manier zu singen vielmehr in Königliche und Fürstliche wolbestalte Capellen gehöret: Für Schulknaben es aber genug ist / daß sie sich befleißigen die *Accentus* über die Noten zu machen / und selbige nach Gelegenheit mit anzubringen / wie auch etliche der leichtesten *Passaggien* / habe ich doch für rathsam erachtet / selbiger *explication* nebest allerhand Exempeln hierbey zu setzen / daraus sie sich zu ersehen haben / worinnen die rechte Musicalische Manier im Singen bestehe (Crüger 1660, pp.19, 21)

Crüger's comments here offer a good insight into the extent of ornamental practice in German performance during the mid-century: the basic school-singer who is competent in figural music should master some of the basic figures, namely the *accentus* family (which Falck likewise singles out as a fundamental of performance), while only those who wish to specialise in music, and those in royal establishments, need be concerned with the more detailed passages. Nevertheless, this does imply that most of the music which concerns us today (e.g. the repertories of Praetorius, Schein, Schütz and Buxtehude, which were indeed composed for the foremost establishments) might well have been sung with considerable embellishment. Moreover, ornamental devices appear in some relatively basic 'middleground' treatises; these will be discussed in the next section.

Praetorius's influence in 'middleground' treatises

Although detailed instructions in Italianate ornamentation are not consistently to be found in the majority of German vocal primers during the seventeenth century, there are enough references in certain 'middleground' primers to suggest that there was an appreciable market for this material.[14] As Crüger implied, it was taught only to the most advanced boys, those who were the concertists for the major figural compositions of the seventeenth century. Nevertheless, Dieterich 1631 and Printz 1671 are exceptional in introducing diminution in elementary 'middleground' primers, that is, in the early stages of music instruction, after clefs, intervals and metre have been mastered.[15] Printz's claim that the first edition of this primer was the official music book for the local school and also used in several other places suggests that, in some areas of Germany at least, diminution was a standard element of practical education.[16]

More normal for a basic primer is Friderici's attitude: coloratura of the Praetorius type is used only in the foremost establishments and is more often appropriate for instrumentalists in any case (see p. 77 above). However, Friderici does include much advice on coloratura in the main body of his singing rules:

> In the bass no coloraturas should be made other than those specified by the composer. (For otherwise the fundament of the song will be mutilated, and the other parts left groundless, then will there be heard nothing other than an annoying dissonance.) Other voices should add coloratura in a way that does not introduce musical faults. (But they can noticeably avoid such when they cease their embellishment on the same note on which they began.) [Example 7]

Example 7   Friderici 1618/1624

aus diesem: also   oder also singen

also   oder also machen

Im *Basso* sollen keine *Coloraturen* mehr gemacht werden / dann die / so vom *Componisten* gesetzet seyn. (Dann sonst wird das Fundament des Gesanges zerreissen / unnd bleiben andern Stimmen bodenloß / und wird nichts denn nur eine verdrießliche *Dissonantz* gehöret.) Andere Stimmen sollen also *coloriren*, daß sie nicht *vitia musicalia* einführen. (Solches aber können Sie mercklich verhüten / wenn Sie in dem *Clave* auffhören zu *colloriren*, darinnen Sie haben angefangen.)   (Friderici 1618/1624, rules 15–16)

It is difficult to determine from the example why the first two solutions are correct and the remainder incorrect; presumably Friderici was judging them on idiomatic, rather than theoretical grounds. He adds futher examples of diminution within the exercises he appends to the end of his treatise. These show systematic diminution of simple scalic note patterns, something which is the staple of Italian diminution treatises (Example 8). In all then, Friderici's attitude to improvised embellishment and diminution is somewhat ambiguous: he gives fairly detailed instruction at two different points in his treatise, yet he asserts that it is not widely practised. As will soon emerge, this ambivalence is also evident in later writings of the seventeenth century. Even when certain writers are cautious about the universal application of diminution, they often seem to be concerned that the singer at least cultivate the facility and become familiar with the conventions. Thus Demantius 1632 lists some of the usual Praetorius manners in the appendix, as if to alert the singer to their existence without offering explicit instruction. La Marche 1656 (p. 22) mentions that the trill should be employed on each dotted note, sharp sign, on alternate notes in strings of quavers and particularly at cadences. If the boy finds the technique difficult, he can become accustomed to it by hitting the throat with the hand.[17]

Example 8   Friderici 1618/1624

11. Exempl. die clausulas finales *diminuiren* zu lernen.

12. *Exemplum* im *ascendiren* etwas zu diminuiren.

Ascensus.   Diminutio

alia

alia

alia

132   Music education and the art of performance

New theories of ornamentation and diminution: the figural system of Printz

Printz, in his later treatises, provided the most detailed information on ornamentation during the entire century. No other author provided such a precise categorisation of the figures constituting passage-work.[18] Indeed it is he who coined the term *Figur* for the motives comprising diminution, something which immediately suggests rhetorical thinking. Just as the rhetorical figure is something of an exception to the norm which gives the oration particular emphasis and style, Printz views the ornamental figure as the 'salt of melody'.[19]

The importance he afforded figures is evidenced by his first surviving singing treatise of 1671, which introduces figures as part of elementary singing tuition (see p. 70 above). In addition to his vastly expanded account of the Praetorius ornaments here, he includes such devices as the *pausa*, a very short space to be inserted between fast notes.[20] Although it is clear from the contents of the book that the pupil will know very little about the rules of harmony, Printz demands that the singer pay attention to the *Fundament* and surrounding voices so that forbidden parallels are avoided.[21] The singer is also enjoined to avoid 'Bauer- oder Bierfiedler *Clausuln*' although it is impossible to infer from Printz's rules the degree of excess which will draw this epithet.

Printz's most detailed exposition of his doctrine of figures appears in the second volume of his composition treatise of 1676–7 and the vocal treatise of 1678. He divides figures into simple conjunct formulae (which include most of the ornaments specified by Praetorius); simple figures which remain on one note; those which leap; 'mixed' figures which are partly conjunct and partly disjunct; trills; and compound figures which combine a variety of simple figures (i.e. passages or diminution). The examples are presumably to be practised as singing exercises which both enhance the technique and cultivate the facility to elaborate pre-existent lines.[22]

Printz gives the clearest account of the relationship between the particular figure chosen and the performance style associated with it:

Here we are in general to be reminded that each figure must have its appropriate *apulsus gutturalis*, that is an attack which must be made in the throat with a natural skilfulness and not with a nasty pressure, hard thrust, bleat, or whinny, so that the singer opens the mouth moderately without making the cheeks hollow, but leaving them as nature has given them, and does not lift the tongue high, or bend it, but leaves it straight and low, so that the free passage of the sound is not hindered; and also holds the mouth still without biting.

Hier erinnern wir ins gemein / daß eine jede *Figur* ihren manierlichen *Apulsum gutturalem* haben müsse / das ist / eine Anschlagen / welches in der Kehle

Ornamentation and the performer and composer 133

gemacht werden soll mit einer natürlichen Geschickligkeit / nicht mit einem garstigen Drücken / harten Stossen / Meckern / oder Wiehern / so / daß der Sänger den Mund mittelmässig eröffne / die Backen nicht hohl mache / sondern sie bleiben lasse / wie sie die Natur gegeben / und die Zunge nicht in die Höhe hebe / noch krümme / sondern gerade und niedrig liegen lasse / damit sie den Schalle nicht den freyen Durchgang verhindere; auch das Maul unbeweglich still halte / und nicht käue. (Printz 1678, p. 43)

Likewise he extends some of the comments on performance specified by Praetorius: the *accentus* is indeed gently formed in the throat, but not so that the voice is completely slurred.[23] The *groppo* is now defined as a turn-like figure (*Kugel*) of four notes, in which the first and third are the same. Its attack is 'moderately sharp' ('mittelmässig scharf', p. 48), like that of all the other running figures. Printz gives the traditional Praetorius/Herbst description (i.e. a modern trill followed by a turn) as a subsidiary definition (p. 49). Several apparently new figures are also added here: *circolo mezo*, a figure like the *groppo* in which the second and fourth notes are of the same pitch; *tirata meza*, a four-note version of the *tirata*. Three new figures in the 'mixed' category (i.e. those that involve conjunct, disjunct motion and repeated notes) are significant enough to sum up the most common motivic material of late Baroque music (pp. 53–5): the *figura corta* (dactylic and anapaestic rhythms and the syncopated short-long-short rhythm); the *messanza* (four-note figures involving both conjunct and disjunct motion); the *figura suspirans* (three-note patterns beginning with a downbeat rest).[24] Printz adds that all running figures can also be performed in a dotted rhythm (p. 56); dotting seems to be the most ubiquitous rhythmic ornament in these seventeenth-century treatises.

Printz's comprehensive survey continues with a study of 'beating' ('schwebende') figures, namely the repeated-note *trillo*, which is learned through retaining the air in the throat, driving the voice with a moderately vehement beating and by imitating singers who can do it already.[25] The 'zusammengesetzte' figures are basically passages of diminution in which Printz analyses the component figures. He concludes his survey with a list of the faults in singing figures. This is compounded with an outline of the faults in singing in general, something which points to the importance of ornamentation as the substance of singing technique *per se*, since Printz clearly saw no distinction between the two categories of *vitia* (see also p. 79 above). The most significant faults are those relating to articulation (*vitia adpulsus*): the singer must avoid excessive articulation and attack of figures; he must not confuse the articulation of one figure with that of another (e.g. by singing the *accentus* with the sharp articulation of the *messanza*); he must pay consistent attention to the *Fundament* and adjacent voices in order to avoid compositional defects; he must never breathe in the middle of figures, or string figures together like a peasant or 'beer-fiddler' (pp. 75–8). Like Friderici, Printz proscribes diminutions in the bass that the composer has not specified, and, predictably, he suggests that imitation of good singers is the surest way to learn the art (pp. 44, 79).

New theories of ornamentation and diminution: Bernhard and his followers

Christoph Bernhard, with his manuscript treatise, 'Von der Singe-Kunst oder Manier' gives perhaps the clearest explanation of the categories of singing.[26] What is particularly important is his division of singing style into two basic fields: that in which simpler ornaments are appropriate and that in which improvised diminution is added (see p. 69 above).[27] The singer should master several ornaments even in the so-called plain singing (*cantar sodo*): the *trillo*, *accento*, several derivatives of the same (*anticipatione della syllaba/nota, cercar della nota*) and *tremolo*.[28] In *cantar passagiato* (or *lombarda*), the more ornamented form of singing, Bernhard gives some detailed advice on the application of diminution (although the constituent figures are not analysed with the detail of Printz).

Mylius's general introduction to singing with figures (1685) gives another illuminating overview of the German tradition, reflecting his consciousness of the history behind the practice and its relation to the contingencies of his own day. He is clearly unacquainted with Printz's writings, but shows the same tendency as Printz to provide the foundations for a practice which is both traditionally based and modernised; Bernhard's practice is, for him, that which is most relevant for his day:

Many distinguished old German musicians took trouble to prescribe rules and regulations of such a kind collected from the famous works of the newest, most authentic Italian and German musicians, in order to create a supply for future generations, particularly the young, by which they might achieve a skilful and elegant way of singing. Among these, Herr Michael Praetorius, in book 3 of *Syntagma Musicum* p. 229, paved the way to this end; he was followed by Herr Johann Andreas Herbst, former Kapellmeister at Nuremberg, who gathered together a good portion of such examples from the aforementioned and furthermore from Herr Daniel Bolli, Claudio Monteverdi, Rovetta, Francesco Rognoni, Adriano Banchieri and other similar famous authors, for which he earned great praise and thanks in his own time. But whether all these ways can also be used nowadays, I will leave to the judgement of reasonable and clever artists, and therefore I will despise no-one: for my part I will follow the recommended outline and good report of my estimable, much-loved and honoured teacher, Herr Christoph Bernhard, instructor to the young honourable electoral Saxon princes and senior Kapellmeister, who wanted to show a good way to follow the same, for the benefit of young people, and so that others too, particularly young people, might have a clue how to achieve an elegant and appropriate way of singing; from such [teaching], as far as it can be done in all conscience, I have extracted some things and gathered them here.

Es haben sich viel vornehme alte Teutsche *Musici* bemühet / dergleichen Gesetze und *Regeln* vorzuschreiben / welche aus denen neuesten bewährtesten *Itali*anischen und Teutscher *Musicorum* berühmten *Oper*en solche Arten *colligir*et / daß der Nachwelt / absonderlich der lernenden Jugend / ein Vorrath hierzu geschaffet / dadurch sie zu einem künstlichen und zierlichen Singen gelangen möchte / unter welchen hierzu Herr *Michael Praetorius, in tomo tertio Syntagmatis Musici fol.* 229. den Weg gebähnet; dem ist nachgefolget Herr *Johann Andreas Herbst*, gewesener Capellmeister zu Nürnberg / welcher aus erst besagten / und hernach aus Herr *Danielis Bollii, Claud. Monteverde, Rovette, Francisci Ragnoni, Andr. Banchieri* und andern dergleichen beruhmter *Autoren* Schrifften einen guten Theil solcher Arten zusammen gelesen / darvon es zu seiner Zeit grossen Ruhm und Danck erworben. Daß aber solche Arten auch heutiges Tages, alle solten angebracht werden können / solches wil ich vernünfftigen und klügern Künstlern zu *judici*ren überlassen / und deßwegen niemand verachten: Meines Orts wil ich auf empfangenen Entwurff und gute Nachricht meines wehrt zu lieben- und zu Ehrenden Lehrmeisters / Hern *Christophori Bernhardi*, Chur Fürstl. Sachs. Hochbestalten Junger Prinzen *Informatoris* und ältesten Capellmeisters / welcher der allgemeinen Jungen zum besten einen guten Weg zeigen wollen / demselben nachfolgen / und damit auch andere / sonderlich die Jugend / eine Spur (zu einem zierlichen und manierlichen Singen zu gelangen) haben mögen; ist aus solchem / so viel sich Gewissens wegen thun lassen wollen / etwas ausgezogen und hieher gebracht worden. (Mylius 1685, ch. 5)

For 'zierliches Singen', Mylius proposes exactly the same categories as Bernhard: *fermo, forte, piano, trillo, accento, anticipatione della syllaba/ nota, cercar della nota, ardire*. The *trillo* is now an alternation of two notes which can be made downwards (preferably) or upwards, and which the boy should learn slowly in order to accustom the breast, neck and throat to the necessary movement. Mylius gives advice on how the trill should be applied: on dotted rhythms in descending motion; in successions of long notes in accordance with the text and where the *Generalbass* has many runs and leaps; in cadential phrases. The most inadvisable application is on the first note of a piece or phrase ('welches ein greulicher Unverstand ist'). He recommends the suave articulation and performance of *accentus* figures, which accords closely with the advice of Printz. To these devices Mylius also adds some of the well-known Praetorius categories which

Bernhard omitted: *tremulo, groppo, tirata, variatio notae*, and *passagio*. He considers these more appropriate for instrumentalists than singers, although they can be a part of *applicatio textus*.

Mylius's opinions are even more clearly demonstrated by his texted examples, in which abbreviations usefully indicate where the fundamental, Bernhardian manners may be employed. For someone who cautions about too much diminution it is remarkable how important he considers the frequent (almost indiscriminate?) application of the simpler ornaments (Plate 3). An interesting corollary to this example is Kuhnau's *ClavierÜbung* (Leipzig 1689/1692) of almost the same time, an engraving peppered with indications for small graces. This not only shows something of the parallels in ornamentation between different performance media but also the ubiquity of the graces, particularly in the case of a composer such as Kuhnau, who was considered quite conservative in his own time.

Mylius's explanation served as the basis for Feyertag's verbose chapter on figures of 1695. Feyertag too notes the importance of the singer's ability to add figures of the *accentus* type:

> These are the most usual and usable forms of the *accentus*, which a scholar should fully impress upon himself, because the composers themselves do not always commit them to paper but suppose it will be the singers who add such according to the manner and art of music, without knowing or understanding where and how they can introduce them.

> Diß sind die gewöhnlichsten und gebräuchlichste *Genera* des *Accents*, welche eine Scholar wohl sich *imprimir*en solle / weiln sie / wiewohln die Herrn *Componisten* selbe / nicht allezeit zu Papier bringen / sondern *Suppon*iren / es werden die Sänger nach Arth und Kunst der Music solche ohne daß wissen / und verstehen / wo und wie sie solche anbringen können. (Feyertag 1695, p. 206)

Stierlein 1691, like Mylius, shows the direct influence of Bernhard's manuscript treatises. The appendix to the first part ('Musica theorica') of this ambitious treatise includes the basic ornaments, *accentus, tremulo, groppo, trillo*. Stierlein's definition of the *accentus* is interestingly taken not from Bernhard's singing treatise but from his composition treatises. Such a harmonic definition is rare in a performance primer:

> *Accentus* or *superjectio* is an upwards or downwards sliding through a second, from a consonance to a dissonance or from a dissonance to a consonance

> *Accentus* oder *Superjectio*, ist ein Auff- oder Abschleiffung *per Secundam*, von einer *Consonanz* in eine *Dissonanz*, oder von einer *Dissonanz* in eine *Consonanz*
> (Stierlein 1691, p. 16)

Ornamentation and the performer and composer 137

Plate 3 Mylius 1685: texted example showing application of ornaments after the manner of Bernhard

138   Music education and the art of performance

Stierlein outlines three further versions of the *doppelter Accent*, which involve more than one added note (neighbour-note figures, slides and turns – all to be performed in a slurred, 'schleiffend' manner). *Tremulo* is now a beating on a single note (i.e. in the modern sense of vibrato).[29] With Stierlein, *groppo* is still in the old form of alternating notes (with ubiquitous dotted rhythm), but Feyertag gives it as the more modern four-note turn. *Trillo* is the modern upper-note trill in Stierlein (with elaborate instructions on how to perform it), but Feyertag describes it more as a fairly violent vibrato.[30] Thus even after a century's tradition of German ornamentation, older and newer definitions seem to survive side by side.

Attitudes towards figured singing at the close of the century: the move from performer to composer

The profusion of complaints about ornamentation and diminution suggest that they were still fairly widely practised throughout the latter half of the seventeenth century. The pastor E. Gruber's elementary primer (1673) stresses that pupils should pay attention to the text and not hinder the edification of the listener with too many diminutions and trills. One of the most vitriolic attacks on florid church music came from the Pietist pastor of Lauben, J. Muscovius, quoted in chapter 2 (see p. 27 above).

Ahle gives a good account of the theologians who have objected to the contemporary performance with passages, quoting Muscovius's amusing attack on coloratura-mongers. His reference to Spener's *Pia Desideria* gives a strong clue as to why there was so much effort to contain, if not abolish, the practice of diminution towards the end of the century: the puritanical influence of the Pietist movement:[31]

Therefore one must not wonder that numerous theologians are so zealously against the present manner of concerting. It is about that which one of them speaks in his reflections on D. Spener's *Pia Desideria*, that the coloratura-making chamber musicians introduced into the church, or rather the Italian caponlaughter, take away from the gravity and the devotion, often throw the temporal in with the spiritual and adulterate the precious gold of serious, Godly truth. Says D. Dannhauer in one place: Away with the supposed nightingales who gladly hear themselves and sing to themselves (and not 'Gloria in excelsis Deo'), who fly more in ambition than in notes!—Away with the new ridiculous Italian leaps and siren songs that aim not at the spiritual heart but at voluptuous worldly pleasures! . . . Because not only the learned men of God noted here but also many more name the present *stylus luxurians* a fleshly, voluptuous, far too colourful and muddled music, that angers those who understand and troubles

Ornamentation and the performer and composer 139

the simple, and indeed neither pleases God nor edifies the congregation; thus they do not wish to tolerate this at all in church either

Darüm darf man sich auch nicht wundern / daß etliche *Theologi* wider die heutige *Concerten*-Ahrt so eifern. Es ist auch an dem / spricht einer in seinem Bedenken über des Herrn D. Speners *Pia Desideria*, daß die *colorirende* in die Kirche eingeführte Kammermusiken / oder vielmehr Italiänische Capaunengelächter / von dem grunde und der andacht abführen / oft zeitliches und geistliches untereinander werfen / und das köstliche gold götlich gravitätischer Wahrheit *adulteri*ren. Hinweg / sagt D. Dañhauer an einem Orte / mit den vermeinten Nachtigallen / die sich selbst gerne hören / ihnen selbst (und nicht *Gloria in excelsis Deo*) singen / einander mehr in Ehrgeitz / als in Noten fugiren!— Hinweg mit den neuen lächerlichen wälschen Sprüngen und Sirenen-Liedern / die nicht nach der geistlichen Herzens, sondern üppigen Welt-Freude zielen! . . . Weil dän nun nicht allein die hier gemelten Gottsgelehrten / sondern auch andere mehr den heutigen *Stylum luxuriantem* nennen eine fleischliche / üppige / gar zu bunte und krauspe Musik / so die verständigen ärgere / und die einfältigen betrübe / ja weder Gott gefalle / noch die Gemeine erbaue; derowegen sie auch solche in der Kirchen gar nicht leiden wollen (Ahle 1704, pp. 81–3)

Many other writers also show a somewhat ambivalent attitude to the performer's unilateral insertion of ornamentation, something which might point to a wide variety of practice and opinion. Mylius's comments on *variatio notae* outline some important developments in the attitudes towards coloratura practice during this period:

Of this there was formerly such abuse that neither singers nor instrumentalists were at all regarded if they could not vary a piece throughout in innumerable ways, but nowadays this is better done by the famous instrumentalists, when they give to one another a theme (a few notes of the bar, making variations over this and varying it a hundred and more times, each mindful to exceed the other), but in singing today it has simply ceased, because such coloraturas or variations of the notes only cause one not to understand the text; thus one should add only the slightest variations in vocal pieces, particularly when a piece is set with simple notes; so I now introduce merely a few examples up and downwards, so that young people have only a foretaste of this, because the remainder are in the composition and cannot be grasped so easily by their understanding.

Vor diesem war hierinnen ein solcher Mißbrauch / daß weder Sänger noch *Instrumentista* etwas geachtet wurde / welcher nicht ein Stücke durchaus auf viel und unzelige Arten verändern kunte / welches aber heutiges Tages, bey denen berühmten *Instrumenti*sten am bessern Gebrauch ist / daß sie einander ein *Thema* (etliche wenige *Tacte Noten*) geben / (über solche *variiren* / und solche zu hundert und mehrmahlen / nach dem einer den andern zu übertreffen gedencket / verändern /) welches aber im Singen heutiges Tages billich abgebracht worden / weil solch *Coloriren* oder verändern der *Noten*, nur verursachet / daß man den

140   Music education and the art of performance

Text nicht verstehet; derowegen man in Singe-Sachen gar wenig *variiren* soll / zumahl wenn ein Stück mit schlechten *Noten* gesetzet ist / daher ich hiernechst nur wenig *Exempla* Auf- und Abwärts beybringen wollen / damit die Jugend hiervon nur einen Vorschmack habe / weil doch das Ubrige in die *Composition* läufft / und mit ihrem Verstand so leicht nicht kan begriffen werden.
(Mylius 1685, ch. 5)

Mylius concludes that if a boy does sing with the kind of variations he prescribes, it should only be done in solo passages or at most when another is singing with him; otherwise, in polyphonic music compositional errors will doubtless arise. The same provisos are necessary for his next category, *passagio*, the diminution of a longer note into smaller ones; it is not entirely clear how this differs from *variatio notae*, other than that it is to be used mainly in cadential gestures. Mylius adds that well-practised singers introduce such passages with much licence and freedom, so that the organist must determine by ear when to play. If other singers are involved they must make trills on their held notes until the virtuoso comes to a close; each should have his turn to show off his art.[32] As usual the bass is excluded from all this glamour, unless of course he is singing solo above a continuo line.

If Mylius's attitude to improvised ornamentation seems somewhat ambivalent – what he gives with the right hand he seems to take away with the left – his attitude is perhaps best summed up in his concern for *applicatio textus*: all other considerations must be subservient to the text. As ever, it is imitation and experience which produce the surest path to a correct application of the various ornaments:

So a boy should take care that, if he is not well led by a capable teacher, or has not learned particular *passages*, to content himself with the *trillo, accent* and the above-mentioned graces, until he hears and understands more and better from others, which he can achieve through the grace of God and the application of diligence.

Daher soll ein Knabe sich hüten / daß / so er nicht von einem tüchtigen Lehrmeister wohl angeführet worden / oder sonderbahre *Passaggien* erlernet / er sich an dem *Trillo, Accent* und obangesetzten *Manier*en begnügen lasse / biß er ein mehrers und bessers von andern höret und begreifft / woran er durch GOttes Gnade und angewenderen Fleiß wohl gelangen kan.   (Mylius 1685)

Two of Mylius' points are typically to be found in late seventeenth-century writing: the renewed concern for the understanding of the text (exactly the reason Praetorius had for introducing these figures in the first place); the growing role of the composer in the choice of coloratura. Ahle (1704), in his discussion of abuses of coloratura practice, even notes that the

Ornamentation and the performer and composer 141

performers are often not so much at fault as the composers themselves, who seldom know the correct time or appropriate place to add figuration.[33] He takes a historical precedent to justify the dominance of the composer, an anecdote about Josquin who complained of singers adding notes:

You ass, why do you add a coloratura here? If I liked that, I would certainly have written it myself. If you want to correct well-composed pieces, write your own and leave mine uncorrected.

Du Esel / warüm tuhstu eine *Coloratur* hinzu? Hätte mir dieselbe gefallen / so wolte ich sie wohl selbst gesetzet haben. Wän du recht ge*componi*rte Gesänge wilst *corrigi*ren / so mache dir einen eigenen / und laß mir meinen ungecorrigirt.

(Ahle 1704, p. 80)[34]

This change of perspective is also evident in Stierlein's account, *De Figuris Superficialibus*. He opens with a modified paraphrase of Bernhard's quotation opening this chapter (see p. 121 above), including the conclusion that today's music (and this is several decades after Bernhard) can be compared to a rhetoric. There is an interesting twist here, though; Stierlein implies that the composers first thought of these devices and that the performers followed suit. Furthermore, he gives an extra justification for the use of figures which stresses their role in serving both consonances and dissonances.[35] Does this subtle editing of Bernhard's original suggest that Stierlein – writing at the end of the seventeenth century – could not conceive that performers may have influenced composers? Certainly this seems to substantiate Mylius's view that the composer was taking over the singer's role in adding ornamentation. Furthermore Stierlein's inclusion of Bernhard's *compositional* account of figures after this passage suggests that performers were being encouraged to learn more about the compositional theory underlying ornamentation. It comes as no surprise that this is precisely the period when theorists were again defining *musica practica* as the art comprising both *musica poetica* (composition) and *musica modulatoria* (performance). Indeed Stierlein's treatise as a whole attempts to give the performer an encylopaedic knowledge of all three fields of music (see p. 35 above).

What is important here then is not so much Stierlein's particular choice of the figures from Bernhard (or indeed his definitions *per se*) but his attempt to show the harmonic justification for certain licenses. He first mentions Bernhard's terms *superjectio* and *subsumptio*, which he does not explain further since these have already been covered by the genus *accentus*. The *passagio* is loosely defined as the countless diminutions over a longer note, which can be made by both composer and singer. *Ellipsis* is the omission of a consonance on the beat, so that the note following the inserted rest is a dissonance: this is obviously similar to Printz's *suspirans*. *Retardatio* is the upwardly-resolving suspension and *heterolepsis* – to be used only in solo singing, with viols accompanying – is the taking of notes which technically belong to another voice (i.e. voice-exchange which would not be allowed in linear counterpoint).[36] *Quasi transitus* is the accented dissonance, often approached by leap, which Stierlein allows only in the recitative style, since here the beat is less strictly observed (another direct quote from Bernhard). Finally *abruptio* is the rather curious ending of a melodic line before the bass reaches the final note of a cadence.

Several writers, accepting the composers' dominance, still recommend that the singer learn something about coloratura:

Although nowadays in singing it is no longer the practice to add much coloratura to the notes where the composer has not indicated it — and it does not lend itself well even to long notes — I have however specified just a few here, and also a few variations on cadences, merely as exercise for the young.

Ob zwar in Singen die *Variationes notarum* heutiges Tages nicht mehr in *Usu*, daß man auf denen Noten viel *Coloratur*en mache / wo sie der *Componist* nicht gesetzt / auch sich solche bey langsamen Noten nicht wohl anbringen lassen; so habe doch nur etliche wenige / wie auch die *Variationes Cadentiarum* zum blossen *Exercitatio* der Jugend / mit anhero setzen wollen. (Beyer 1703, p. 60)

Thus coloratura is to be practised merely for the technique and facility it affords. As Fuhrmann implied, the performer's task is primarily one of recognition:

Truly one could complain here that the various graces specified in this chapter need to be understood not at all by the vocalist but only by the composer. Answer: it is true, but whoever does not peer with only one eye, sees without my reminder that I have cited these poetic delicacies for the good of the student, so that the same may learn to understand, at the side of the composers, something of their language, if they label these graces with Italian names. For if a singer sings away at a piece with enjoyment, but does not know how the virtuosi name this or that grace, it is rather like the case of a peasant who devours a delicately prepared concoction with great appetite, but does not know what type of dish he has eaten, if one were to ask him.

Zwar möchte hier jemand einwerffen: Es wären in diesem Capitel unterschiedliche *Manier*en *specificirt*, so ein *Musicus vocalis* gar nicht / sondern nur ein *Musicus Poëticus* verstehen müste. Antwort: Es ist wahr / aber wer nicht *coch*sch gucket / der siehet ohn mein Erinnern / daß ich diese *delicias Poëticas* einem *Tyroni* zum besten mit angeführet habe / damit derselbe bey Zeit der *Compon*isten ihre Sprache in etwas verstehen lerne / wenn dieselbe diese *Manier*en mit

Italiänischen Namen *exprimi*ren. Denn wenn ein Sänger ein Stück schon mit Lust wegsinget / weiß aber nicht / wie die *Virtu*osen diese und jene *Manier* darin nennen / so gehets ihm fast eben als einem Bauer / der eine *delicat* zugerichtete *Potage* zwar mit grossen *Appetit* hineinschlinget / weiß aber nicht / was er vor ein Gericht gegessen / wenn man ihn fraget. (Fuhrmann 1706, p. 71)

Presumably Fuhrmann's general intention is to cultivate the skill of recognising figures – thus to perform them in the appropriate manner – and to give the singer the capability for adding them if necessary. His *vitium multiplicationis* makes clear his assumption that ornaments are now generally on the paper: singers who add as many figures as those already notated often create graces that fit the *Generalbass* as well as a fist in the eye.[37] As Ahle stressed with his anecdote from Josquin, Fuhrmann notes that if the composer had desired such elaboration he could easily have composed it.[38] Nevertheless, in Fuhrmann's condensed version of this treatise in 1715 (from which one can learn music in six days) he not only reprints his chapter on coloratura but expands it with some of the figures from the Printz tradition (e.g. *corta, messanza* and *suspirans*).[39]

Eighteenth-century developments

After the first decade of the eighteenth century there seem to be far fewer treatises addressed specifically to the Lutheran cantorates. However, the influence of the earlier writings is still evident in Mattheson's chapter 'On the art of singing and playing with graces' (1739). It is here that he outlines the basic requirements and common deficiencies of a good singer (see p. 86 above), which suggests that matters of technique and performance style were still indissolubly associated with matters of ornamentation. He notes that the distinction between graces for singing and those for instruments has not sufficiently been emphasised in the past, although singing should always form the basis for all musical interpretation.[40] In his study of *modulatoria* (cf. Printz's title of 1678), he alludes to the somewhat ambiguous situation that was becoming evident at the end of the seventeenth century: the singer should observe the composer's intentions, yet at the same time perform with ornament and artistry:

True, it is not necessary that a singer, as such, would compose his melodies himself, which is what the word 'modulate' would mean to many; but it is necessary that he knows how to perform a pre-composed melody not only without the slightest offence against the directions but especially with much grace, ornament, and artistry: the first is bad reading; the second is reading with expression and good style. (trans. Harriss 1981, p. 265)

Zwar wird nicht erfordert, daß ein Sänger, als solcher, seine Melodien selbst mache oder setze, wohin ihrer viele das Wort, Moduliren, deuten wollen; sondern daß er eine bereits verfertigte Melodie sowol ohne den geringsten Anstoß nach der Vorschrifft, als insonderheit daß er dieselbe anmuthig, geschmückt und künstlich herauszubringen wisse: das erste ist schlecht lesen; das andre mit Nachdruck und guter Art lesen. (Mattheson 1739, p. 110)

Quoting Finck from the mid sixteenth century, Mattheson stresses that 'the matter is not merely determined by rules but more so by usage, long practice and experience'. The ornaments he specifies are those that are everywhere in favour and not simply determined by one's individual experience. Thus just like Praetorius over a century before, Mattheson implies a normative approach to musical expression and elaboration.

Mattheson begins predicatably with the *accentus*, now often called *appoggiatura* and *port de voix*. Since so many textbooks have already dealt with the conjunct varieties, Mattheson concentrates on leaping appoggiaturas. Unable to cope with the concept of historical change in matters of definition, he considers any view that the *tremolo* is a two-note ornament – in particular Printz's – to be wholly erroneous and states that it basically means a vibrato. To his mind, most earlier writers have also confused the *tremolo* with the *trillo*, the trill in the modern accepted sense. The *groppo* he defines as a large circling figure, the *circolo mezzo* as a similar figure of half the size (again in contradistinction to earlier writers). He continues with *tiratas* and smaller slides, *ribattuta* (the accelerating dotted alternation of two notes) and *transitus* (the passing note), the definition of which probably goes back to Bernhard's theories of dissonance. The last two terms belong more to the eighteenth century than to the German tradition: *mordant* (prefigured in Praetorius's *tremolo*) and *acciaccatura*, which Mattheson curiously defines as a mordent on a whole tone. He omits any explanation of those figures which he terms 'very large and long', such as the *passaggi*, *bombi* and *mistichanze* since these are the domain of the composer rather than the performer.[41]

In all, then, Mattheson's definitions and terminology show the survival of the seventeenth-century ornamental tradition but they are adapted to the contingencies of his own age. Some of the older ornaments also survive in Kürzinger 1763 (e.g. *groppo*, *tirata*) but most writers after Mattheson base their definitions solely on the newer Tosi/Agricola tradition (see p. 88 above). The *Vorschlag* and its compounds (*Nachschlag* and *Doppelschlag*) is the principal grace (similar to the old *Accentus*) for Kürzinger, Doles, Marpurg and Petri. Almost as important are vibrato (*Tremolo/Bebung*) and trills.

Only Marpurg (1763) enters into a detailed examination of the

Ornamentation and the performer and composer 145

relationship between ornamental devices and the fabric of composition, with his chapters on passages and manners. He separates 'mechanische Setzfiguren', which comprise the 'willkührliche Auszierungen' – optional improvised ornaments for the performer – from the 'Manieren', the standard notated graces (*Vorschlag, Schleifer, Triller* etc), which he terms 'wesentliche Manieren' (essential ornaments). In other words he is making a distinction between the basic figures of diminution which constitute passages in music and can sometimes be improvised by the performer, and the 'essential' graces which are more a matter of good taste. Something of this distinction was evident in Bernhard's differentiation of 'plain singing' (which did in fact include some ornaments, notably the *accentus*) and singing with passages.

It is with Marpurg that we sense a more modern conception of ornaments as something distinct from the basic fabric of the music. His comments on passages and their component figures hardly prescribe what the singer should add; rather they provide the basis for analysis of the music. Just as with Beyer and Fuhrmann, it is the recognition of the figures which is most important:

The *mechanical set figures*, which one simply calls *set figures* and which have in their use a certain affect, originating in the *rhetorical set figures*, are made either in the tying together or in the diminution of the beats.

Die *mechanischen Setzfiguren*, die man schlechtweg *Setzfiguren* nennet, und in deren Anwendung auf einen gewissen Affect, die *rhetorischen Setzfiguren* ihren Grund haben, nehmen entweder aus der Zusammenziehung oder der Verkleinerung der Tacttheile ihren Ursprung. (Marpurg 1763, p. 144)

Here then Marpurg is continuing the German tradition in compositional theory, going back to Bernhard, in which most elements of the musical surface (i.e. anything other than beat-by-beat movement) are explained in terms of certain figures. The reference to the rhetorical basis for this style of ornamentation has its origins in traditional German compositional theory, something which is also evident in Praetorius's seminal instructions on singing. Marpurg's terminology also shows the same mechanistic thinking that is evident in Bernhard's compositional theory: for instance, notes which come between the 'Hauptnoten' are defined as 'neighbour-notes' ('Nebennoten'), both harmonic and melodic (i.e. consonant or dissonant); a neighbour-note which sounds on the beat in place of a structural note is a 'changing note' ('Wechselnote'); a harmonic neighbour-note which comes as a *Nachschlag* is an 'escaped note' ('durchgehende Note'; Marpurg 1763, pp. 144–5).

Tosi and Agricola represent the new 'specialised' level of singing, something which was no longer directly associated with liturgical music. It is significant that while they document detailed improvised passages, mid eighteenth-century school primers do not. Petri does however give some tantalising evidence of a form of improvisation which may have had a long tradition: improvised harmony in chorale singing. There are virtually no references to this practice in the standard school treatises of the previous century,[42] but Petri's comments imply that it was still a well-ingrained tradition in the mid eighteenth century (indeed he still refers to this practice in his extended treatise of 1782, p. 211):

> How can one ensure that, when a choir sings well-known church chorales without music, as must often happen, there are not such terrible transgressions against a pure harmony in the bass and middle voices? And is it possible that many heads in a choir can have a single mind? . . . One teaches each and every one the most necessary rules of harmony and makes them acquire, through frequent repetition of faults, a distaste for the same

> Wie ist dem Uebel abzuhelfen, daß ein Chor, wenn es bekannte Kirchen-Chorale ohne Noten singet, wie oft geschehen muß, im Basse und den Mittelstimmen nicht so schreckliche *Vitia* machet gegen eine reine Harmonie? Und ist es möglich, daß viel Köpfe eines Chores einerley Sinn haben können? . . . Man lehre allen und jeden die nöthigsten Regeln der Harmonie, mache ihnen durch öfteres Wiederholen der *vitiorum* einen *degoût* vor denselben
>
> (Petri 1767, p. 63)

After giving a few rules of thumb on how to avoid the worst problems, Petri states that the technique of singing improvised harmony is best learned by initially using a figured bass line. What seems clear from his description is that, in his time at least, many improvised in this fashion without really understanding the rules of harmony.

If, as this study has suggested, the composer gradually took over the singer's prerogative for adding the freer, improvised ornaments, but the singer was increasingly encouraged to understand the composer's newly-acquired art, one may question whether the average German singer *ever* understood the fundamentals of composition, especially during the time when he was still freely elaborating the composer's work (i.e. up to the late seventeenth century). In other words, did the concept of *musica practica* involve anything of the art of *musica poetica*?[43] Certainly Praetorius, himself a first-rate composer, notes at the outset of the German Baroque that the singer must not only have the natural gift of a good voice, 'but also must have a good understanding and complete knowledge of music.'[44]

Ornamentation and the performer and composer 147

However, it is clear from the context here that the 'complete knowledge of music' is a knowledge of the ornaments and coloratura that he is about to demonstrate. He does add that the singer cannot apply these anywhere, but only at the appropriate place and with regard to the rules of music. These points he probably intended to demonstrate in the third section of the chapter ('Exercitatio') which he never wrote. Herbst likewise breaks off his narrative at the same point and merely adds examples. Perhaps his *Arte prattica & poëtica* (1653), which gives rules on counterpoint, improvised 'contrapunct à mente' and *Generalbass* (mostly plagiarised from Italian sources), is designed to provide the necessary instruction for specialists.

Friderici and Bernhard imply that the singer must have some regard for the rules of music, since they recommend that diminutions in the bass (as the 'fundament') be avoided and that all elaborations should return to the prescribed notes. Printz warns the singer to be particularly cautious in polyphonic pieces, and pay heed to the 'fundament' in solo pieces (Printz 1678, p. 44). However, like Praetorius and Herbst, these authors do not state that the singer should understand composition; these rules merely ensure that the notated composition is not ruined. The reference to the bass as the 'fundament' clearly reflects the thinking of the 'thoroughbass age': diminution is the melodic corollary to the arpeggiated elaboration of a specific chord.

Tutors which give 'complete' singing instruction from rudiments to ornamental figures also show that the latter could be learned without a formal grounding in composition: for Dieterich (1631), coloratura was the fourth body of skills to be learned after clefs, note-lengths and Italian terms (which comprise only *forte* and *piano* here). Crüger introduces ornamentation immediately after dealing with intervals and the various signs used in music; he recommends that the singer discern to which *trias harmonica* the piece belongs, but he does not seem to require any deeper awareness of the harmonic structure (Crüger 1660, p. 18). Printz introduces figures in the second part of his *Compendium* (1689), after a discussion on the pronunciation of text; this sequence of tuition is essentially the same as that in his first vocal treatise of 1671 (Printz 1689, pp. 42f). Evidently, if Bernhard was correct in observing the influence of performers on compositional practice, the influence flowed only one way. There seems to be no evidence that improvising German performers were necessarily acquainted with the rules of composition. Ornamentation and diminution seem to have been treated merely as elements of performing style. Ironically, it is only in the later seventeenth century – when singers were enjoined not to disturb the composer's notated ideas – that there are attempts to educate the performer in the rules of composition. Here then it is appropriate to examine sources on *musica poetica* – treatises which offer instruction in composition – to determine whether the composer indeed absorbed the performer's art, as Bernhard affirmed.

ORNAMENTAL FIGURES IN COMPOSITIONAL THEORY AND PRACTICE

Bernhard's assertion, opening this chapter, is significant as a retrospective view of the early years of the Baroque era. His theory was designed to show that music of the tradition begun by Monteverdi (i.e. the *seconda prattica*) could, by means of reductive analysis, be reconciled with the traditional rules of counterpoint which were still fundamental to compositional instruction (i.e. the *prima prattica*). This he may have developed in response to the polemics of Artusi, with which he probably became acquainted during his visit to Italy.[45] Artusi's complaints focus precisely on that which 'charms the ears' rather than reason, and on composers who adopt the *accenti* (usually upper neighbour-note ornamentation) traditionally improvised by singers (preferably with discretion and judgement at that).[46] Dahlhaus suspected that the *Figurenlehre* of Bernhard was a Germanic apology for Italian vices, one which did not necessarily accord with the motives or theoretical concerns of the Monteverdi school. Nevertheless Bernhard's comment does resonate with that purely sensual (and thus anti-mathematical) view of music propounded by Vincenzo Galilei, which Dahlhaus considered so important to Italian musical aesthetics at the outset of the seventeenth century (Dahlhaus 1986, pp. 141–50).

Bernhard's historical assertion that performers influenced composers and compositional style is well substantiated by Newcomb's penetrating study of the madrigal at Ferrara: the virtuoso style of the celebrated women singers both necessitated the notation of diminution in order to avoid clashes between the polyphonic parts and inspired composers to use diminution as part of their regular language (Newcomb 1980, vol. I, p. 59). Several Italian works published in the 1580s show diminution used 'not merely as an incidental feature in a single voice but as an essential and identical feature of the thematic material in several voices' (*ibid.*, p. 76).[47]

That Bernhard's theories were still significant in German-speaking lands for several decades after his death is reflected by the numerous copies of his treatises (for instance by Kuhnau and Stierlein),[48] and by the fact that his figural treatment of dissonance was assimilated by writers located as far apart as J. B. Samber and Mattheson. Particularly interesting is the appearance of substantial passages from Bernhard – including that opening this chapter – in J. G. Walther's *Praecepta* of 1708, perhaps the most significant theoretical source of compositional theory for the early environment of J. S. Bach.

As has been noted above (see p. 141) the only treatise aimed specifically at performers which contains a version of this statement is Stierlein 1691. Nevertheless, Kuhnau's introduction to his publication of keyboard sonatas, *Frische Clavier Früchte* of 1696, shows the close relationship between his views as a practising composer and performer and his opinions as a theorist, the latter seemingly derived from Bernhard's comment. This gives us a very useful insight into the way a composer of the late seventeenth century may have thought about his art and its relation to history:

Now and then something can be seen which appears to correspond little with the rules of the old composers. For I have written many movements or passages of which I myself would have approved little a few years ago in the works of other authors, however famous, and which often struck me like sour grapes or other premature fruit. But the authority of the same practised virtuosi at that time brought me to other thoughts, and allowed me to consider that the nature of their works was rather like that of the so-called Ritter or green pears: these are in appearance almost never ripe; but however suspect this fruit may be on account of its colour, how ripe and delicious it can nevertheless be. And so I beg forgiveness of these new artists from my heart . . . and recognise that they have not sinned against the rules of the ancients at all but have merely sought in accordance with reason to conceal the simple and natural mixing of the consonances and dissonances as it were under the figures of oratory; or in imitation of many gardeners, who wish to know the trick of producing a foreign and lovely colour in common flowers.

Es lässet sich zwar hin und wieder etwas blicken / welches mit denen *Regulen* der alten *Componisten* wenig übereinzukommen scheinet. Denn ich habe manche Sätze oder Gänge gemachet / die ich vor etlichen Jahren in anderer / wiewohl berühmter *Autorum* Wercken selbst nicht *approbi*ren wollen / und sind sie mir öffters wie Herlinge / oder ander unzeitiges Obst vorgekommen. Allein die *Autor*ität selbiger *exercir*ten *Virtuos*en hätte mich damahls sollen auff andere Gedancken bringen / und erwegen lassen / daß es mit ihren Wercken fast die Beschaffenheit habe / wie mit denen so genandten Ritter- oder grünen Birnen: Diese sind dem Ansehen nach fast niemahls reiff; Doch so verdächtig als dieses Obst wegen seiner Farbe ist / so reiff und wohlgeschmack kan es hingegen seyn. Und also bitte ich es diesen neuen Künstlern in meinem Hertzen . . . wieder ab /

150   Music education and the art of performance

und bekenne / daß sie wider die *Regul*en der Alten durchaus nicht gesündiget / sondern bloß gesuchet haben / die schlechte und natürliche Vermischung der *Consonanti*en und *Dissonanti*en gleichsam under denen *Oratori*schen *Figur*en vernunfftmäßig zu verstecken / oder es etlichen Gärtnern nachzuthun / welche das Kunst-Stücke wissen wollen / denen gemeinen Blumen eine frembde und liebliche Farbe beyzubringen.   (Kuhnau 1696, foreword)

The conception of the compositional style as heavily influenced by ornamental figures is certainly an interesting view of the relationship between the roles of composer and performer in the German Baroque. If the music can indeed be viewed from the standpoint of its status in that relationship, modern concerns for historical performance can more profitably be directed towards that which lies notated in the music itself. Analysis would play a more important part in the determination of a legitimate interpretation, since much of the desired historical performance style lies already encoded in the music, itself a distillation of 'original' performance practices.

Do the ornamental figures described in treatises specifically directed towards *composition* reflect Bernhard's view that the composers were absorbing and synthesising the mannerisms of performers? If so, was this a literal annexation of the figures concerned, affixing them to an existing musical structure, or were ornamental devices to be integrated more tightly into the compositional fabric? A study of selected compositions showing composers consciously notating ornamentation derived from performance practice – and particularly those providing a simpler, unornamented version concurrently – will help to establish how closely the theories correspond to compositional practice.

While some Italian theorists (e.g. Zacconi and Diruta) do to some extent absorb diminution into their treatises on counterpoint, the newer dissonances are never really explained, only exemplified (see Gallo, Groth, Palisca and Rempp 1989, pp. 288–90 and 347–8). All German writings on compositional theory during the seventeenth century are essentially manuals on late Renaissance counterpoint. Therefore any concern with figuration or diminution is secondary and never evident in the chapters dealing with the fundamentals of composition. What is remarkable in the context of this study is that most references to ornate composition correspond closely to their counterparts in the singing tutors. Lippius 1612 introduces the matter of florid composition – as Praetorius did for the singer – with reference to the nature of the text and the effect of the music on the listeners; the composer can use these ornaments to polish his harmonic oration. Coloratura is reserved for the upper voices, while the bass proceeds slowly. Just as Bernhard was later to observe, Lippius notes that 'in this style ordinary musicians often embellish a basic composition when appropriate, using pleasant elegance like an elaborate scriptural flourish' (see p. 47 above).

Crüger 1654 falls into three parts, the first dealing with the rules of harmony, the second with the ornamentation of melody and the third with thoroughbass. The second section is essentially a Latin translation of Praetorius's instructions to singers (which Crüger later incorporated into his singing tutor). Clearly, then, the composer was to assimilate the techniques used by performers (both ornamental figures and thoroughbass) in order to perfect and refine his style. Praetorius's comment that singers must not overstep the 'laws of music' and ruin the work with too much coloratura is repeated, again without any real indication of how this is to be achieved. Presumably the composer's study of counterpoint, his knowledge of the text and experience in oratory will prevent him from succumbing to the worst excesses of singers.

Printz's most detailed study of ornamental figures appeared in the second part of his *Satyrischer Componist* (initially published in 1676–7, one year before the vocal tutor of 1678, and after that of 1671), a treatise in composition which, exactly like Crüger's, ends with an explication of thoroughbass. As he states in the introduction to *Figuren*, the material is equally useful for the composer and singer.[49] The chapter is designed expressly for composers who, although skilled in their art, lack their own *inventiones*; working with these figures as elements of 'variation' will not fail to stimulate the imagination. Given the title of the chapter – 'Tractatus de Variationibus & Inventionibus' – Printz clearly views variation and invention as being two sides of the same coin. He schools the composer in the arts of ornamenting pre-existent lines, and creating new ones out of the available formulae. The only difference between this text and that of his singing treatise of 1678 – for the most part the two are identical – is the greater attention Printz gives here to the statistical possibilities opened up by the use of each particular figure. There is something rather mechanical about Printz's approach to figures: the number of permutations for each is meticulously calculated, leading to the remarkable conclusion that a single crotchet beat can, using figures comprising quavers and semiquavers, be varied in 2,897 ways (Printz 1696, part 2, p. 61). The composer proceeds in just the same manner as a singer schooled by the exhaustive examples in Italian diminution treatises. To Printz the figure was something which was added to melodic invention, somewhat in the manner of salt to food.[50]

It is not precisely clear how the composer is to use these figures since Printz does not relate them to the rules of dissonance in composition (these having already been covered in the first volume); the main intention is to stimulate invention.[51] The prospective composer should proceed from figure to figure; after weeding out those figures which have 'too great an ambitus' or 'some other defect', he must thereafter

take one after another of the same, and add on to each another suitable figure, first on just the same pitch as the last note of the first figure, as far as it is appropriate, since few such figures can prettily be employed in vocal pieces; after that in all the other suitable intervals, both ascending and descending.

Hernach nimmt er eine nach der andern von denenselben / und setzt zu ihr eine jewede andere schickliche *Figur*, erstlich in eben der *clave*, in welcher die letztere Note der ersten *Figur* stehet / wofern es sich nur schicken will; sintemahl wenig solche *Figuren* in *Vocal*-Sachen hübsch angebracht werden: Darnach in allen andern geschickten *Intervallen* / so wohl auff- als absteigenden.
(Printz 1678, p. 66)

Therefore the composer assimilates figures originally used in performance, and employs them during the actual process of composition.

The Leipzig cantor Johann Kuhnau gives a vivid picture of a composer working with figures, along the lines of Printz's theories. In the introduction to his cantata cycle of 1709 his primary intention is to explain word-setting as a catalyst for invention and variation; however, he shows that 'invention and variation' can be understood in another – specifically musical – sense too:

Certainly the discussion here is not about the art and manner of variation and invention, which I have considered in another place, namely how, for example, four notes of a single quantity can be varied in such a way according to the precepts of the art of combination 24 times, and five notes 120 times, and so on, in that one multiplies the last product with the following number of notes to be varied in arithmetic progression, so that soon each combination has a different effect in the heart of the hearer. Such variations would be almost unending, if one wished at the same time to change the quantity of notes somewhat.

Zwar ist hier nicht die Rede von der Art und Weise zu variiren und inventiren, davon ich an einem andern Orte gedacht, wie nehmlich, zum Exempel, vier Noten von einerley Quantität nach denen Praeceptis artis combinatoriae 24. mahl, und 5. Noten 120. mahl, und so fort, da man das letzte Productum mit dem in Progressione Arithmetica folgenden Numero Notarum Variandarum multipliciret, solcher gestalt können verwechselt werden, dass bald jede Combination einen andern Effect in dem Gemüthe der Zuhörer operire. Welche Variation fast unendlich seyn würde, wenn man an der Quantität der Noten zugleich etwas changiren wolte. (Kuhnau 1709, in *MfMG*, 1901, p. 150)

In this elaboration of Printz's system Kuhnau perhaps comes as close as any author to suggesting the affective connotations of the note combinations comprising diminution. However, it is clear that he is working from a hypothetical standpoint; so infinite are the combinations and the concomitant stirrings of the soul, that it is virtually impossible to describe or analyse them, not to speak of relating them to a verbal language.

Just as Printz the theorist shows clearly that the art of variation is shared by composers and performers alike, so one of Kuhnau's predecessors as Leipzig cantor, Tobias Michael, adds diminution (or rather substitutes simpler lines with diminution) in the manner of the singer in some of the vocal lines for the second part of his *Musicalische Seelen-Lust* (1637). The preface to the *Quinta vox* shows that he is very much of the opinion that coloratura is the privilege of singers. He is openly apologetic for having included lines of coloratura, since, in his experience, talented singers perform better if they are given free rein in adding diminution, and he cannot agree with those who want to tie everything down to one manner.[52] His patently formulaic coloratura (following 'Kapsberger's style') is provided as an alternative for certain parts of the extant lines and is included merely by way of example to assist the inexperienced (Example 9). Here he may have been following his predecessor as cantor of the Thomasschule, J. H. Schein, who had likewise added some passages in a publication (*Diletti pastorali*, Hirten Lust 1624), in full awareness of the fact that composing was the duty of the composer, 'passaging' the privilege of the singer. Schein notated the diminution – following the example of other 'foremost composers' – because many German singers were still not particularly familiar with the contemporary Italian style of singing.[53]

Despite Michael's claims that performers could have done this just as easily, it is difficult to conceive how they could have improvised so freely from the notated line (preserving only the first and last notes of the original) without knowledge of the bass part, or, in the case of b. 31, of each other's line. This consideration aside, Michael gives little attention to the musical implications of the figured versions, just as if he were a singer applying his favourite figures: in bb. 25–7 the rhythmic and melodic elements of the original imitation are obscured by the diminution; the diminution of b. 31 more successfully (and necessarily) relates the simultaneous vocal parts of the original, although the contrary motion is abandoned.

One of the most interesting commentaries on the relationship between performing and composing practice in the latter part of the century is to be found in J. G. Ahle's *Musikalisches Gespräche* (1695–1701). In two of the

154   Music education and the art of performance

dialogues, Ahle (his Latinised name thinly disguised by the anagram 'Helianus') answers a student who complains of forbidden parallels caused by the figuration in the music. His response is that if such a figure were removed, the singer would surely add it (since figures of the *accentus* variety are so often added in progressions involving thirds). Such notes

Example 9   Tobias Michael, *Musicalische Seelen-Lust*, part 2. No. 34, 'Kommet her zu mir' (from the print of 1637; clefs modernised)

are so short in time that they cannot cause offence. Why should one forbid in notation that which is common in singing and playing? If performers give such elegance and gracefulness with the various figures (here there is a list of references to many of the vocal treatises already encountered) how can it be wrong if the composer does the same? (Ahle 1695, pp. 32–4). Helianus later substantiates this argument by observing that 'intrinsically short dissonances' can neither mitigate an error nor cause one.[54]

Here the composer is explicitly recommended to imitate performers, since much is to be gained from the style therein and any passing parallels can be tolerated just as they would be in performing practice. J. G. Walther – who also borrowed Bernhard's comment (p. 149 above) – quotes Ahle on this matter, adding that figures must be employed with a respectable moderation, so that any illegal consecutives pass by without the ear noticing.[55] Obviously singers had made their mark on musical style with their expressive devices (of which diminution practice was a component) and composers were anxious not to lose their share of the credit.

It is significant that Ahle's later comments (1704) added at the end of an enlarged edition of his father's singing treatise of 1673 suggest that complaints about coloratura practice should be addressed not so much to performers as to the composers themselves, who so seldom understand the correct time and suitable places to add the 'figures of music' (see p. 141 above). Although this could imply a contradiction in Ahle's thinking – i.e. the references to the 'correct time' and 'suitable places' might suggest that the performer/composer should assiduously avoid errors of musical grammar – it is more likely he is concerned with the appropriateness of such devices to the text, and that the work is not deformed and rendered unrecognisable. As a poet laureate, Ahle was greatly concerned with text setting and the transfer of poetic rhetorical devices to music. Strictness of musical grammar was perhaps subservient to the affect and meaning of the music, matters which were understood innately and learned by example rather than through theory:

Whoever has a musical ear and good judgement, and understands the musical passions, he will know well when, how, and where he should use dissonance.

Wer ein Musikalisches Gehör und gutes *judicium* hat / und die *Pathologiam Musicam* versteht / der wird die *Discordanzen* wohl zugebrauchen wissen / wän / wie / u. wo er sol. (Ahle 1699, p. 39)

It is not difficult to find composers of Ahle's era who give little attention to the harmonic accuracy of coloratura. Example 10 shows two extracts

156   Music education and the art of performance

Example 10   Johann Schelle, *Christus, der ist mein Leben* (text from *Johann Schelle: Six Chorale Cantatas*, ed. Mary S. Morris, Recent Researches in the Music of the Baroque Era, 60–1, Madison, 1988)

from the florid instrumental parts in the cantatas of Johann Schelle, yet another cantor at the Thomasschule, Leipzig. Clearly this is the sort of notated coloratura which Ahle excused: the harmonic problems could be mitigated by the speed at which they pass (but the composition hardly seems perfected to the degree we might expect from Schütz). On the other hand this may provide us with a good notated example of the kind of coloratura improvised by performers of the period.

What is significant, if not unexpected, about these theoretical and practical views of composition, is that they not only substantiate Bernhard's point that composers had in the past absorbed the devices of performers but also imply that composers of the present should behave exactly as if they *were* performers: much was to be gained by adopting the latters' 'mannerisms'. Only Printz (and to a certain extent Kuhnau) went so far as to suggest that figures might be the catalyst for invention, but this is merely a possibility opened up by the study of figures, one which is essentially identical to that offered to performers.

However, as the overview of vocal tutors has revealed, the composer seemed to be gaining precedence over the performer towards the end of the seventeenth century. Werckmeister – somewhat more cautious than Ahle – was quite unequivocal in his distaste for composers contravening the fundamentals of musical grammar:

One always seeks that which is new, which is good, but there must be a reason for it . . . Whoever understands the firm progressions and true resolutions of dissonance, will also introduce the graces cautiously. Therefore no one should show off until he has first a certain grounding in his art.

Man suchet immer was Neues / ist wohl gut / aber es muß ein Grund dabey seyn . . . Wer die Säße / *progressiones*, und rechte *resolutiones* der *dissonantien* verstehet / der wird auch die *Mani*ren behutsam anbringen. Darum prale doch ja niemand / er habe denn erstlich einen gewissen Grund von seiner Kunst.

(Werckmeister 1700, p. 18)

As a writer who still saw all arts as grounded in the order of nature, according to God's plan, Werckmeister saw dangers in adopting diminution practices which contradicted the fundamentals of composition.

Obviously the German composers whom we now consider to be the greatest of their age employ figuration in a manner which reflects Werckmeister's concern for the integrity of the compositional style. The one school of compositional theory which did attempt to account for composers' use of figures in terms of traditional compositional procedures was that of Bernhard himself. Bernhard's work on figures – 'a certain manner of using dissonances so that these do not sound repulsive, but much more pleasant, and bring the composer's art to the light of day'[56] – is well documented in modern literature. All manners of dissonant licence are discussed, so ornamental figures of the kind encountered in practical tutors form only one part of Bernhard's wider survey of 'figures' (which, for example, also covers the resolution of dissonances by other voices, and chromatic progressions). Although the two treatises in composition are designed as prescriptive methods for the student composer, it is quite clear that Bernhard's treatment of figures (particularly the *figurae superficiales* which are used in the modern *stylus luxurians*) is essentially analytical, an account of how the figuration in the compositions of his age could be explained in terms of a background adherence to the rules of dissonance prescribed by the *prima prattica*. Many examples show how certain passages make sense musically when they are understood in terms of the proposed reduction (Example 11).

Federhofer's study of 1989 and an earlier one by Rifkin (1972) have convincingly shown that Bernhard's methods are a viable method of analysing music of the Schütz era (especially in view of Schütz's own prescription of strict counterpoint for the incipient composer, in the preface to the *Geistliche Chor-Music* of 1648) in a manner which would not merely permit any random succession of notes to be justified according to strict rules of counterpoint. Bernhard's approach is unique in taking

Example 11   Christoph Bernhard, *Tractatus*, Chapter 33 (Müller-Blattau 1926/1963, pp. 81–2; clefs modernised)

   Stehet natürlich also:

the figured version as the starting point rather than as the elaboration of a simple version. The reduction (as in Example 11) reflects the composer's subconscious absorption of the fundamental contrapuntal rules and is therefore not necessarily a proposed compositional sketch which must have been written first. He thus shows how many composers of his age were creating music of greater depth than that purely derived from the conventions of performing embellishment.

However, it is significant that Bernhard still frequently notes that figures of embellishment and diminution originated in performance practice; indeed in the second treatise he introduces *figurae superficiales* with the historical conception of figures opening this chapter. Furthermore, many of the figures (i.e. methods of using dissonance) are exactly those which he also specifies in his treatise on singing (i.e. methods of

Ornamentation and the performer and composer 159

embellishment). The first figure in both compositional treatises is the *superjectio* or *accentus*, shortly followed by *subsumtio* or *cercar della nota* and *variatio* or *passagio* (Müller-Blattau 1926/1963, pp. 71–5, 147–50). In the last category, intervals – beginning with the second – are embellished in turn, exactly in the manner of an Italian diminution treatise. Bernhard even goes so far as to suggest that the composer remain alert to current fashions in performance, avoiding variations that are too old-fashioned.[57] He carefully explains passages of diminution in terms of figures he has already described:

it is clear that variation upon the third is nothing other than the *transitus* . . . that upon the fourth originated from the *quasi-transitus*. The rising or falling fifth, since it is naturally composed of two thirds, is therefore varied in the same manner as thirds are – that is with the true *transitus*.

NB. Aus diesem Exempel erhellet, daß die *Variation* der *Tertie* nicht anders ist, als ein *Transitus* . . . daß die *Variation* der *Quarte* aus dem *Quasi-Transitu* herfließe. Die steigende oder fallende *Quinte*, wie sie natürlich aus 2 *Tertien* bestehet, also wird sie auch wie die *Tertien variiret* und ist daher ein wahrer *Transitus*.
        (Müller-Blattau 1926/1963, pp. 73–4)

As has already been noted, Bernhard's method of analysing the figures used in composition was adopted by several later theorists: (e.g. Stierlein, Samber, Walther, Heinichen, Mattheson and Marpurg). As late as 1752 Ruetz remarks that the quantity of figures in the music of his day is that which most distinguishes it from that of earlier generations. However the requirements of perfection ('Vollkommenheit') – perhaps more of a concern to mid eighteenth-century aesthetics than to those of Bernhard's time – demand that the more varied the figuration adopted, the more necessary it is that everything be united and directed to one end.[58]

Although Bernhard's theory clearly acknowledges the influence of improvised diminution on compositional practice, the figures are viewed from the standpoint of an experienced composer, immersed in late Renaissance conventions. This rather contradicts Ahle's view that composers should loosen their pedantic rules of voice-leading in favour of the immediacy of expression achieved by singers. R. P. M. Spiess (1745) effects, to some extent, a compromise between the two views, since he separates the figures constituting the *decoratio* of music into two types: those which are notated by the composer and those to be improvised by the performer.[59] It is difficult always to discern a clear distinction between these two fields, since general figures of ornamentation are common to both; however, the figures specified for the composer are of a more rhetorical nature, relating to the poetic effect of the music (*abruptio*, *anabasis* etc) rather than to the specific motives employed.[60]

In sum, there are two basic attitudes to notated figuration in seventeenth-century Germany, both of which clearly acknowledge the influence of performance conventions. First, there are the writers and composers (Michael, Printz, Ahle and Schelle) who take over the performer's art wholesale and recommend that the composer apply it in his written compositions, as a free embellishment of a simpler structure. Secondly there are those (Bernhard and his followers) who – while adopting many motivic patterns used in performance – give more attention to the role and development of the figuration concerned, justifying it in terms of an underlying system and ultimately changing the norms of the compositional language itself. Clearly the actual state of affairs is hardly likely to be clear-cut, but the hypothetical distinction is a useful tool by which to gauge the attitude of any particular composer to the task of composition.

THE RELATIONSHIP BETWEEN COMPOSER AND PERFORMER: MUSICA POETICA AND PRACTICA

The most interesting cases of notated ornamentation are those where the composer seems to be taking over the performer's art, but tends to use the figures in a manner which could not possibly have been achieved by the improvising performer. Praetorius's notated coloratura in his *Polyhymnia caduceatrix* (1619) is an obvious attempt to introduce the 'latest Italian manner' into German church music and is, as such, the corollary of his vocal tutor. He clearly states in his 'Ordinantz' that the 'simplex' version has been added above the more elaborate lines so that boys, especially in schools, can still perform the works if they are unfamiliar with diminution practice.[61] He clearly considered his ornamented lines as the 'official' text and the simpler versions as a means of rendering the settings more usable; this is quite the opposite of the case in Tobias Michael's publication (some twenty years later) where the composer seemed almost embarrassed to specify coloratura (see p. 153 above). Praetorius remarks that boys can use the given examples as models by which to simplify other passages; as a rule of thumb, the first note of diminution over the syllable of text is usually the principal note for the simple version. All this suggests that Praetorius composed the versions with diminution first.

On the other hand, since most of the works are chorale-based, much of the diminution was obviously composed around the notes of the

Ornamentation and the performer and composer 161

original melody; indeed Praetorius states in the introduction to no. 14 'Wir gläuben all' that 'your humble servant has somewhat diminished the Chorale in the vocal parts in the current Italian fashion'.[62] However what is significant is that in some places the diminution presents a rather more coherent musical structure than that of the simplified version. In the second part of no. 15, 'Aus tiefer Not' the ornamentation links the parts in bb. 9–10 by sequential movement in thirds (Example 12). This produces a far more unified texture than that of the simplified parts which bear no melodic relation to each other and lack the sequential

Example 12   Michael Praetorius 'Aus tiefer Not', part 2 (*Polyhymnia caduceatrix*, 1619). Bar numbers from *M. Praetorius: Gesamtausgabe*, ed. Friedrich Blume (Wolfenbüttel, 1928–40), xvii; music text revised from original print of 1619.

162   Music education and the art of performance

movement. Likewise, in no. 24, 'Siehe wie fein und lieblich ist', the imitation from the word 'und' is more consistent than that in the simpler version (Example 13). In the third part of this piece the two ornamented voices imitate each other in short phrases; however, the simplified version in slower note values often lacks this consistency, since literal imitation would have led to awkward dissonances.

Significant conclusions can be drawn from the case of Praetorius. First, as a composer, his practice was more sophisticated than that advocated by the compositional theorists who suggested merely that the composer imitate singers. The very act of notating coloratura caused its nature to

Example 13   Michael Praetorius, 'Siehe wie fein und lieblich ist' (*Polyhymnia caduceatrix*, 1619). Bar numbers from *M. Praetorius: Gesamtausgabe*, ed. Friedrich Blume (Wolfenbüttel, 1928–40), xvii, music text revised from original print of 1619

change, from added ornament to musical substance, something which was also evident in the Italian repertory in the last decades of the previous century.[63] It may well be the composers' assimilation of figures of diminution and the – probably unconscious – subjection of them to the standard processes of composition which accounts for some of the basic compositional changes during the German Baroque. The increasingly authoritative use of figures by composers has also been amply demonstrated by the comments in vocal treatises of the late seventeenth and early eighteenth centuries. However, this process was clearly not a linear historical development, since composers can be found in both categories throughout the period concerned: while the role of the *figurae superficiales* might be equivocal in Praetorius, dispensable in Michael and questionable in Schelle, it is difficult to see the notated figuration in the music of J. S. Bach as optional or capriciously formed; here diminution is indispensable and (as Printz recommended) the very substance of the 'invention'.

However, this does not mean that performers were to give up their responsibilities in understanding the figuration. Several writers in the latter part of the period stress – quite to the contrary – that the performer must be familiar with the art of composition too (see p. 141 above). Werckmeister's distaste at incompetent diminution is supported by a large quotation from Kuhnau's *Der musicalische Quacksalber* which centres on the qualities of the true musician. A performer who does not know the rules of composition is no better than a bird; likewise a composer who does not understand practice is like a dumb orator.[64] Niedt similarly suggests, in the preface to the second part of his *Handleitung* (1706), that 'A true musician's equally composer' (Poulin and Taylor (trans.) 1989, p. 60). The vogue for relating music to rhetoric (as is evident in the quotation from Bernhard at the opening) may also have played a part in this association of composer and performer: he who writes a speech must equally be capable of delivering it, and vice versa.

There may also be a strong social case for the closer association of composers and performers and the growing versatility of musicians in the latter part of the seventeenth century in Germany. First, the cantor's role was moving from that of schoolmaster or musical instructor towards that of a more purely practical musician who was expected both to compose ever more demanding music and to direct the performance (see p. 17 above). Secondly, the roles of organist and cantor were drawing closer together, so that such posts could be – and often were – filled by someone capable of fulfilling both roles (consider the careers of Buxtehude and J. S. Bach). Thirdly, the cantor, as a more practical musician, often achieved higher status as town music director (J. S. Bach) or even opera director (Telemann). Such increased mobility contributed to a greater mingling of musical functions and styles. A glance at the achievements of the pupils of Bach and the surviving testimonials he wrote for them give a remarkable insight into the versatility expected of the more talented practical musicians: most sang, played several instruments and also composed.

The growing importance of thoroughbass is another symptom of this development: composition was increasingly learned through the most *practical* method, one which cultivates fluency in both composition and performance. It is interesting that in the early eighteenth century composition was taught in the sequence thoroughbass – strict counterpoint (e.g. Niedt, Heinichen, and later, Kirnberger) while in the preceding century the sequence was precisely the reverse (e.g. Herbst, Crüger and Printz). The interaction between composer and performer is also reflected in some of the definitions of music from the latter part of the seventeenth century. Printz and Walther define *musica practica* as an art encompassing both *musica modulatoria* (performance) and *musica poetica* (composition) while earlier German authors tended to reserve *musica practica* for performance alone (Printz 1676 (vol. I)/1696, p. 17; Walther 1708, pp. 14–15). The definition of Printz and Walther persists in the writings of Murschhauser 1721 (p. 1) and Maier 1741 (p. 23).

Performers of German Baroque music today are obviously no longer the composers. However, this study has suggested that much of the musical style itself derived from the continuous and changing dialogue between composer and performer. Indeed many major issues in performance practice can be reduced to the basic inquiry into the bias of any particular text or repertory toward composer or performer. Is the performer expected to add coloratura? If the composer has notated it, has he done so as a casual performer or has he reformed the figures concerned and integrated them into a deeper imitative structure? Modern performers may also alter their attitude to their task when they appreciate how the composer probably gained just as many ideas from what he heard performed as from what he had formally learned as a composer; thus as performers we must learn from the composer what 'we' originally taught him. Differences and subtleties in interpretation will reside in the subjective assessment of the details of a simpler 'background' and of how each ornamental figure relates to it.

Ornamentation and the performer and composer

The performer also has a variety of historical opinions to choose from: while many vocal tutors – particularly the earlier ones – imply that he was a 'blind' elaborator of the composed musical structure, some of the later theorists suggest both that the notated music is becoming more didactic and that the performer should understand the essentials of composition. There is an interesting dichotomy here: the performer appears in one category as a 'composer' who need not understand composition, while in the other he is purely an 'interpreter' who is expected to understand the whole theory of composition and the relationship between the figural texture and the contrapuntal and chordal structure. Perhaps then, as musical compositions became more 'fixed' in notation at the outset of the eighteenth century, it became crucial that performers did not lose the interpretative colour that improvisation would formerly have lent their performances; they still had to view the music from 'inside' in order to bring across its rhetorical properties.

6

The decline of the Lutheran cantorates during the eighteenth century

This study has thus far centred on the musical period commonly termed the Baroque; as chapter 2 suggested, this is the era of the greatest flowering of Lutheran church and school music. Nevertheless, both the changes in educational stance and the internal developments of music as a specialist art, growing away from its academic roots, sowed the seeds for the eventual demise of this rich tradition. This final chapter examines the literature relating to this period of decline, from three angles: evidence for the stagnation and decline of many cantorates; new developments in performance practice and pedagogic stance and their influence on the more secure establishments (and thus a continuation of chapters 4 and 5); and finally, a consideration of changing attitudes to the function and status of music (thus concluding the study of such topics in chapter 2).

DECLINING STANDARDS OF PRACTICAL MUSIC INSTRUCTION

There are many indications that the standards of singing both in school and in German musical life had declined precipitously by the mid eighteenth century. One first-hand report even suggests that the choir of the Thomasschule in Leipzig was virtually non-existent in the last years of J. S. Bach's life (see Fröde 1984); Quantz alludes to the general poorness of singing in German schools (1752, ch. 18/80),[1] and Agricola states at the outset of his translation of Tosi's renowned singing treatise that the Germans have not perfected singing to the same level as the Italians. His extensively annotated translation of 1757 is clearly an attempt to remedy a situation for which the decline of the basic music education in schools must partly have been responsible. Burney's chronicles also paint a grim picture of indigenous German singing in establishments less exposed to Italian performers, such as the Leipzig playhouse.[2]

The situation is well illuminated by a consideration of the life and writings of the most notable figure in German music education during the latter half of the eighteenth century, Johann Adam Hiller. To begin with, he spent much of his career outside the traditional church and school establishment.[3] Indeed he was instrumental in fostering the concert tradition in Germany, and founded the first German music conservatory, that institution which was to replace the Latin school as the central authority in practical music instruction. His departure from the norms of the conservative church/school tradition is shown even more clearly by his advocacy of the musical education of women, who should have every right to sing church music; the fact that it was traditional to exclude women from church music was, in itself, no good reason.[4] He became cantor of the Thomasschule, Leipzig only at the end of his career, revitalising an old (but still venerable) institution with the hindsight of the more modern systems of music education.

The introduction to Hiller's first singing treatise gives perhaps the clearest picture of German singing in the 1770s and its relation to the school environment. The author opens with the bold statement that, while everyone sings, the vast majority sing badly.[5] And, although he considers German composers superior to Italian ones, German singing is significantly backward, primarily because of the standard and style of tuition in schools. Here Hiller uncovers what he sees as an unthinking attitude towards learning, one that evidently seemed anomalous in the Age of Enlightenment; now young people had to understand the structures underlying any system of rules before they could transfer and apply those rules in other circumstances.

In singing I enjoyed instruction, communally along with others, from my twelfth year onwards, as is usual in schools. To be sure, pitching and rhythm were certainly the goal towards which we had to run; but the way was so uncertain and uneven that it took much time before one learned to go without stumbling. The example of this or that interval, written on the board according to the succession of scale degrees, was always soon learned; but if one of these intervals should be given out of order, we were like the honourable Corporal Trim in *Tristram Shandy*, who knew the fourth Commandment very well; but only when he could begin with the first. Of the good use of the voice, of the comfortable drawing of breath, of a pure and clear pronunciation, however essential these elements of singing were, little or nothing was mentioned.

Im Gesange habe ich, von meinem zwölften Jahre an, den Unterricht, wie er auf Schulen gewöhnlich ist, mit andern gemeinschaftlich genossen. Treffen und Tact

168   Music education and the art of performance

> war freylich wohl das Ziel, nach welchem wir laufen mußten; aber der Weg war so unsicher und Holpricht, daß viel Zeit dazu erfordert ward, ehe man ihn ohne Stolpern gehen lernte. Die nach der Stufenfolge der Tonleiter an eine Tafel geschriebenen Exempel dieses oder jenes Intervalls waren immer bald gelernt; aber wenn eins dieser Intervalle außer der Reihe angegeben werden sollte, so gieng es uns, wie dem ehrlichen *Corporal Trim* beym *Tristram Schandy*, der das vierte Gebot sehr gut wußte; aber nur, wenn er beym ersten anfangen durfte. Vom guten Gebrauche der Stimme, vom bequemen Athemholen, von einer reinen und deutlichen Ausspruch, so wesentliche Stücke sie auch beym Gesang sind, ward wenig oder nichts erwähnt. (Hiller 1774, 'Vorrede')

Clearly some cantors in the mid eighteenth century were still teaching singing in exactly the same manner as outlined by the primers from nearly two centuries before.[6] Secondly, the advances in performance technique and details of interpretation which became more prominent in the 'middleground' seventeenth century treatises seem to have all but disappeared. Certainly it has already been noted that the sixteenth-century format – and indeed treatises such as Faber's – survived well into the Baroque period and that there seemed to be a noticeable decrease in publications during the first decades of the eighteenth century. As Quantz observed in 1752, German school choirs sang with a uniform volume of tone, knew nothing of uniting the vocal registers and aspirated much of the passage-work, creating a choppy, unrefined style (Quantz 1752, ch. 18/80).[7]

In 1781 Hiller made explicit his opinion that the backwardness of German singing lay in an unthinking, mechanical attitude to the art, an opinion that might well be shared by a modern reader of much of the literature relevant to the present study:

> Good voice production, clean and clear pronunciation, smooth breathing is nowhere thought of, though everything depends on it. One sees from this that the study of singing is as deficient as ever in Germany. The endeavour of most is directed purely towards the achievement of great mechanical dexterity.
>
> An gutes Tragen der Stimme, an reine und deutliche Aussprache, an bequemes Athemholen wird überall nicht gedackt, worauf doch alles ankömmt. Man sieht daraus, daß das Studium der Musik immer noch mangelhaft in Deutschland ist. Das Bestreben der meisten ist blos auf eine Erlangung einer großen mechanischen Fertigkeit gerichtet.
>   (Introduction to Hiller's *Duetten* 1781, quoted in Weimar 1795, p. 4)

The situation that Hiller describes may have developed because the better musicians (such as himself) were no longer attracted to service in school and church, and because the authorities were turning away from the appointment of musically outstanding cantors (see p. 189 below). Many supported the appointment of cantors of the traditional 'academic' type who taught music along very conservative, if not archaic lines.[8]

Hiller was aware of the extent of the German pedagogic literature on singing in schools and how this far exceeded the amount published in Italy.[9] He reckoned that this vast corpus of literature was not properly used and did not in any case give sufficient practical instruction (he even criticises Marpurg's treatise for its dearth of practical examples). However, he does admit that the Germans are better at sight-singing than the Italians, since they learn instruments as well. Furthermore, since church musicians had to sing so much for the regular services with little time for adequate preparation, they often became reliable choir singers even if they were not fine soloists.

Here it seems appropriate to ask why earlier writers did not anticipate Hiller's views. Certainly many of the earliest Lutheran primers were designed to cultivate nothing more than fluency of reading. But, as has been shown, there was a growing number of writings which did introduce elements of voice culture. However, most elements of technique were related to other, more pressing concerns, namely ornamentation, expression and the presentation of the text. By Hiller's time, singing technique was being studied in the more modern sense as a 'Wissenschaft' in itself. As music evolved as less of a functional, unquestioned part of education and society, its component techniques became more abstracted. Significantly Hiller divides the art of singing into two separate treatises: the first concerns 'Richtigkeit' ('correctness', 1774), the second 'Zierlichkeit' ('grace', 1780).

Petri's expansion of his 1769 treatise in 1782 is another good testimony to the changing circumstances, attitudes to, and demands for music. Petri was still actively engaged as a school cantor, but he notes at the outset that the enlarged treatise addresses the 'Verbesserung der Kirchen- und Konzertmusik' ('improvement of church and concert music'). It is essentially an encyclopaedic work offering the incipient musician as many facets of performance as possible. While pupils should be trained so that they can sing music directly according to the intentions of the composer and conductor, they should also gain some critical knowledge themselves so that they can avoid the provincial and ignorant attitudes of many teachers (Petri 1782, foreword).

Like Hiller, Petri recommends that singing be taught with more practical emphasis and he believes that even without Italian-style conservatories, music in schools could be so much better if it were taught with knowledge and understanding.[10] Petri later outlines some specific reasons why the church choirs sing so poorly: if the ensemble and pronunciation are poor, the cantor is at fault; cantors also often let soloists perform without adequate ornaments or conversely permit chorus singers to perform with them. Citizens do not pay enough to secure good music and the young performers are lazy, often singing from memory (Petri 1782, p. 209).

Some twenty years later, the second volume of Forkel's *Allgemeine Geschichte der Musik* (1801) provides the most comprehensive and devastating account of the decline of singing instruction in German schools. Forkel notes that chorales used to be taught in schools and that cantors once paid great attention to the purity of tone and intonation in singing, bringing melodies to those who were ignorant of them.[11] The status of church music had greatly changed by the end of the eighteenth century:

Thus it has come to pass that [chorale singing] in most churches has for the most part lost its edifying quality, there is often more howling than song, and the standard has sunk to that which Luther even in his time named lazy chorale singing, in which no life, no confidence, in short, no expression reigns.

Daher kommt es denn, daß er jetzt in unsern meisten Kirchen seine Erbaulichkeit größtentheils veloren hat, oft mehr Geheul als Gesang, und zu dem herunter gesunken ist, was Luther schon zu seiner Zeit den faulen Choralgesang nannte, worin kein Leben, keine Zuversicht, kurz kein Ausdruck herrscht.
(Forkel 1801, p. 15)

Forkel is quite scathing of the general ignorance of teachers, who know little about 'true works of art' and teach little more than dance, folksong, ariette, or at most a sonata of the same kind.[12] Thus even if some schoolmasters were still interested in teaching music, it seems it was entirely for secular pleasure.

LATER DEVELOPMENTS IN EDUCATIONAL STYLE AND CONTENT

Some writers, even late in the eighteenth century, preserve a remarkably conservative format and educational style. Nopitsch's treatise of 1784 was addressed to complete beginners, specifically the lower classes of the *Trivialschulen*. The format is roughly that of traditional 'middleground' treatises, covering all the basics of notation in the first part and issues of performance and interpretation in the second. However, unlike most writers, he introduces correct pronunciation of vowels and consonants as the content of the opening chapter. Later he stresses the supreme importance of coupling the sense of the text with the appropriate musical expression:

> If he attains these indispensable principal parts of art – if his voice, his performance matches exactly the sense of the words – then the text set to music receives its true life, and it achieves a completely irresistible power over the nervous system of a sensitive listener.
>
> Erlangt er diese wesentlichen Haupttheile der Kunst – trift seine Stimme, sein Vortrag, mit dem Sinn der Worte genau überein, so bekommt der in Musik gesezte Text sein wahres Leben – und eine ganz unwiderstehliche Kraft, bei einen empfindsamen Zuhörer auf das seinere Nervensistem zu würken.
> (Nopitsch 1784, p. 35)

Thus, just like the writers from the outset of the Baroque period, Nopitsch sees music as primarily a medium for textual expression, and one with a quantifiable affective power.

Wolf (1784), more than any other contemporary writer, shows a strong adherence to the German school tradition. Although he acknowledges the influence of many recent writers (Marpurg, Hiller and Tosi/Agricola), he was also indebted to Printz, that seventeenth-century writer who seems most to endure in the next century. Not only are Printz's recommendations on lifestyle clearly evident but his advice on choir organisation is reprinted in its entirety. It is interesting that the division of singers into concertists and ripienists still seems to pertain.[13]

Wolf also preserves traditional methods of learning notation: boys should take turns to point out on a board the notes being sung.[14] The rules on forming the voice in the throat rather than between the lips, the avoidance of singing through the nose, and the direction to sing the higher notes quietly, could easily have been written a century before. Wolf's teaching format is likewise remarkably traditional: he proceeds with instructions on scales and staves, vocal ranges, intervals (best learned with the help of a keyboard), and how to sing a simple song with note names and Graun's syllables. The first part concludes with note values, rests, the signs used in music, keys and metre. Predictably, part two, in the traditional manner, concerns the art of graceful singing: appoggiatura-type ornaments, trills, mordents and slides. Next Wolf discusses correct pronunciation of the text, breathing and the various styles required for different musical genres and different places (church, concert, theatre).

While the majority of cantors apparently gave little attention to the standard of singing and other elements of practical music in the latter part of the eighteenth century, the better teachers kept abreast with the recent developments in singing technique and educational philosophy. Indeed the approach can be quite radically different from that of the first two centuries of the Lutheran tradition, something which underlines the vast changes in culture and thought during the latter half of the eighteenth century.

Already, Marpurg's treatise of 1763 shows great attention to the structure and ordering of instruction, even though the initial stages correspond quite closely to traditional methods (compare with the plan, p. 56 above). The pupil should first sing with the letter names of the notes or solmisation syllables, without the text. Then the teacher should proceed with slow, even note values, steadily introducing more complex rhythms and metres. The principal departure from the traditional Lutheran methods is the introduction of keys after this point, arrayed in a circle of fifths. Pupils must learn to beat time (in rehearsal only) and, above all, accustom themselves to singing from notation and not from memory (Marpurg 1763, pp. 3–8). Given that the early Lutheran primers seemed intended for rote-learning (see p. 8 above), something which was a feature of education *per se*, it may be that memorising of information, texts and music was still widespread in the mid eighteenth century. In Marpurg's age the excessive reliance on memory was evidently seen as an inhibition to true understanding.

Marpurg includes several points of practical advice which are seldom to be found in earlier treatises: the pupil should not hold the score in front of his mouth; the singers should be rehearsed alone and in pairs before singing together as a group; pieces should be practised at several speeds, presumably so that the pupil can cultivate flexibility and confidence in performance. He still sees the tremendous advantage in using canons and fugues for preparing the pupil for all musical styles (including even the *galant* idiom – Marpurg 1763, pp. 8–9).

Marpurg also distinguishes the concept of a teacher from that of the virtuoso (it is the implication of most previous authors that the outstanding musician will naturally be an outstanding teacher, since so much was learned by direct imitation). The teacher should have a good sense of intonation and pronunciation, a knowledge of harmony and 'good taste'. He should be clear and understandable, introducing the right amount of material in each lesson, with an ability to distinguish the easy from the difficult. Again, in traditional German teaching the writers give no indication of which fundamentals are likely to require more time (although some lay great stress on the importance of experience and practice in the field of diminution and ornamentation). Foremost among the cantor's qualities should be honesty, enthusiasm, patience and praise of industry (Marpurg 1763, pp. 11-13).

The principal development is the utilisation of the pupil's own rationality within the learning process (although the seeds of this attitude are evident in the early seventeenth century; see p. 66 above). Marpurg outlines how a teacher can cure a seemingly incurable block in pitching the notes of the scale with a little insight into the mental processes of the pupil (p. 14). Like several earlier authors, he insists that the pupil learn the keyboard and later the rules of harmony, presumably so that he gains an awareness of the entire context surrounding the line he sings (p. 15). Exactly the same point is made by Hiller a few years later.[15] All this complements the movement observed in the latter part of the Baroque era (chapter 5): the pupil was encouraged to delve deeper into the rules of composition and understand something of the creative processes underlying the notation.

Some of this new approach to educational method was doubtless inspired by the growing philanthropic movement, influenced by the naturalistic philosophy of Rousseau. Some schools, for example in the Palatinate, show this influence directly (Finkel 1978, pp. 258, 280-3): all teachers should know all the arts, aesthetics should be a primary element of education, and music should be treated as a beautiful 'Wissenschaft' rather than as a craft. Methods of instruction were often remarkably imaginative: Christmann's *Elementarbuch der Tonkunst*, for instance, employed many mnemonic techniques, including the use of colours to learn notes (*ibid.*, p. 283; see also Schünemann 1928, pp. 255-76). The philanthropic movement was one of the only aspects of Enlightenment thought that contributed to an improvement in school music education. However, it could not directly revitalise the cantorates, since it was primarily secular in nature and not directly related to the traditional establishments of church and school. Furthermore, it tended to favour the cultivation of instrumental over vocal performance (Schipke 1913, p. 52).

The most radical break with traditional methods of 'mainstream' school singing comes with Hiller's treatise on 'correct' singing of 1774, which (given that Hiller was yet to become cantor of the Thomasschule) was more of a prescription than a reflection of actual practice in school music. It doubtless reflects Hiller's experience as a teacher in his own music conservatory. Like Marpurg, he stresses that the length of time spent on each lesson (each chapter of his book is called a 'lesson') should correspond to the singer's achievement and not be restricted to the confines of a single hour. Again, singing from memory is to be discouraged, and the pupil should work from an example book, published simultaneously with the main treatise at a cost which each pupil can afford. The examples comprise two basic categories (a distinction never observed in earlier writings): those which function as explanations and those which are to be used in practice to cultivate facility in the matter in hand; both are to be studied industriously so that singing becomes not a mechanical art or profession but a 'Wissenschaft', an art that requires the same degree of rationality as a science.

Hiller considers that all fourteen lessons may be learned in six months with four lessons per week (he may have been thinking of the unusually liberal allocation of music lessons at the Leipzig Thomasschule here);[16] even if this took a year, it would still be short compared with the courses of Italian conservatories, which lasted three to four years. Of the recent publications on singing he recommends Agricola's translation of Tosi, but he notes that it is not really designed for the beginner in school. Furthermore, Marpurg does not include enough practical examples (indeed this author had stated at the outset that the cantor would do best by choosing these from his own store).

Despite the originality of his pedagogic approach, much of Hiller's advice on the qualities of a suitable singer conforms surprisingly well to the German tradition: by nature he or she should have a sense of pure and clear pronunciation, good intonation and rhythm, a sense of 'correct' expression and elegance; singing through the nose is, as usual, proscribed and the falsetto register is of use only as an extension of the natural range. Hiller's recommendations on diet and lifestyle likewise seem to be based directly on those of Printz from nearly a century before (Hiller 1774, p. 13).

Hiller does make some use of solmisation syllables (Graun's system of 'da, me, ni, po' etc), but not until lesson 6, and then for the primary reason that they use all the principal vowel sounds. His method of teaching intervals is more subtle than traditional solmisation (perhaps because of his own experience as a pupil, see p. 167 above): the simpler, triadic intervals appear in lesson 7, fourths and sixths in lesson 8, sevenths and ninths in lesson 9, and larger, compound intervals in lesson 10.

Given that this first volume of Hiller's singing method is addressed to 'Richtigkeit', it is remarkable how many ornamental devices are presented. *Vorschläge* (i.e. the successors to the *accentus* ornaments) appear in lesson 7, trills (originally introduced in lesson 1) are dealt with in greater detail in lesson 12 and the following lesson concerns passages. In other words, certain elements of ornamentation are relevant even at a comparatively early stage, before 'Zierlichkeit' is officially introduced. This primacy of ornamentation is not unlike that often observed in some seventeenth-century treatises: while Bernhard, Crüger and Mylius reserved ornamental passages for a particular, advanced style of performance, they all regarded the relatively simple ornaments of the *accentus* type as fundamental to the simplest style of singing (see chapter 5).

While some of the later seventeenth-century treatises show that the performer's role in adding coloratura was declining and that notation was becoming more specific, it is noticeable that certain figures, particularly of the *Vorschlag*/appoggiatura type and trills, are common in sources from the mid eighteenth century onwards (for Marpurg, Petri and Doles, see p. 144 above). This undoubtedly reflects the renewed influence of Italian singing, particularly with the publication of Tosi's treatise and its expanded translation by Agricola. Furthermore, Italian singers themselves were increasingly to be found in important operatic centres (e.g. Hamburg and Dresden) from the 1730s onwards.[17] In this light it is interesting to examine Scheibe's critique of Bach, namely his opinion that the composer indicated too many things in the notation which were the privilege of the singers. Clearly it was common for singers to be responsible for a certain amount of expressive embellishment during the late 1730s, so perhaps Bach's didactic notation (and indeed his compositional personality) reflected more the trends of the turn of the century, when, as is suggested in chapter 5, the composer was taking over much of the performer's prerogative.[18]

The greatest innovation in Hiller's method is the division of material into 'lessons', each of which introduces the pupil to a variety of material (rather than taking one subject at a time and studying it exhaustively): for instance, in lesson 1 the pupil learns about vocal ranges, the notes, their names and the system. But he also learns the fundamentals of the *trillo*, so that he can begin practising this from the very beginning of his studies. In other words, one of the most difficult techniques, one which is indispensable to the interpretative style of the age, is ingrained even before many of the more basic fundamentals are encountered. Lesson 2 likewise introduces the concept of long and short notes as a form of musical expression (i.e. 'good' and 'bad' notes) together with the upper tetrachord, intervals, the major and minor modes and an extensive introduction to metre. The succeeding lessons also introduce 'musical' points and elements of technique: a fundamentally legato articulation, conservation of breath, where to take breath and the *messa di voce*, an ornament which is not only musically useful but also a good means of cultivating breath control.

Hiller thus seems to show a deep insight into the learning process – or, rather, his method conforms to a more 'enlightened', psychological awareness of the pupil's natural learning abilities. Several techniques and dimensions in performance – musical rudiments, singing technique, matters of musical style – are introduced a little at a time, so that the pupil's understanding, facility and insight are developed simultaneously during the course of several lessons. As we have seen, most primers in the German tradition tend to introduce the rudiments separately in a specific order and only then (if at all) cultivate elements of performance technique and interpretation.

To generalise, this entire study has shown the change from an impersonal, 'uninterpretative' and memorised learning method to one which fosters the pupil's understanding, facility in performance technique and rhetorical awareness. Some of the seeds for this change were laid in the seventeenth century with the pedagogic approach of such reformers as Comenius and the widening of the definition of *musica practica*; however, the changes after 1750 are that much more striking. It is hardly a simplification to suggest that this development is paralleled in attitudes toward the function of music and in the changes of musical style itself.

With the second volume of Hiller's singing course, that concerned with 'Zierlichkeit' (1780), the subject is almost entirely musical expression and ornamentation. Now that the singer is more advanced, Hiller abandons his division into lessons and follows the more usual chapter format. He shows the influence of recent Italian writers, particularly Mancini, and is fully conversant with the practices in Italian conservatories. In contrast to the German treatises on ornamental singing from the previous century, Hiller lays great stress on the thoroughness of Italian music education; the principles of music and harmony, and knowledge of the keyboard are absolutely mandatory if good taste in expression and ornamentation is to prevail. Predictably, ornaments of the appoggiatura variety form the basis of good ornamentation, 'arbitrary embellishments, which for our taste have become a necessity'.[19] Like Agricola, Hiller believes that there is no harm in the composer indicating some of these (Tosi's scorn notwithstanding), since not all singers can be expected to have the same ability and knowledge.[20]

The introduction of unnotated dotted rhythms is another feature that can be traced back to the Italianate ornamental methods of the early Baroque. Hiller introduces progressively more complex forms of the appoggiatura: e.g. simple and double *Nachschläge* and sliding figures; varieties of the trill. The one-note *tremolo*, which was the principal trill a century before, is now considered old-fashioned, though still worth practising (Hiller 1780, pp. 65–6). The expressive *Bebung* remains important, however, as does the cultivation of dynamic flexibility on long notes.

Following Tosi (and indeed Bernhard from the mid seventeenth century), Hiller includes a chapter on the various genres within which vocal ornamentation is appropriate: the most sober style is appropriate for church, while the character and affect of the part define the style for the theatrical singer; the singer must be most brilliant in the context of the concert (a relatively new phenomenon, for which Hiller's pioneering work as an impresario was partly responsible).

A glance at the basic format and complexity of this second treatise shows that Hiller was hardly addressing the average cantorate here. Like Agricola, in his translation of Tosi, Hiller was concerned with the more advanced, potentially professional singer, in an attempt to raise the general standard of singing in Germany. Petri 1782 notes that Hiller's method was strongly influenced by Agricola and that Hiller's 1774 treatise is more useful for individual singing lessons than for choral preparation (Petri 1782, p. 195). Furthermore, he notes that even Hiller's carefully planned example book is too advanced in places for the beginner. On the whole, Petri himself retains the traditional format of instruction, from staves, clefs and notes to diatonic scales and intervals. After learning Graun's syllables in order to attain pure pronunciation of vowels, the pupil can progress to chorales in numerous keys, then to small canons, fugues and motets.

Wolf 1784 finds fault with the major singing treatises of his time; Marpurg's is incomplete, Hiller's is too expansive and rambling. His primary complaint with the latter method concerns just that element which made Hiller so revolutionary, the mixing of several topics within a single lesson. Wolf was not alone in his criticism of Hiller's format. Reichardt believes that Hiller's unsystematic (but perhaps psychologically progressive) approach clashes with the traditional tenets of the Enlightenment:

This work of Herr Hiller appears to me good enough as a practical instruction; I find conscientiousness and experience therein. Only it still has something of the error of the majority of our teaching books: when regarded specifically as practical instruction, there is not enough order or conciseness in it.

I understand the fully systematic succession of things in the former just as little as the compactness of style in the latter. I would have wished to avoid the mixing of materials that should simply follow one another, and the verbosity.

Mir scheint dieses Werk des Herrn Hillers, als ein praktischer Unterricht recht gut zu seyn; ich finde Fleiß und Erfahrung darinn. Nur hat's immer noch einen

178   Music education and the art of performance

Theil der Fehler der mehresten unser Lehrbücher: es ist selbst als praktischer Unterricht betrachtet, nicht Ordnung und Kürze genug darinnen.
    Ich verstehe unter jener eben so wenig die völlig systemathische Folge der Dinge auf einander, als bey dieser das Gedrungene des Styls: Nur Vermischung der Materien, die schlechterdings aufeinander folgen sollten, und Weitschweifigkeit, die wünschte ich vermieden.   (Reichardt, quoted in Boecklin 1790, p. 44)

In 1792 Hiller – now cantor at the Thomasschule at Leipzig – produced a further singing treatise, specifically designed and condensed for tuition in town and village schools. Although he claims that his treatise of 1774 is still the most complete and best commentary on singing, he abandons the lesson format and writes in a sequence of topical paragraphs. Such are the constrictions of the school schedule that Hiller seems to have returned to the more traditional format for German school treatises. Ironically, he places 'Treffen' and 'Tact' (pitching and rhythm, Hiller 1792, foreword) at the head of his priorities, just those elements which he saw as being the overriding concern – to the detriment of everything else – in his own early education (see p. 167 above). However, he also includes the subjects of 'Vortrag' and 'Vorbereitung' (performance and preparation) as equally essential issues.

The format of Hiller's school primer follows fairly predictable lines. Although the mixing of subjects which made the first treatise so revolutionary is no longer evident, Hiller is careful to introduce pertinent elements of technique at an early stage. He introduces the notion of saving breath and holding the tone through to the end of each note when the pupil first learns to sing scales.[21] Hiller introduces the trill – 'the most necessary ornament of singing'[22] – directly after scales, and, probably in direct emulation of Printz (see p. 79 above), recommends that the pupil practice trills during the singing of chorales.[23]

Particularly interesting are Hiller's recommendations on the singing of passages (which come directly after the subjects of rhythm and metre):

A singer who wishes to have a flexible throat, must industriously practise the same [passages]. Furthermore they [passages] do not always comprise continuous, scalic figures, but sometimes circular, broken, even leaping figures. Clear performance demands that the first note of such a figure should always be completely clean; for if this is not the case, the following ones will be even less so. Also it is greatly beneficial to clarity when the first or even the first two notes of four or eight notes are strengthened with a gentle pressure.

Ein Sänger, der Fertigkeit der Kehle zu haben wünscht, muß sich fleißig in denselben üben. Auch bestehen sie nicht immer in grade fortlaufenden Figuren, sondern bisweilen in zirkelförmigen, in gebrochenen, auch in aus Sprüngen

The decline of the Lutheran cantorates   179

zusammen gesetzten Figuren. Der deutliche Vortrag fordert, daß immer die erste Note einer solchen Figur vollkommen rein sey; denn wenn diese es nicht ist, so werden es die folgenden noch weniger seyn. Auch trägt es zur Deutlichkeit viel bey, wenn von vier oder acht Noten, die erste, oder auch die beyden ersten Noten durch einen gelinden Druck verstärckt werden.
(Hiller 1792, pp. 49–50)

While Hiller might have drawn the directive to emphasise the first note of a metrical grouping from Tosi/Agricola,[24] the reference to the variety of figures and the clear delineation of each recalls precisely the advice of Printz over a century before (see p. 132 above). This advice seems extraordinary in the context of late eighteenth-century music; it is also to be found in Hiller's long treatise on 'ornamented' singing (1780) and might reflect his conscious emulation of previous authors of German school books.[25]

Nevertheless, Hiller was clearly not blindly copying his predecessors in this treatise, since so many elements of his teaching are directly applicable to the needs of his age. He introduces the student to the principal genres of church music: chorales, choruses, arias and recitatives (Hiller 1792, pp. 67–74); he covers the essential trills and appoggiaturas in considerable detail. Particularly conscientious is his advice on coordinating breathing with the syntax of the text, ensuring that breaths are taken after a strong beat and never before (*ibid.*, p. 57). His careful blending of tradition with innovation and his sensitivity to the contingencies of his age are shown in his choice of examples in the closing pages of the treatise: new chorale melodies, arias and songs appear side by side with canons and fugues.

Hiller's concise treatise for school singing did not lie unused. In 1795 G. P. Weimar produced a book of practical exercises to supplement Hiller's advice. Weimar believed that Hiller's examples on pitching and intervals required amplification and he added much advice on the actual practice of teaching intervals in class. Again it is interesting to note that canons still form a significant part of basic classroom practice.

It would be grossly incorrect to assert that these thorough and 'enlightened' treatises mark the end of the German singing tradition. Significant methods (e.g. Lasser 1798; Schubert 1804) were soon to be written, and singing at both amateur and professional levels blossomed during the course of the ensuing century. Indeed Bach's vocal works might never have come to light without the remarkable developments in amateur choral singing. However, Hiller's treatise of 1792 is the last major work in a literary tradition connected with Lutheran school education, one which reached back over two hundred years.

CHANGING ATTITUDES TO MUSIC IN CHURCH AND SCHOOL

The early eighteenth century

The increasing 'artistry' in practical music and the adoption of an ever more elaborate notated style by composers had engendered many complaints towards the end of the seventeenth century (see p. 25 above). Orthodox Lutheran music theorists were not slow to respond. Werckmeister reaffirmed the Pythagorean perspective of the God-given priority of music as a reflection of the cosmic order, something which was not revoked by worldly misuse. The following comment was still in print during the latter half of the eighteenth century:

But just as a trumpet contains in itself the entire order of harmony, C c g c e g c, and no others [notes] can be used in between, so God has wished to show with this, that we cannot do other than lead and regulate our lives and religion in harmony according to the order and will of God . . . But because the Devil is the enemy of the holy order and wisdom of God, he always rouses evil people who must misuse this creation and use it for all kinds of voluptuous songs and frivolous dances; indeed all the multifarious misuse cannot be described. Therefore devout hearts must also take care not to despise this wisdom of God on account of the misuse, to detach music from public worship and pour out the baby with the dirty bath water . . . We will nevertheless sing and maintain the *Harmony* and the eternal *Holy*. Music is and indeed remains good if the intention of the musician is solely good and holy; likewise with the pure instrumental music . . . which thrived in the first church.

Wie aber eine Trompete die ganze Ordnung der Harmonie C. c g c e g c in sich hält, und keine andere darzwischen können gebracht werden; also hat GOtt hiermit andeuten wollen, daß wir nicht anders, als nach der Ordnung und Willen GOttes in der Harmonie unser Leben und Religion halten, und anrichten sollen . . . Weil aber der Satan der heiligen Ordnung und Weißheit GOttes feind ist; so erwecket er immer böse Leute, die dieses Geschöpfe müssen mißbrauchen, und zu allerhand üppigen Liedern und leichtfertigen Tänzen gebrauchen, ja der vielfältige Mißbrauch ist nicht alle zu beschreiben. Darum haben sich auch fromme Herzen vorzusehen, daß sie nicht wegen des Mißbrauchs diese Weißheit GOttes verachten, die Musik von dem öffentlichen Gottesdienste absondern, und das Kind sammt dem unflätigen Bade ausschütten . . . Wir werden doch die *Harmonie* und das ewige *Heilig* singen und behalten. Die Musik ist und bleibet doch gut, wenn die Intention des *Musici* nur gut und heilig ist; auch die blosse Instrumentalmusik . . . welcher in der ersten Kirche gelebet.   (Werckmeister 1700, in Steffani 1699, ed. Albrecht 1760, pp. 30–1)

Werckmeister's outlook matches closely that in Niedt's treatise (published at virtually the same time) which is especially celebrated for its direct influence on J. S. Bach.[26] Although Werckmeister stresses the importance of the human intention in guaranteeing the divine status of music, it can be inferred that the mere substance of *any* music can reflect the Godly order. As Niedt and Bach remark, it is the good use of music, together with its perfect crafting according to the seemingly eternal laws of thoroughbass, which are of foremost importance. The question of the devout intention of the musician points to another level of musical significance: the affective status of music and consequently its power to influence the listener. A pious composer/performer will communicate – quasi-mechanically – the state of his soul to the congregation.

Albrecht reiterates in a later footnote (1760) that many use evidence of the misuse of music as a weapon against church music *per se*;[27] the content and grounds of the debate seem just the same as they were at the turn of the century. Indeed the debate can be traced throughout the first half of the eighteenth century. In 1703 and 1708 Motz produced lengthy books defending church music against the attack of the Pietist pastor Christian Gerber. Armed with a predictable array of Biblical quotations in support of music, Motz addresses each of Gerber's points in turn. When, for instance, Gerber complains that many establishments are infested with musicians from divers religions and nations – in particular papist Italians – Motz replies that the identity of the singers is irrelevant provided that what they sing is not contrary to Lutheran teaching.[28] He similarly castigates Gerber for objecting to the presence of ordinary citizens such as labourers in the choir, merely because their virtue is not to be guaranteed; Motz observes that much the same can be said for the congregation as a whole, and this would hardly be a reason to ban the singing of chorales (Motz 1703, pp. 32–3).

Regarding the nature of music itself, Motz affirms that elaborate music does not chop up the text; indeed repetitions contribute to the essence of the text (just as in Psalm 136).[29] As has already been noted (see p. 26 above), the Pietists laid great emphasis on the precise wording and original meaning of a verbal text, since it is from this that the reader acquires the correct sense. Orthodox theorists, however (and to these belonged the most enthusiastic supporters of elaborate music), tended more towards essentialist thinking: words allude, perhaps imperfectly, to eternal truths which the human being can experience through several forms of communication and artistic creation.

The influence of Pietist thought is evident for instance in the ordinances of Schleswig-Holstein: in 1745 singing of the Gospel and Epistle was banned, in the following year the singing of the Creed and Gloria (Detlefsen 1961, p. 240); musical pieces were banned from the communion in Freiberg in 1729 (Krickeberg 1965, p. 116). In Calvinist Prussia, King Friedrich Wilhelm even published an edict for the preachers in his state (1739), stating that they could not go far enough in their proscription of music.[30] Instrumental music in church was particularly vulnerable at this time; according to Gerber it was banned by the king of Denmark in 1730,[31] and Mattheson noted a papal ban during the 1740s (see p. 185 below).

The introduction of musical forms deriving from operatic practice during the first decades of the eighteenth century has already been observed (see p. 44 above). While some writers (e.g. Scheibel) were eager for the expansion of this practice, others, including Gerber, were quite incensed by the development (see Stiller 1970/1984, pp. 263–5). Meyer's desire to return to the practices of the early church immediately recalls the prescriptions of Vockerodt, in the last decade of the seventeenth century (see p. 26 above):

For the sake of this I have referred to ancient times, those of the Jewish churches as well as even the heathen and subsequently the first churches, and wish to demonstrate, having observed through their example and uses of their church music, that they always had a loathing for theatrical music in their services, and especially saw to it that the hearing was not so much flattered as the glory and praise of God was broadcast, and that the enlivening of the listeners' devotion might be achieved.

Ich habe mich um des willen auf die alten Zeiten so wol der Jüdischen Kirchen / als auch so gar der Heyden und nachgehends der ersten Kirchen beziehen / und durch deren Exempel und Gebräuche / so sie bey ihrer Kirchen-*Music* beobachtet / erweisen wollen / daß sie jederzeit einen Abscheu vor der *Theatral*ischen *Music* bey ihren Gottesdienst getragen / und vornemlich darauf gesehen / daß damit nicht so wol dem Gehör geschmeichelt / als die Ehre und das Lob Gottes ausgebreitet / und die Ermunterung der Zuhörer Andacht bewircket werden möchte. (Meyer 1726, p. 4)

Meyer proceeds to discuss the origin of what he terms 'Cantaten', and how the new works banish the Scriptures and render the texts incomprehensible (Meyer 1726, p. 53). In all, this sort of criticism stands in a direct line from that at the end of the seventeenth century. Whereas the complaint before was about the florid coloraturas of singers in the seventeenth-century concerto style, the attention is now drawn to the new integration of secular cantata forms. In other words, the earlier fears that church music was becoming too operatic were more than substantiated by the subsequent developments in musical style itself.

The defences of church music likewise greatly resemble those of the previous century, showing that, as far as basic attitudes were concerned, nothing had changed:

Singing is an art and science of singing all kinds of arias, cantatas and songs in an artistic and ingratiating way according to the prescribed notes at the correct pitch and with a measured beat, to an accompanying instrument. The singing is a particular component in the church service, which contributes greatly to the enlivening of the heart. Those who completely abolish the songs and their singing and believe that it does not make sense that when one asks something of God, one steps out and sings something with a beautiful sound, are mistaken.

Singen, ist eine Kunst und Wissenschafft allerhand Arien, Cantaten und Lieder auf eine künstliche und schmeichelhafte Manier nach der vorgeschriebenen Noten in richtigem Tone und abgemessenem Tacte, in ein darein spielendes Instrument abzusingen; Das Singen ist ein besonderes Stück bey dem Gottesdienst, welches zu der Ermunterung des Hertzens sehr vieles beyträgt. Es irren also diejenigen, welche die Lieder und deren Absingen gänzlich verwerffen und meynen, es reime sich nicht, wenn man was bey GOtt erbitten wolle, daß man hintrete, und in einem lieblichen Tone etwas hersinge.
(Zedler vol. XXXVII, p. 1,656)

Scheibe is another illuminating source on adverse attitudes to church music in the late 1730s. While he is usually celebrated as a figure who criticised Bach's music – particularly his supposedly unmelodic style – Scheibe was quick to come to the defence of church music *per se*. In his article for 24 March 1739, he asks why so many have such an unreasonable view of music, considering it to hinder all spiritual matters (Scheibe 1739, pp. 281–6). Like Luther, he states that the inclination towards music was implanted by God himself, and that music both inspires piety and soothes the person burdened by worldly affairs.[32] In acknowledging that music is often misused, Scheibe does not concur with those who are wary of its associations with the theatre and inns: indeed he affirms that the theatre can be a school of virtue and that there is hardly a Godly ban on enjoyment in itself. Just like his colleagues in the previous century, Scheibe stresses the distinction between the instrinsic value of art and its misuse.

Scheibe's article for 15 September 1739 gives a useful account of the functions of church music as he saw it. In focussing on the recent proscription of music on a penitential day, he seemingly ignores the fact that music was traditionally excluded from fasting periods and days of penitence; for him it is 'a necessary and indispensable component of a reasoned and well-ordered church service'.[33] He notes that we no longer

184   Music education and the art of performance

live in a time of sackcloth and ashes and that the New Testament has come; in any case the Old Testament itself contains psalms of penitence, which were obviously sung. Although organists and church musicians often leave much to be desired, this does not mean that music cannot lead to greater devotion on all occasions.

In his study of the origins and age of music, published in 1754, Scheibe tackles another prejudice about music, affirming that many educated people now consider music to be beneath them:

In short, almost all our scholars today, with only a few exceptions, know little or nothing about music . . . Thus it has come to pass that they are even ashamed of themselves if they read musical writings or books

Kurz, unsere heutigen Gelehrten fast ingesamt, nur wenige ausgenommen, wissen wenig oder nichts von der Musik . . . Daher kommt es denn, daß sie sich so gar schämen, musikalische Schriften oder Bücher zu lesen
(Scheibe 1754, foreword, p. xxiv)

Scheibe's assertion immediately engenders questions concerning the status of music as an adjunct to general education during the eighteenth century. The Bendeler dispute of 1706 centred on the somewhat ambiguous jurisdictional relationship between the cantor and rector within the school hierarchy (see p. 31 above). This conflict seems to have been uncannily replicated with the dispute between cantor J. S. Bach and rector J. A. Ernesti during the 1730s. Both cases can be seen as evidence of the direct confrontation between the old Lutheran orthodox view of music as an essential component of education and worship and the educational stance of the early Enlightenment, which saw music more as an optional luxury.[34] Indeed Ernesti's Saxon school ordinance of 1773 contains no mention of music at all (Schünemann 1928, p. 227). Doles and Hiller, both of whom gained great renown for their work as cantors of the Thomasschule in the later years of the century, experienced very similar difficulties in their relations with certain rectors (Schering 1941, pp. 396, 657).

The mid eighteenth century

While Bach's dispute with Ernesti is that which is best remembered today, the most celebrated pamphlet war of the time was that instigated by the publication of J. G. Bidermann's *De vita musica* in 1749. School and church music had flourished in Freiberg under the leadership of J. F. Doles and this had almost inevitably led to conflicts between the cantor and rector Bidermann (for an extensive summary see Banning 1939, pp. 17–40). Matters came to a head in 1748 when the pupils of the Freiberg *Gymnasium* performed a Singspiel to celebrate the centenary of the peace of Westphalia. The text was prepared by Bidermann and the music by Doles, but the latter's work achieved far more renown than the former's (Mattheson 1749, p. 8; Banning 1939, p. 24). Bidermann's insulting underpayment of Doles for his part in the venture may well point to his chagrin, and, if Mattheson is to be believed, Bidermann's pamphlet was the direct result of his envy.

De vita musica is startlingly similar to Vockerodt's writings from the end of the previous century: the programme affirms that music can easily lead to an unsavoury lifestyle and examples from antiquity, such as Caligula and Nero, only go to show how true this is; therefore the young cannot adequately be warned of the ruinous influence of the art. It was no coincidence that Mattheson published his *Mithridat wider den Gift einer Welschen Satyre* later in the same year (1749). He took as the main text for his polemical commentary the anti-musical satire by the Italian landscape painter Salvator Rosa, *La musica*. Into this he wove many pertinent comments on the status of music in contemporary education and worship:

Now there are great goings-on concerning sacred music, which, sadly, has been made by very many godless peasants of the Christian Church into a stone to be cast away; whereas it is no small cornerstone of godly veneration.

Nun gehet es mit aller Macht über die geistliche Musik her, welche, leider! von sehr vielen gottlosen Bauleuten der christlichen Kirche zu einem Stein gemacht wird, der verworfen werden soll; da er doch kein geringer Eckstein göttlicher Verehrung ist.   (Mattheson 1749, p. 54)

He cites several examples of this attitude (in addition to Bidermann): the present pope has recently banned all musical instruments from the church (*ibid.*, p. 75); a certain Leipzig professor has excluded music from the seven liberal arts (*ibid.*, p. 189). One anecdote might well refer to Bidermann himself: recently a man, taking his son to a certain Gymnasium, asked the rector whether any of the pupils played the harpsichord: 'Yes', replied the rector, 'there are such strummers here, but I wish there weren't.'[35]

Among the many other pamphlets published during this dispute is the *Christliche Beurtheilung des von Herrn M. Bidermann edirten Programmatis de Vita Musica*, prepared by the Nordhausen organist and theorist C. G. Schröter at the end of 1749. According to a contemporary, Georg Einicke, this response was commissioned by J. S. Bach (a fellow member of Mizler's elite music society) during the last months of his life. Furthermore

Bach – despite his reported protestations to the contrary – apparently altered and embellished the text in several ways while preparing the pamphlet for publication, much to Schröter's disapproval (see Banning 1939, pp. 33–4, *Bach-Dokumente* II, pp. 461–4).

Schröter affirms that it is not the fault of music itself if it is misused by its practitioners. This defence reads very like those of the late seventeenth century (see p. 180 above); indeed the author even refers to the pamphlet war between the Gotha rector Vockerodt and J. Beer. He shows that music has a respectable origin in Scripture, since Jubal's father, Lamech, was a pious and brave man; in any case, as Mizler has argued, music is neither more nor less noble, on account of its inventor and his father. Furthermore, if music is ordained by God through Scripture as a vehicle of his praise, it cannot be godless, unless God himself has ordained something godless.

Bach's presumed additions include the title, 'Christian Judgement . . .', something which incensed Schröter, since it was not suitable for the matter concerned.[36] Schröter's review is, after all, one attacking the structure and logic of Bidermann's argument rather than one centring on Christian dogma. Bach (?) also adds, in a more mundane tone, that music is also ordained by the *Kirchen-Ordnung* of the prince of the land. Furthermore, if no one studied music, as recommended by Bidermann, how would the church music, opera and royal establishments be furnished? And finally he asks – somewhat cryptically – what would those collecting tax on liquor have to say about this?[37]

Bidermann wrote a scathing response to all these criticisms in 1750, terming Schröter's text a 'Mißgeburt' ('misbirth', p. 11) and reminding his readers that he was not critical of music in and of itself, but merely of its misuse. In this respect he strikes a note very close to that of the Pietist critics of music who were writing in the last decade of the previous century (see p. 28 above).

The most comprehensive analysis of the status of church music in the middle of the eighteenth century is offered by the Lübeck cantor C. Ruetz in the three volumes of *Widerlegte Vorurtheile* (1750–3). The first volume contains a protracted discussion of the importance of music in both Old and New Testaments, followed by a survey of more recent developments. Ruetz is particularly complimentary of the stylistic developments of recent years which have greatly increased the affective power of music (see p. 44 above). The second volume is a prescriptive survey of contemporary musical style and the requirements of unity and perfection. It is the third volume which gives the most vivid picture of the contemporary situation. He first points out the importance of the choral foundation for its nurturing of the future citizens, just as Schröter/Bach did in 1749:

Indeed the Lübeck choir has been, so to speak, the vegetable garden in which not only did there grow learned men, who were skilled to serve the church and the public good, but also through which many musical services for the church were furnished with capable people. The good Lord has used you through this, most worthy fellow citizens, to be tools of his providence, to maintain the music as the ornament of our worship, and not a little to contribute to the building of the kingdom of God here and abroad.

Ja der Lübeckische Chor ist, so zu sagen, der Pflantzgarten gewesen, darinn nicht allein gelehrete Männer, die der Kirche und dem gemeinen Wesen zu dienen geschickt waren, erwachsen, sondern auch daraus viele musicalische Kirchenbedienungen mit tüchtigen Leuten besetzet worden. Der liebe GOtt hat Sie, Wehrteste Mitbürger, hierdurch zu Werckzeugen seiner Vorsehung gebraucht, den Schmuck unsers Gottesdienstes die Kirchenmusic aufrecht zu erhalten, und zum Bau des Reiches GOttes hier und an auswärtigen Orten nicht wenig beyzutragen. (Ruetz 1753, introduction)

He observes that the Lübeck choirs have never been in such a state of decline; it was as if Satan had had his way and the most dire prophecies of God had been fulfilled.[38] Not only does Ruetz present a long discussion of common complaints against music, he also gives attention to the effect music has on the listener, cultivating hearing and enjoyment, awaking and stilling the affects (Ruetz 1753, pp. 32–3). While he believes that the grounds for music's power are largely hidden from human understanding, he notes that certain musical progressions relate to certain affects. Above all, the musician should follow one of the most important rules of oratory: he who wishes to move others must himself experience the same affect.[39] Ruetz's treatise is lavishly illustrated with biblical examples justifying the use of music in church, something which was typical of so many writings from the previous century.

The end of the eighteenth century

Already it is becoming clear that music as a regular component of education was losing its battle against the reformers. The testimony of Forkel in the second volume of his *Allgemeine Geschichte der Musik* (1801), gives a good perspective of the decline in church and school music during the latter half of the century. Forkel's four reasons for the decline of the entire fabric of church music begin, interestingly enough, with the 'all

188 Music education and the art of performance

too frequent use of music in general'. Sensing that music had changed from a necessity into an object of mere superficial pleasure, he inveighs against the easy tastes of the 'Liebhaber':

The little which the unpractised amateur knows of music belongs purely to the superficial beauties of the same, whose charms soon pale and induce satiety, if the inner beauties do not stand by them and serve as support. This last class of musical dilettantes has at all times been the most numerous and is so still. It is also actually that which has always in the main stood against the true perfecting of the art, and because its knowledge is much too superficial for it to be able to raise itself to the height of the style of a worthy composition, it is also in particular that class which has most harmed the reception of church music, and has, little by little, brought it as low as it is now. Its satiation with purely outward beauties has altogether cooled its inclination towards [church music], so that in particular good church music, which can least satisfy its pampered and degenerate taste with adventurous novelty, must be either of no consequence, or even entirely repugnant and unpleasant to it.

Das Wenige, was hingegen der ungeübtere Liebhaber von der Musik kennt, gehört bloß unter die äußern Schönheiten derselben, deren Reitze bald stumpf werden, und Ueberdruß erwecken, wenn ihnen nicht innere Schönheiten zur Seite stehen und zur Unterstützung dienen. Diese letztere Classe der Musikliebhaber ist zu allen Zeiten die zahlreichste gewesen und ist es noch. Sie ist auch eigentlich, die von jeher hauptsächlich der wahren Vervollkommung der Kunst entgegen gestanden hat, und weil ihre Kenntnisse viel zu seicht sind, als daß sie sich bis zur Höhe des Styls einer würdigen Composition erheben könnte, so ist sie auch insbesondere diejenige Classe, welche dem Aufnehmen der Kirchenmusik am meisten geschadet, und sie nach und nach soweit herunter gebracht hat, als sie es nun ist. Ihre Sättigung an den bloß äußern Schönheiten hat ihre Neigung dazu überhaupt erkaltet, so daß insbesondere eine gute Kirchenmusik, die ihren verwöhnten und ausgearteten Geschmack durch abentheuerliche Neuheit am wenigsten befriedigen kann und darf, ihr entweder gleichgültig, oder gar widerlich und unangenehm seyn muß.

(Forkel 1801, pp. 20-1)

Of course Forkel was reflecting the aesthetic stance of his own age when he conceived of the inner, eternal beauty of great art. Yet his perception of the growing 'amateurisation' of music does contain a grain of truth: music as an object of personal choice and fashionable enjoyment was anathema to a system which saw music as an indispensable component of education and worship.

Forkel's second diagnosis of the decline in church music is the general lack of knowledge. While music had been an important element of education since the Middle Ages, music teachers now were interested in little more than secular trifles. The widespread ignorance of music led many to become suspicious of the art, maintaining that it would destroy the inclination to study other subjects; again this was entirely contrary to Luther's prescription that all our strengths and abilities should be developed to the full (Forkel 1801, pp. 21-3).

Forkel's third reason is already a familiar one: the misuse of the art. Organists often use something out of the newest comic opera for their preludes; modern church musicians know little about the differentiation of affects; musicians are often appointed for their technical facility rather than for the substance of their art (*ibid.*, pp. 23-5). His fourth and final reason is the thriftiness of the authorities. While there are many biblical precedents for paying musicians well and the Catholic churches still put much money into church music for special festivals, nothing of the kind happens in the Protestant churches (pp. 26-7).

Forkel's view might partly derive from the changing attitudes towards vocational music; in his opinion the performer must spend much of his time practising, so he should avoid earning his bread through other means which will consume his valuable time; the composer should have a 'free spirit' untroubled by living problems and other employment.[40] This trend towards the specialising musician can be traced back to the seventeenth century with the metamorphosis of certain cantors into the *Director Musices*, and the tendency for the more active musicians to turn away from their traditional academic duties. Forkel, as a pioneering music historian, shows a remarkable awareness of the changes in the cantorate since the time of the Reformation, the expansion of music in church and the increasing demand for novelty and fresh composition. However, cantors of the later eighteenth century were still being paid well below the rates for the leading musicians of their age, and were moreover treated as traditional schoolmaster-cantors with only a trivial interest in music (*ibid.*, pp. 28-31).

Forkel is also aware of the social importance of the dying cantorate tradition. The money for school choirs came from various individuals and endowments, and this tradition produced the majority of great musicians in all walks of life. Furthermore, the pupils themselves grew up to be more charitable and to encourage the education of their successors in a similar manner. Forkel sees this system as having evolved over many years, and thinks that it is far easier to destroy than to build (*ibid.*, pp. 31-3). Indeed he believes the decline will bring with it many other unforeseen consequences, including the destruction of many benefits in traditional education.[41] Hiller likewise alludes to the social value of school music in the preface to his singing treatise of 1780: not only does it support poor pupils, it also invites endowments out of which teachers' salaries are paid. Forkel proceeds with a remarkable defence of the somewhat Spartan street-singing tradition ('Currende'): it strengthens the constitution and personality of the pupils through its very hardship (*ibid.*, pp. 34–40).[42]

In all Forkel sees school music as the principal means of caring for poorer children and believes that its decline reflects a general inclination to give less attention to poor children than to the offspring of the rich.[43] It may well be that Forkel's stance was influenced by the recent demise of the choir at the Michaelisschule in Lüneburg, from which he had acquired his own musical education.[44] Many other cantorates were abolished around this time.[45] Indeed Hiller stated in 1793 that Dresden was about the only town in Germany that retained church music of the quality of Leipzig.[46]

On the other hand, Forkel also offers extensive prescriptions for the improvement of church music, believing that there is hope for this since only in a few of the larger towns has music already been abolished and reduced to the standard of the village church; the Enlightenment has brought improvements in all aspects of worship except music (*ibid.*, pp. 48–9). Furthermore, he considers that good church music is crucial for the edification of the uneducated masses, since only the more educated classes have the option of attending concerts. In other words, the church should lay the foundations for beauty as well as goodness.[47] This he sees as being the case in Italy, despite the perfidious influence of *opera buffa* (pp. 49–52). Forkel's obvious conservatism notwithstanding, it is clear that he views church music with an Enlightenment conception of intrinsic beauty rather than from the more traditional rhetorical and affective viewpoint.

The foremost priority is the appointment of good cantors, and as a prerequisite for this, the choice of more musically informed school officers, competent to make a satisfactory appointment. Furthermore the cantor must be relieved from teaching duties, since wherever the musical and teaching duties are separated, the standard of music has improved immeasurably. Forkel illustrates this point with the examples of Calvisius, Kuhnau, Telemann, J. S. and C. P. E. Bach (p. 56). Once a suitable cantor has been acquired, the singers must be drawn from the locality, since those from distant places cost too much and are not supported by local parents (p. 57). Forkel advocates a restoration of the original Lutheran practice of educating all pupils in singing (even figural singing), since it is more useful than any other art and encourages people to be

The decline of the Lutheran cantorates 191

joyful and skilled in many other activities (pp. 57-61). All this contributes to better public chorale singing and also to a better body of potential teachers who will, in turn, choose better cantors. He adds the frequently encountered opinion that singing aids all the other practical musical arts. Moreover, far from discouraging the pupil to study of other subjects, music cultivates many skills which are transferable to other activities.[48]

Forkel's second approach to the improvement of musical standards is to ensure a good selection of music, music which is appealing both to experts and to laymen. Forkel demands a 'noble simplicity' of style:

One must understand this simplicity of style to be not that simplicity which arises out of the lack of competent artistic knowledge and is actually nothing other than an empty, low wretchedness, but rather that noble simplicity which can only be the fruit of the highest culture in the art of music . . . Nothing other than the highest culture in the art, the most correct taste and the most correct concepts of the means and purpose of holy music can lead to this.

Man muß aber unter dieser Simplicität des Styles nicht jene Simplicität verstehen, welche aus dem Mangel an hinlänglicher Kunstkenntniß entsteht, und eigentlich nichts als leere, niedrige Armseligkeit ist, sondern jene edle Simplicität, welche nur eine Frucht der höchst Cultur in der musikalischen Kunst seyn kann . . . Nichts als die höchste Cultur in der Kunst, der richtigste Geschmack und die richtigsten Begriffe vom Wesen und Zweck der heiligen Musik kann dahin führen.
(Forkel 1801, p. 66-7)

Just as writers throughout this study have exhorted the singer to choose the 'correct' ornaments, or to cultivate the appropriate affect, Forkel assumes that the correct choice from the increasingly wide range of styles is self-evident to the discerning musician. Likewise typical of his age is the supremacy he accords to the chorus in church music: choruses are suitable both for relatively inexperienced singers and for the common listener, particularly if he can understand the words; but arias are 'too personal' for general use in church, and recitatives are unappealing and unedifying (Forkel 1801, pp. 67-8).

It is striking that Hiller (at the outset of his school treatise of 1792) also voices concerns for the type and quality of music that the singer is expected to perform:

But it is less pleasing to me when I see a good man wasting his industry and time that he does not have to spare on such platitudes and miserable doggerel, out of which the majority of our so-called church cantatas are constituted. May I here, most beloved friends, give you some good advice? Do as I do. Abolish, for the most part, recitative from church. Draw from your Sunday sermon an inference, look in your store [of music], or write for it a suitable chorus and aria and then append to this an appropriate and meaningful chorale verse; thus will you certainly have the best church cantata.

Unangenehmer aber ist es mir, wenn ich sehe, daß ein guter Mann seinen Fleiß und seine Zeit, die er nicht übrig hat, an solche Plattitüden und elende Reimereyen verschwendet, aus denen die meisten unserer sogenannten Kirchencantaten bestehen. Darf ich Ihnen hier, *theursten Freunde*, einen guten Rath geben? Machen sie es wie ich. Schaffen Sie die Recitative größentheils aus der Kirche weg. Ziehen Sie aus Ihrem Sonntagsevangelio ein Resultat heraus, suchen Sie in ihrem Vorrathe, oder schreiben Sie ein dazu passendes Chor und Arie, und hängen noch einen schicklichen und bedeutenden Choralvers daran, so haben Sie gewiß die beste Kirchencantate. (Hiller 1792, foreword)

Treatises from the German Lutheran tradition do not usually provide a critical or normative commentary on the type of music to be performed (although seventeenth-century writings might make a point of preparing the pupil for the 'new Italian style'). The comments of Hiller and Forkel imply several changes: church music was now subject to a wider and more 'aesthetic' criticism; it was no longer an elevated craft involving a relatively narrow spectrum of styles; as it was no longer central to the music life of the age, it was prone to be musically inferior to more important genres; the recitative style, so enthusiastically introduced at the beginning of the eighteenth century, was now considered inappropriate. Particularly significant is the much greater emphasis placed on communal singing (Hiller's own performance of Handel's *Messiah* in 1786 involved several hundred performers),[49] and it was indeed the amateur choral society which would, during the ensuing decades, preserve some of the most impressive Lutheran church music. But, in creating this new breeding-ground of musical culture, it was the same Enlightenment – with its secular leanings, its cultivation of music as an aesthetic, non-functional art – which had also brought about the demise of the tradition within which some of the newly-canonised 'masterworks' were written.

Notes

1 The establishment of Lutheran musical practice in the sixteenth century

1 For a more detailed survey, see Schünemann 1928, pp. 76–82; Niemöller 1969, p. 617.
2 *An die Radherrn aller Stedte deutsches lands: dass sie Christliche schulen auffrichten und halten sollen* (Wittenberg, 1524); WA XV, pp. 9–53.
3 These ordinances, and the many others that succeeded them are to be found in R. Vormbaum, *Evangelische Schulordnungen*, vol. I (Gütersloh, 1860), pp. 1, 8.
4 That Luther himself saw music as an element of the *trivium* is suggested in WA Tischreden V, no. 5603: 'S. Maria ist mehr celebrirt worden in der Grammatica, Musica und Rhetorica, denn ihr Kind, Jesus.'
5 Clearly there is a close terminological relationship between *Musica choralis* and the genre which in English is usually termed chorale. However, while Luther took many of his chorale melodies from the existing repertory of Gregorian hymns, he and his contemporaries generally used terms such as *Lieder* and *Gesänge*; moreover these pieces were printed in the measured notation of *musica figuralis* rather than the chant notation of *musica choralis*. Nevertheless, the fact that chorales were generally sung monophonically by the congregation and came to take over much of the role of Gregorian chant suggests that they could have been considered a part of *musica choralis* too.
6 For a further study of the negative influence of humanism on music-making, see Bremer 1976, especially pp. 6–7. While there was (and still is) a popular belief that the Lutherans advocated the complete abolition of Latin, it was rather the case that Luther encouraged the use of the vernacular *together* with Latin (see, for instance, his alternative versions of the Mass, the Latin *Formula missae* and the German *Deutsche Messe*). Not only did Latin remain the principal language of education right through to the eighteenth century, but Latin was still retained for many parts of the liturgy.
7 'und die musica mit der gantzen mathematica lernen'.
8 'Musica ist eine halbe Disciplin und Zuchtmeisterin, so die Leute gelinder und sanftmüthiger, sittsamer und vernünftiger machet.'

194 Notes to pages 3–14

9 'Auch bleibet alle Lehre viel fester im Gedächtnis, so sie in den Gesang gefasset ist.' Niemöller 1969, p. 619.
10 See Bremer 1976, especially pp. 37–40.
11 'Mus der Cantor in Figural die knaben vorsuchen, ihrer fünff vnd fünff lassen zusammen ein stück singen, damit er zur nott zugleich an zweien orttern konne die Cantorey bestellen.' Schünemann 1928, p. 87.
12 Niemöller 1969, pp. 709–10, lists all the known references to specific published books in sixteenth-century ordinances.
13 'habe ich gedacht / die selbigen auffs aller kürtzte und leichtest / als ymmer zuthun müglich / allein der Jugent des gantzen Deudschen lands zu gut und nutz / ynn unsere rechte Deudsche muttersprache zubringen'; Agricola 1528, foreword.
14 Agricola 1532, ch. 6: 'Der Tact odder schlag / wie er alhie genomen wird ist eine stete und messige bewegung der hand des sengers.'
15 'Und ist solche Musica der art und aygenschafft / das die Kinder daraus lernen singen / contrapunct setzen / auff der Lautten / Geigen und Pfeyffen / auch ander instrument'; Singer 1531, fol. 2r.
16 'Nun ist zu mercken / welches vicia sein das ist / welches eine übelstandt ist oder nit / und welcher das nit waiß / der klumpert und lürlet umher hin / vermaint wenn er nur vill colores / das ist / vill lauffwercks mach / so sey er güt / so doch die Componisten den gesang woll möchten zu reissen uñ coloriren / das mancher nit vil lauffens machen möchte / so er nit die vicia vermeyden wolt / und die holtseligkeit und süssigkeit süchet im gesang.' Singer 1531, fol. 7r.

2 The role of practical music in education c.1600–1750

1 'The Italians or instrumentalists, violinists and cornettists can perform sixteen semiquavers to a beat better than the Germans. Indeed they even manage thirty-two demisemiquavers to the beat.' ('Sechtzehen *semifusas* auff einen Schlag / können die Welschen oder Instrumentisten / Geiger unnd Zinckenbläser besser Musiciren als etliche Deutschen. Ja / sie setzen noch *semisemifusam* 32. auff einen Tact dazu'; Quitschreiber 1607, ch. 5.)
2 'Music ist ein nicht geringes Ornamentum und Zierrat dieser Stadt'; Krüger 1933, p. 6.
3 'die edle *Music* oder Singe-Kunst / welche man billig eine recht Himmlische / ja Göttliche Gabe oder Geschenck kann nennen / allen Traur- und Freuden-Spielen weit / weit sey fürzuziehen'; Rist 1666, p. 157.
4 'die Musik . . . in Kirchen und Schulen Ein schönes Ornament und Wohlstand . . . so . . . Ein sonderbahres condimentum der Studien sein Pflegt'; Finkel 1973, p. 328.
5 'Ich sehe sehr gern / das die Jugend . . . unterrichtet und geübet wird / nicht allein GOtt den HErrn damit zu ehren / sondern auch / weil mancher armer Schüler sich mit der Cantorey / in diesen so kümerliche

Zeiten / durch die Welt reiset / sein *Panem propter Deum* ersinget / beym Studiren erhalten / und letzlich zu einem feinen gelehrten / Kirchen unnd Schulen wolanständigen Mann wird'; Büttner 1625, foreword.

6 'Also wil [der Teuffel] auch die edle Musicam ausrotten / Wie ers dann bey den Calvinisten schon so weit bracht / daß sie *Musicam figuralem* abgeschafft'; Rosinus 1615.

7 'So ist nun die Music in der Christlichen Kirchen auch heutiges tags nicht nur ein feiner Christlicher Wolstand / sondern auch ein nutzliche ubung'; Anwander 1606, p. 28.

8 'Das Hertz des Menschen sey der Organist / welcher durch des himlischē Capel-Meisters des h. Geistes Gnad und Krafft den Gesang Gott gefällig fuhren und regieren müsse.'

9 See also Kalb 1965, pp. 146–7, who quotes a similar analogy between musical performers and heavenly order, made by Saubert in his sermon for Cantate Sunday 1623.

10 'was für Stücke zu dem recht-zierlig und künstlichen Singen gehören'; Preussner 1924, p. 418.

11 'die itzige, neue Art und wie dieselbe in Chur- und Fürstlichen Capellen heutiges tages hergerichtet wird'; Krickeberg 1965, p. 108. It is interesting to see that the Leipzig school ordinance of 1634 recommends that the cantor strike a balance between old and new styles, following the tastes of the city officials and citizens rather than being solely influenced by those desiring only the most modern music: 'In den *Cantionibus sacris* sol er auch einen Unterscheid halten / und weder die newen so gar offt einführen und gebrauchen / noch auch der alten *Moteten* gantz vergessen / Sondern sich hierinn mehr nach den Bürgern und Einwohnern / als nach den jenigen / so allein die *moderna* belieben / richten.' Leipzig *Ordnung* 1634, ch. 6/5.

12 'auch ettwa 7–8 Knaben in der Lateinischen Schul, welche er dazu qualifizirt vnd tüchtig befinden werde, gutwillig und ohne einige Accompens in der Musica vnd mit allem Fleiß underrichten'; see Allerup 1931, p. 19n.

13 'denn es stehet schlimm / wenn der Organist klüger als der Cantor . . . ist'; Fuhrmann 1706, pp. 12–13.

14 Even in Leipzig, though, other musicians were sometimes responsible for certain musical parts of the service: at the Neue Kirche the cantor of the Thomasschule provided boys only to sing chorales and motets, while the organist was permitted to direct the 'modern' figural music (see Stiller 1970/1984, p. 193).

15 'Bey denen Stifftern ist auch der Name *Cantor* bekannt, welches eine besondere würde ist.'

16 'Er sey im Choro Musico oder nicht'; Krickeberg 1965, p. 138.

17 Leipzig *Ordnung* 1733, p. 13.

18 'durchs Musicieren manche schöne Lehren und Glaubenssprüche sowohl den Singenden als Anhörenden bekandt werden und ins Hertze dringen'; J. C. Lange, quoted in Preussner 1924, p. 429. Demelius's (undated) treatise even includes Latin grammar as the text to vocal exercises (Preussner 1924, p. 429).

Notes to pages 21-6

19 'Und heut zu Tage wird die Musica in Schulen fleissig geübet / und in vielen wol destalten Kirchen dieser Lande hat und findet man beydes *Musicam vocalem ac instrumentalē*'.
20 'wofern er nicht *capabel* zur *Vokal-* doch zur *Instrumental-Music* könte gebraucht werden'; Gradenthaller 1687, 'Nutzlicher Vorbericht'.
21 Indeed the sons of rich parents in Leipzig usually went to the Nicolaischule and therefore did not have any of the singing commitments of the Thomasschule pupils (Krickeberg 1965, p. 117).
22 'denen Knaben so wohl in Schulen / als in der *privat-information* . . .'
23 'dieweil sichs aber offt zuträget / daß der *Cantor* wegen fürfallender Leichen die *ordinari* Singestunden nicht halten kan / auch ohne das nicht müglich / daß in einer Stunde alle und jede absonderlich gehöret und *informiret* werden / welches gleichwol / wann sie zur *perfection* kommen sollen / von nöhten / als wird der *Cantor* dorauff bedacht seyn / daß er auch zur andern jhm bequemer Zeit einen und den andern / bevorab die jenigen / welche feine *naturalia* und lust zu singen haben / erfordere / und *privatim in Musicis* höre und unterweise.' Leipzig *Ordnung* 1634, ch. 6/1.
24 'Alle zu solchen *Cantorey*en gehörige Schüler sollen täglich, um die gesetzte Stunde, sich in *Musicis* fleißig üben, diejenigen aber, welche von solcher Sing-Stunde weg bleiben, von dem *Cantore*, oder wer dessen Stelle vertreten mögte, bestrafet werden.' Leipzig *Ordnung* 1723, p. 74.
25 'In der dazu verordneten Singstund sol der *Praefectus* mit seinen Chor-Schülern so viel möglich alle / oder doch zum wenigsten die unbekantesten und schweresten Stücke / so er die Woche über singen wil / versuchen / und nur diejenigen gebrauchen / die ohne einigen Fehler getroffen werden.' Printz 1678, p. 4.
26 'Die Verächter der wunderschönen Musickunst / solten nur das gruntzen der Säw und das Geschrey der Esel hören.' Büttner 1625, foreword.
27 'Es hat die liebe Music fast vor allen andern Künsten und *Disciplin*en nun etzliche Jahr her wunderliche Abwechselung / Ab- und Zunehmen gehabt'; Michael 1637, preface to *Quinta vox*.
28 'Ey die meisten lieben und lernen nur gern solche Künste / die den Beütel schmücken und füllen / oder sonst einträglich seyn'.
29 See Kalb 1965, pp. 149-50.
30 See *Ibid.*, pp. 142-9 for a discussion of the reservations within Orthodoxy.
31 There is a certain amount of confusion in the literature concerning the definition of Lutheran 'Pietism', particularly when J. S. Bach's faith is the issue. Above all it seems important to preserve a distinction between 'Pietism' as a movement and 'piety' as a description of personal devotion. For a clear exposition of the movement (which began c.1675) specifically within the Lutheran Church, see Leaver 1991.
32 It is interesting to note here that Anwander's organ-dedication sermon of 1606 is based on Paul's letter to the Ephesians 5:19, with the text 'singet und spielet dem HERREN in ewerm Hertzen' (Anwander 1606, p. 7); however he later admits that the German text strictly reads 'singet und psalliret' (*Ibid.*, p. 15).

33 'Also sehen die lieben Herren Musicanten / daß ich so wohl die Stimmen- als Zeug-Music NB in ihrem rechten Gebrauch viel höher und werther halte / als sie selbst'; Muscovius 1694, p. 28.
34 'Ist nun die Music ernsthafft / ansehnlich und fein / so sind auch die Leute ernsthafft / haben eine gute Autorität / und befleißigen sich der Erbarkeit'; *Ibid.*, p. 29.
35 'todte Pfeiffen / und etliche künstliche Stimmen-Dreher'; *Ibid.*, p. 36.
36 'und geklaget haben / daß sie gerne mit singen wolten / wenn sie vor solchen unerbaulichen / ja ärgerlichen Musiciren dazu gelassen / deutsche Lieder / dazu die Orgel zugleich mit geschlagen / langsam und andächtig gesungen würden'; *Ibid.*, p. 37.
37 'Was dem *Caligulae, Claudio* und *Neroni* geschadet hat / das schadet allen Fürsten. Nun hat das *Musici*ren / Tantzen und die Lust-Spiele *Caligulae, Claudio* und *Neroni* geschadet / ergo schadet *musici*ren / tantzen und die Lust-Spiele allen Fürsten.' Beer 1697, p. 15.
38 'so bald die Predigt angehet / aus der Kirchen lauffen / und wenn die Predigt geschlossen wird / erst zu ihren Brausen wieder kommen'; Muscovius 1694, p. 45; see also Selle's comments about the Hamburg musicians (p. 23 above).
39 See K. Snyder, 'Scheidt, Samuel', in *NG XVI*, p. 605.
40 'Derowegen bey *reception* und Auffnehmung der Knaben / ungeacht eines oder des andern *commendation*, billich dohin zu sehen / daß dieselben / wann sie über das zwölffte Jahr sind / und in dieser Schul sich auffzuhalten begehren / *in arte Musica* nicht *rudes*, sondern deroselben guten theils erfahren / und ein Stück fertig und artig *musiciren* können.' Leipzig *Ordnung* 1634, ch. 7/1.
41 'und do er auß Mangel der Stimme zur *Musica* entweder gantz nicht tüchtig / oder auch selbige nicht lernen wolte / Sol . . . nach gelegenheit seiner *profectuum*, eine gewisse Zeit gesetzt werden / binnen welcher er seiner Stell / so er in der Schulen gehabt / *resigniré*, damit also durch ihn und seines gleichen die Bestellung der *Musica*lischen Chor nicht verhindert / auch andere / so in dem Singen geübt / und damit der Kirchen unnd Schulen dienen können / darvon außgeschlossen werden.' *Ibid.*, ch. 7/4.
42 'Dann es ist ja eine bey allen vernünfftigen Menschen ausgemachte Sache; daß derjenige / welcher das Hauptwerck zu verwalten hat / selbiger auch das Haupt in derselben gantzen Sache sey. Die Kirchen-Music aber ohnwidersprechlich das Haupt aller *Musiquen* ist: so ist auch der Cantor nach dem Zeugniß des Gewissens aller vernünfftigen Menschen / sie mögen heissen Christen / Jüden / Türcken oder Heyden / das Haupt der Musici und nicht der Rector.' Bendeler 1706, p. 2.
43 'Und gesetzet / es *in*formirete der Rector die Schüler auch in *Musicis*, wie man denn bißwellen *Rectores* findet / welche die Music verstehen; so reichete es doch / wie aus obigen gnugsam zu ersehen / bey weitem noch nicht hin.' *Ibid.*, pp. 5–6.
44 'Dafern nun dem *Cantori* die Macht einen Chor-Schüler zu *excludi*ren gelassen würde / so könnte er demselben die *Subsistenz* beynehmen / daß er genöthigt

würde die Schule zu *quiûren* / dadurch denn viellecht der Rector eines guten *Subjecti* beraubet würde. Der Schüler komme hauptsächlich üm der Schule willen in die Stadt / oder nicht / gnug / daß er ein Chor Schüler / und nicht wegen der Schule; sondern wegen der Kirchen-Music hauptsächlich in Chor genommen wird.' Bendeler 1706, p. 23.

45 'Jedoch kan ein Rector wider des *Cantoris* Willen keinen *Praefectum* bestellen / weil der Cantor von seiner *Capaci*tät in der Music zu *judici*ren / und einen haben muß / der in Nothfall seine *vices* zuvertreten tüchtig'; *Ibid.*, p. 9.

46 'Die Musicalischen Aufwartungen sind eine Sache für *Concertisten. Concertisten* aber als *Concertisten depend*iren nicht vom *Rectore*; sondern vom *Cantore*, als von welchem sie lediglich zur *Concert* angenommen und angewiesen werden.' *Ibid.*, p. 10.

47 'die Bestellung der Music dem *Cantori privativè* zustehet'; *Ibid.*, p. 11.

48 'In Stierlein's definition *Musica theorica* refers to all the rudiments that are generally discussed within the standard primers. An extensive section on ornamentation and diminution forms a protracted appendix to this 'theoretical' section (one which, incidentally, relies extensively on Bernhard's composition treatises – see p. 136 below). *Musica practica* is an introduction to thoroughbass, that art which so succinctly links the practice of performance and composition ('Der *General-Bass* ist das beste und vortrefflichste *Fundament* / nach welchem sich ein gantzes *musicali*sches Stuck / so wohl in der *Composition*, als Auffführung und Machung desselben richten muß'; Stierlein 1691, p. 24).

Stierlein's definition of *musica poetica*, however, is totally absurd: it is little more than a proposed system of notating music with a system of numbers (i.e. in the manner of a tablature) and, despite Stierlein's frequent use of the term *componiren*, it has absolutely nothing to do with the art of composition.

49 Magirus 1596; Gumpelzhaimer 1600 (an amplified translation of Faber); Calvisius 1602; Orgosinus 1603; Eichmann 1604; Kretzschmar 1605; Demantius 1607; Kraft 1607; Quitschreiber 1607; Crappius 1608; Harnisch 1608; Beringer 1610; Walliser 1611 – to cover merely the first decade or so.

50 Hase 1647; Zerleder 1658; Stenger 1659 (with the amplification of Hizler, almost word for word).

51 Ulich 1682; Lange 1688 (with Hizler's addition); Falck 1688 (which adds the playing of instruments to singing); J. G. Ahle 1690 (a reprint of J. R. Ahle 1673).

52 '*qui benè cantat, bis orat*, wer wol singt ist so viel / als wenn er doppelt bettete', a maxim which was commonly attributed to St Augustine.

53 'Die Musik ist eine Wissenschaft und Kunst, geschickte und angenehme Klänge klüglich zu stellen, richtig an einander zu fügen und lieblich herauszubringen, damit durch ihren Wohllaut Gottes Ehre und alle Tugenden befördert werden.'

54 One later source, Anton 1743, offers an unusually scientific definition concerning the nature of sound, the composition of melody and harmony and the practice of the same. But despite this latter-day union of the three ancient arts of music, the treatise itself covers only the rudiments of notation.

Notes to pages 38–44   199

55 'welcher alles geordnet hat mit Maß / Zahl und Gewichte'; Ahle 1690, 'Anmerkungen', p. 2.
56 'Wer (lieber Gott!) erfrewt sich nicht? Wer lässt die Ohren nicht begnügen / Wenn er so viel Gethön hört fügen In rechte Maaß / Zahl und Gewicht?' Ribovius 1638, foreword.
57 'die Natur / als *mater sonorum*, und die Kunst des Tohnmeisters oder *Musici*.' Ahle 1690, 'Anmerkungen', p. 2.
58 'die Bewegung des Menschen zur Tugend / und zu mäßiger Fröligkeit / wie auch dienlicher Traurigkeit'; *Ibid.*, p. 3.
59 Feyertag 1695, p. 3.
60 e.g. Friccius 1631, pp. 53, 56: 'des Menschen Seele sey eine *Harmonia*'.
61 'Ob auch öffters eine starcke *Dissonans* sich ereignet in Creutz und Absterben / so bringts der HERR JESUS doch wieder zur Ordnung.' Hack 1676, introduction.
62 The eternal qualities of music are also mentioned by Herbst in the introduction to his primer on Italian manners; for him these qualities place music above all the other free arts (Herbst 1642/1653, Introduction).
63 'Ich habe die Weise / wo gute Noten bösen Text haben / da gebe ich solche Noten einen guten Text'; Friccius 1631, p. 34, quoting D. Erasmus Alberus.
64 The fact that Printz recommended the use of a monochord to learn intervals (Printz 1678, p. 23) suggests that the pupil still had an awareness of the mathematical basis of musical intervals (something which was probably emphasised in mathematics lessons too). Nevertheless, the subject does not seem to have been consciously studied within the context of practical music instruction.
65 'So begreift derselbige in sich zehen zu dieser *Action* gehörige *Concerten* . . . Insonderheit aber darbey mit stillschweigen nicht zu übergehen ist, daß der *Author* dieselben in Druck heraus zu geben dahero Bedencken getragen hat, alldieweil Er vermercket daß außer Fürstlichen wohlbestälten Capellen, solche seine *Inventionen* schwerlich ihren gebührenden *effect* anderswo erreichen würden'.
66 'Das gantze Gemüth des Menschen wird durch Gesang regieret und geführet'; Friccius 1631, p. 87.
67 Anwander similarly describes good music as acting like a magnet on the human heart (Anwander 1606, p. 18).
68 'so mus man sich wundern / warüm doch die *Componisten* in den Kirchensachen nicht den *Stylum recitativum* . . . brauchen: maßen ja derselbe mit der natürlichen Aussprache am besten übereinkömt / und den Text gar deutlich und annehmlich macht.' Ahle 1704, p. 83.
69 'Die Music aber hat in dem Jahrhundert, darin wir leben, eine merkliche Veränderung zu ihrem größten Vortheil und Aufnahme erlitten'; Ruetz 1750, p. 78.
70 'Da nun aber die itzige *status musices* gantz anders weder ehedem beschaffen, die Kunst üm sehr viel gestiegen, der *gusto* sich verwunderens-würdig geändert, dahero auch die ehemalige Arth von *Music* unseren Ohren nicht mehr klingen will . . . Es ist ohne dem etwas Wunderliches, da man von denen teütschen *Musicis proetendiret*, Sie sollen *capable* seyn, allerhand Arthen von

Music, sie kommen nun aus *Italien* oder Franckreich, *Engeland* oder Pohlen, so fort *ex tempore* zu *musiciren*'; *Bach-Dokumente* I, p. 63.

It is interesting that Bach's Leipzig predecessor, Johann Kuhnau, in the introduction to his cantata cycle of 1709, still saw fit to avoid the new styles (their advantages in grace notwithstanding), on account of their theatrical connotations: 'Nichts desto weniger bin ich doch bey der einmahl gefasten Resolution geblieben, und zwar um so viel mehr, weil ich, indem ich ietzo von dem Madrigalischen Stylo, der in Arien und Recitativ bestehet, nichts sehen lasse, dem Verdachte der Theatrischen Music desto leichter zu entgehen gedencke.' Kuhnau 1709, in *MfMG* 1902, p. 149.

71 'Die Musik allein aber ist unbeseelet, und unverständlich, wenn sie nicht an Worte hält, die gleichsam für sie reden müssen; damit man wisse, was sie haben will.' J. C. Gottsched, *Auszug aus des Herrn Batteux Schönen Künsten* (Leipzig, 1754), p. 207.

72 See N. Frye, *Anthony of Criticism* (Princeton, 1957/1900), p. 245: 'Rhetoric has from the beginning meant two things: ornamental speech and persuasive speech. These two things seem psychologically opposed to each other, as the desire to ornament is essentially disinterested, and the desire to persuade essentially the reverse.'

73 '*Optimus Orator est vir canorus, qui in dicendo animus aodientium delectat, & permouet.* Cosi, ricercasi al modern cōpositore di Musiche nell'esprimere vn Madrigale Motetto ò quali sieno altre parole, dene operare imitando con l'armonia gi'afetti dell'Oratione, accio che nel cantare habbino diletto non solo il proprio conpositore, n'aparimente gli cantori & audienti'; Banchieri 1614, p. 166.

74 'es sey dann / das es *viva Praeceptoris voce & ope* geschehe / und einem vorgesungen und vorgemacht werde / darmit es einer vom andern / gleich wie ein Vogel vom andern *observiren* lerne.' Praetorius 1619, p. 237.

75 Dating according to Hilse 1973, p. 8; this was the time that Bernhard directed the choirboys of the Dresden court chapel.

76 Feyertag (1695, p. 234) defines *Coloriren* as a combination of singing according to the words (*Moderiren*) with *Diminuiren*, added diminution.

77 For an application of this hypothesis to the case of J. S. Bach, with regard to his notated articulation, see Butt 1990.

3 *The contents, layout and style of instruction books*

1 See for example, Feyertag 1695, introduction: 'Dahero ich dieses Büchlein auß denen vornehmsten *musicis* zusammen getragen und fast nichts neues / weder sehr zierliche noch hochtrabende Wörten darinnen gesetzet'.

2 Demantius 1592 was replaced by a new version in 1607 which was republished at least until 1684, Vulpius 1608 was printed several times up to 1665, Friderici 1618 until 1677, Hizler 1623 was reprinted in 1628, Herbst in 1642, 1653 and 1658, Quirsfeld 1675 until 1717. Printz 1678 was rewritten in 1689 and republished in that form until 1714 (for a full list of surviving editions, see *RISM* catalogue).

3 e.g. Bernhard, Burmeister, Calvisius, Crüger, Herbst, Praetorius.

4 For instance the title page of Praetorius 1574 notes that the book was used in the schools of Lüneburg; Gumpelzhaimer 1591 records the author as cantor at Augsburg; Harnisch 1608 ends with rudiments specifically addressed to the *quarta* class at Göttingen; Beringer 1610 introduces the author as cantor at Weissenburg; Friderici 1618 is dedicated to schools in Rostock; Trautmann 1618 was used in the schools of Lindau; Hase 1657 was written for the school in Osteroda. Even in the eighteenth century a published treatise might be designed for schools of a specific locality: e.g. Anton 1743 was written for students in Bremen.

5 'Newe und zuvor nie erfundene Singekunst / dadurch Manns- und Frawenspersonen alle Gesänge leichtlich singen lernen können'.

6 My inquiry to the editors of *RISM* for a list of manuscript treatises of the Baroque era was answered with the statement that they intended to make no such catalogue, since there were so few unique manuscript treatises which never at some point appeared in print.

7 'In dem *Compendio Theologico, Dialectica, Rhetorica* und andern Künsten / so den Knaben gelesen werden / Sollen sie die *Praecepta* unnd *Regulas* leuchtlichen nicht ändern / Sondern eben dieselbige Wort behalten ... Auch insonderheit darauff sehen / domit die Knaben die nothwendigen *Praecepta* und *Exempla* ... so in gewisse *qvaestiones* und *Responsiones* verfasset seyn / fleissig außwendig lernen / solche offt mit sich selbst *repetiren*'; Leipzig *Ordnung* 1634, ch. 3/13.

8 The anonymous *Kurze Anweisung* of 1752 is likewise designed for the use of the teacher or the pupil himself.

9 Hase 1657 (p. 26), Crüger 1660 (p. 14), Hoffmann 1693 (p. 30) and Feyertag 1695 (p. 18).

10 'Ists derwegen an der *discretion* eines *Directoris* gelegen / daß er / nach dem die Worte des *Textus* es mit bringen / den *Tact* so wol in *Tripla* als in *sesquialtera*, langsam oder geschwinde schlage'; Friderici 1618/24, ch. 6.

11 'wird aber heutiges Tages von vielen nicht in Acht genommen'; Hoffmann 1693, p. 10.

12 'doch in Ansehung des *Accords* und Zusammenstimmung kommt es alles auf die *Tertia* des *Basses* an'; Wesselius 1726, p. 9.

13 The same point is later taken up by Printz 1671, ch. 1.

14 'sind also nicht gar ungleich einem trunckenen Manne / der zwar in sein Hauß kommen ist / weiß aber nicht / welchen Weg er gegangen sey'; Hase 1657, p. 7.

15 The well-known anonymous *Wegweiser* includes elements of a lost treatise by Carissimi and was reprinted many times between 1689 and 1753; other Catholic treatises include Eisenhut 1682 (reprinted 1702 and 1732); Münster 1748; Schmelz 1752.

16 'Welche in einer einfachen oder auch mehren Sing-Stimmen, ohne *Instrumenten* bestehet; wie zum Exempel unsere Kirchen-Gesänge sind.'

17 Schneegass 1591; Quitschreiber 1598; Burmeister 1601; Calvisius 1602; Leisring 1615; Friderici 1618, to cover the first two decades.

18 e.g. Gengenbach 1626; Demantius 1632 (an addition to his earlier tutors); Sartorius 1635.

Notes to pages 61-7

19 '*Signa Soni Lati* Die sind zur Zeit noch nicht verhanden / die Italianer gebrauchen an ihrer statt viel verwirrete / und beydes den Sängern und Druckern unbequeme Wörter / unter welchen hier nur *Forte* und *Piano* zu mercken ist.' Dieterich 1631, p. 12.
20 'so sollen die Knaben mercken / sonderlich welche auff dem Clavichordio oder Instrument lernen wollen / daß man wegen der Höhe oder Tieffe / jeden Gesang eine Quart oder Quint höher oder tieffer setzen könne'; Quitschreiber 1607, ch. 10.
21 See Moyer 1992, especially pp. 25, 27.
22 *Ibid.*, pp. 71-3.
23 Demantius 1632 contains one hundred canons, some in seven voices; Stenger 1659 contains sixty-seven.
24 'in theils Schulen ist man gewohnt / bey ihrer alten Manier noch zu verbleiben / damit die Jugend noch mehrer verhindert / als befördert wird / *tribuli*ren dieselben so lang mit allerley *characteribus* und *signis*, damit sie der *Music* müssen gram werden / da doch der Jugend mit viel leichterer Müh kan und mag geholffen werden / vermittelst Göttlicher Hülff.' Gradenthaller 1687, 'Nutzlicher Vorbericht'.
25 Comenius's program for a universal education recommended a much closer attention to the coordination of the pupil's readiness and ability to learn with the various stages of instruction. All components of a subject should be linked with what was previously learned and the teacher should search for suitable examples, precepts and stimuli. Particularly important was the cultivation of a favourable environment for learning, with the subject so arranged that the pupil studies 'as if' of his own accord. See J. E. Sadler, *J. A. Comenius and the concept of universal education* (London, 1966), especially pp. 196-206; also Petzoldt 1985, p. 13 and Rainbow 1989, pp. 83-5.
26 'Gegen die Knaben sollen sie freundlich seyn / und dardurch bey ihnen zu förderst rechte Liebe der *Praeceptorum*, und so dann Lust und Frewde zum Studiren erwecken / dargegen aber alle Unfreundligkeit und tyannische Gebärde meiden / und die Jugend damit von den *Studiis* nicht abschrecken.' Leipzig *Ordnung* 1634, ch. 1/6.
27 'die solle ein *Discipulus Musices* alle und jede erstlich recht lehrnen verstehen / darnach von Wort zu Wort . . . auswendig lernen / und stehts in frischer Gedächtnuß behalten.' Hizler 1623, Introduction.
28 'Die *Musicque* nimmet ihren Platz gleich neben der *Theologie*, und stehet über den übrigen Künsten und Wissenschafften allen.' Eisel 1738, Vorrede.
29 'Sie ist auch eine nöthige Wissenschafft; indem Sie unter die Requisita eines *galant-Home* gezhlet wird, und können die in Italien, Franckreich und andern Königlichen und Fürstlichen Höfen *Europae* befindlichen *Virtuosi* zur Genüge bezeugen, daß sie auch eine nußliche und einträgliche Wissenschafft sey.' Maier 1741, p. 2.

4 The development of performance practice and the tools of expression and interpretation in the German Baroque

1 Indeed the tradition of regarding singing as something rather more than accurate pitching can be traced back as far as Conrad von Zabern (1474) in the German writings; see Ulrich 1973, p. 18.
2 'NB. Wer keine Beliebung zu der Abwechselung mit pian: und fort: träget / kan solche in folgendem Stück wol ubergehen.' See Adrio 1961, p. 117. Ribovius 1638 describes changes of dynamic and tempo as musical *figures*, in other words exceptions to the norm which are neccessitated by the contingences of the text (Ribovius 1638, pp. 131–2).
3 The German writers reflect the situation in many Italian writings: Avella 1657, a sizeable compendium on the rules of music, including composition, contains but two pages on vocal technique, pp. 33, 127. Even a treatise as comprehensive as Banchieri 1614 concentrates primarily on matters of ornamentation. The description of head and chest voice is the only additional technical information on vocal production; see Cranna 1981 (translation of Banchieri), p. 302.
4 Praetorius 1574, ch. 5/3: 'Vocem etiam verbis conformare studeant, ita ut in re hilari hilarem, in tristi tristem concentum promant, & auditorum animos suauiter afficiant, & ad affectum aliquem traducant.'
5 See Allerup 1931, pp. 32–4; Bartels 1989, p. 31 apparently mistakenly attributes these comments to a 1645 edition of Calvisius's work. Although *NG* dates this treatise to 1594, the *RISM* catalogue shows no surviving exempla before that of 1602; in any case Calvisius died in 1615.
6 Allerup 1931, p. 33; Mattheson 1739, remarks that this good advice was generally forgotten by his own generation.
7 'Haueranno etiandio li Cantori questo auertimento, che ad altro modo si canta nelle Chiese, & nelle Capelle publiche, & ad altro modo nelle Priuate Camere: Imperoche ini si canta a piena voce; non però se non nel modo detto di sopra; & nelle Camere si canta con voce piu sommessa, & soaue, senza fare alcun strepito.' Zarlino 1558, p. 204.
8 Friderici's statement that cantors should not sing with the uppermost voice if they have no 'false voice' suggests that singing with falsetto was a fairly common practice: 'Those unskilled cantors therefore err not a little, who, when they cannot sing *fictâ voce* with the discantists, will sooner take the octave and make a tenor out of a discant part and introduce not a few faults of [parallel] fifths.' ('Irren derowegen die ungeschickten *Cantores* nicht wenig / Welche / wenn Sie bey den *Discantisten* nicht können *fictâ voce* singen / alsbald zur *Octava* greiffen / und einen *Tenorem* aus dem *Discant* machen / und nicht wenig *vitia* von *quinten* einführen'; Friderici 1618/1624, ch. 7 rule 14.) Erhardi implies that a falsettist – or a castrato – might be employed in an emergency when the alto is missing: 'Zu weilen muß man auß der Noth eine Tugent machen / und in Ermanglung eines *Altisten* / dieselbe Stimme von einem *Discantisten* / *Falsetisten* / oder *Eunucho, in octava superiore* singen / und musiciren lassen.' Erhardi 1660, p. 103.

204 Notes to pages 74–81

9 Caccini's *exclamation* describes a lowering of the voice followed by an increase (see trans. in Strunk 1981, vol. III, pp. 22–3). Either Praetorius misunderstood Caccini's definition, or he modified it for his own purposes.
10 Friderici's rules are translated into Latin as the final chapter of J. Praetorius 1629; Zerleder 1658 contains a virtual word-for-word copy of Friderici's rules, showing that his treatise was transmitted at least as far as Bern.
11 For the purposes of this study we follow the orthography of the later 1649 edition.
12 'Auch welche ruffen und schreyen / daß sie gantz schwartzroth wie ein Kalkuhnischer Hahn'; Friderici 1618/1624, ch. 7, rule 1.
13 Demantius 1607; Walliser 1611 (exhaustive study of each interval); Gengenbach 1626 (exercises for intervals and varied note-values).
14 The fact that an early hand has added Praetorius's rules at the end of a 1649 edition of Friderici preserved in the Staatsbibliothek zu Berlin-Preussischer Kulturbesitz, only goes to reinforce the impression that vocal ornamentation and diminution played an enormous part in the vocal performance practice of the age (see chapter 5).
15 His other singing treatises include the precursor (1671, probably first published in 1666) and the shortened version of Printz 1678 published in 1689, and still in print in 1714.
16 He later remarks that trills and *trilletti* can be added to long notes and that this is preferable to the common mistake of restriking every division of a long-held note (p. 22).
17 See Foreman 1969, p. 28 and Ulrich 1973, p. 10.
18 Mylius 1685, performance rule 7, gives a graphic description of the problems of those who have difficulty in mutating to bass at the time of the voice-change. They make appalling gestures and shout unnaturally like the tooth-breaker: 'noch daß er im Gesichte und mit dem gantzen Leibe keine heßliche Geberden und garstige Verstellungen von sich blicken lasse / dergleichen dieienigen am meisten von sich spüren lassen / welche zum *Bass muti*ren / da sich die Stimme noch nicht recht gesetzet / und mit grossem Zwang gern tieff singen wollen / da es unmüglich ist / und in der Mitte wie die Zahnbrecher unnatürlich schreyen / als wenn sie gespisset werden solten / welches denn ein heßlicher Ubelstand ist.' See also Mattheson 1739, p. 84 below for an attempted physiological explanation of the relationship between the 'increasing ardours and humours' and the voice-change.
19 Most Italian sources stress, like those in Germany, that runs must be formed in the throat. Maffei 1562 seems to be the only writer who actually describes the action of the glottis. See Greenlee 1987, pp. 50–1.
20 'Wenn der Knabe einen Gesang anfähet / soll er nicht alsobald mit vollem Halse schreyen / sondern Anfangs fein linde / und hernach immer stärcker und stärcker; doch also / daß er die Stimme nicht wieder sincken lasse / sondern biß aus Ende in gleicher stärcke behalte.' Quirsfeld 1675/1688, pp. 27–8.

21 'auch der Singer die Stimm also *moderiret* / daß sie bald starck / bald schwach / bald lustig / bald traurig &c. an gebührenden Orten / sich vernehmen lässet'; Falck 1688, p. 89.
22 'Solche Wissenschafft war in alten Zeiten von der Erheblichkeit, daß man eine eigene Profeßion daraus machte. Itzo kennen viele Ton-Meister kaum den Nahmen, geschweige dessen rechte Bedeutung; obgleich die Welschen Sänger, und zwar, so viel mir wissend, dieselben schier allein, noch ein wenig davon beibehalten, und bisher gewisser maassen, nicht ohne Nutzen, gebraucht haben.' Mattheson 1739, p. 95.
23 'denn die Grade der Schwäche und Stärcke menschlicher Stimmen sind unzehlich, und ie mehr einer davon zu finden oder zu treffen weiß, ie mehrerley Wirckungen wird er auch in den Gemüthern seiner Zuhörer zu Wege bringen'; *Ibid.*, p. 97.
24 'Die Sache nicht bloß auf Regeln, sondern vielmehr auf den Gebrauch, auf grosse Uibung und Erfahrung ankomme'; *Ibid.*, p. 112.
25 See *Beiträge zur Bach-Forschung* vol. VII, ed. A. Schneiderheinze (Leipzig, 1989) for a full text and commentary.
26 Indeed Petri still refers to Printz's advice on diet in 1782, p. 215.
27 'durch Stärke und Schwäche der Stimme'; Doles, in Schneiderheinze 1989, p. 68; Petri 1767, p. 61.
28 '*Pian, submissè*, weñ sie die Stiñe *moderiren* und zugleich gar stille intoniren uñ Musicirē sollen. Sonsten ist *Pian* so viel / alß *placidè, pedetentim, lento gradu*: daß man die Stiñen nicht allein messigen: sondern auch langsamer singen solle.' Praetorius 1619, p. 132.
29 'Diesem *Chor* kan auch der *Capellmeister* / oder wer sonst das Werck *dirigiret*, beywohnen / und einen rechtmessigen langsamen *appropriirten* tackt / (darinnen gleichsam die Seele und das Leben aller *Music* bestehet) darzu geben.'
30 'Gegen das ende des Gesanges / *in penultima consonantia*, das ist / ohn eine / der letzten Noten / so da klinget / sollen alle Stiñen außhalten / und ein sanfftes / fein messig gezogenes *Confinal* machē / und nicht also bald dz *final* dem Gesange anhengen. (Denn solches den Zuhörenden gar verdrießlich und unangenem zu hören vorkömmt. Und nimmt auch dem Gesange eine gutes theil der lieblig- und anmutigkeit hinweg / wenn man also bald den Gesang abbricht / und kurtz abreist.)
    Sonderlich wol aber zieret der *Bass* den gesungenen Gesang / weñ Er vor andern Stimmen / so wol im *confinal* als im rechten *final* ein wenig länger *protrahiret*, und ein wenig zuletzt absonderlich / doch fein gelind und sanfft / mag gehöret werdē. (Sol demnach ein *Cantor* seinen Knaben im *Discant* und *Alt* nicht gestatten / am lengsten außzuhalten.)' Friderici 1618/1624, rules 20-1.
31 Staden 1648 adds that the penultimate notes stands outside the measure to allow for the improvisation of cadential figures. See Dammann 1967/1984, p. 392.
32 'und nicht selber mit dem Fuß oder Hand *tactiren*.' Hoffmann 1693, p. 3.
33 'Es ist aber der *Tact* eine gewisse richtige Bewegung des Arms, oder auch des Fußes, wodurch die *Music* in genauer Ordnung gehalten wird.' Anton 1743,

p. 28. 'Wünscht man, zumahl bey stark besetzten Musiken, ein äuserliches Kennzeichen zu sehen, nach dem sich alle Musicirende in der strengsten Richtigkeit des Tacts . . . zu achten haben, so ist das mäsige Auf- und Niederschlagen der Hand oder des Fusses des, der die Music *dirigirt*, das Bequemste. Das Niederschlagen macht die 1ste Hälfte, das Aufheben die zwote Hälfte jedes Tactes . . . in der ungeraden Tactart aber, ist die Zeit des Niederschlags noch einmahl so lang als die Zeit des Aufschlags.' Doles, in Schneiderheinze 1989, pp. 57–8.

34 'Er thut am besten, wenn er den Musikdirector bittet, ihm sein *piano* oder *forte* bey jeder Note vor zu schreiben'; Petri 1767, p. 46.

35 Quitschreiber's advice on giving the singers their starting-notes clearly formed the basis of a similar passage in Leisring 1615.

36 Friccius suggests that church pieces be sung at a low pitch, not only because this makes it easier for the singers and listeners, but because it evokes the appropriate 'lowliness': 'so müssen wir allhie im niedern Chor unser Lobsagen nicht aus hoffärtigem sondern demütigem Hertzen verzichten'; Friccius 1631, p. 269.

37 'Die *Transposition* ist zwar unterschiedlich; *Ordinariè* aber / geschichts in ein *quart* oder *quint*.' Gradenthaller 1687, p. 27. The author proceeds to specify how the performer can effect a transposition by changing the clefs.

38 'Der vornemsten *Musicorum* Meynung ist diese; Man soll den Gesang (wenn die *Transpositio* nicht nothwendig) wie der *Componist* derselben gesetzt / am sichersten / *sine transpositione* behalten.' Erhardi 1660, p. 113.

39 'Vox alia aliam non obtundat, Sed sint omnes in aequabili intensione, & inuicem ad alias attendant.' Calvisius 1602, rule 3.

40 It is interesting that the call for a strong bass line is still heard in the mid eighteenth century: according to Petri the bass should be strong but proportioned to the rest of the music ('Der Baß sey stark, aber doch der übrigen Musik *proportion*irt'; Petri 1767, p. 42).

41 'Wo die Gelegenheit des Ortes und der *Adjuvant*en es leiden wil / können die Stücken / in welchen *Capellen*, *Symphonien* und dergleichen zu finden / also ausgetheilet werden / daß die *Symphoni* an einem besondern / die *Capell* an einem besondern und zunähest zu dem Wercke oder Orgel / die *concertirenden* Stimmen auch besonders / und sonderlich der *concertirende Bass* von dem Bass. Contin. etwas weg und an einen besondern Ort gestellet werde / zu welchen allen sehr dienlich ist.' Michael 1637, preface to *Quinta vox*.

42 'In *disposition* und Anordnung der *Capellen* so zwey Chörichts / kan man in acht nemen / daß die Chor creutzweiß gestellet werden / und daß *Capella 1.* dem andern *Coro Fauorito*, und hingegen *Capella 2.* dem ersten / etc. am nechsten sey / so werden die Capellen den gewündschten *effect* erreichen.'

43 Indeed Praetorius observes that the terms concerto, motet etc. are often used indiscriminately by Italian composers themselves; Praetorius 1619, p. 6.

44 'Diewel dieser *Chorus* fast meistentheils zugleich mit einfället / wenn die andern Chor alle zusammen kommen'; Practorius 1619, p. 133.

45 Praetorius's suggestion that the cantus and tenor, alto and bass parts sometimes be printed in the same book so that the two singers harmonise better with each other, also implies that he had only a few – if not single – singers in mind; Praetorius 1619, p. 90.
46 'Es habe ihn aber hierzu sonderlich bewogen / dieweil er gesehen / daß offtmals eine *Mutet* von 5.6. oder mehr Stimmen in die Orgel gesungen worden / der Sänger oder *Cantorn* aber / sonderlich in den Klöstern / selten uber zwey oder drey gewesen / und also aus mangel der andern Stimmen der *Symphony* an Lieblikeit und Zierde viel entzogen / sonderlich / weil die außgelassene Stimmen mit *fugis, Clausulis, & c.* (Welchen in den andern Stimmen / so mit *Musicanten* bestellet / lange Pausen zu *respondiren* pflegen) erfüllet seyn', Praetorius 1619, p. 4.
47 '*Chori favoriti* sind / welche mit den besten Vocalisten und Instrumentisten bestellet werden sollen / da denn entweder nur eine Stimme allein . . . gesungen wird / oder zwey / drey / oder vier miteinander *certiren*, und also guten *favor* und Ruhm zu erlangen / sich bemühen.' This advice is repeated – almost word for word – in Falck 1688.
48 'Aus diesen sechs *Concertat* Stimmen können ferner (wo da Wort *Capella* stehet) sechs andere Stimmen / biß auff die nechstfolgenden Strichlein / abgeschrieben / und also noch ein absonderlicher *Chor* oder *Capella* mit angestellet und eingeführet werden.'
49 'So seyn die . . . *Complementen*, in vier absonderlichen Büchern / zu befinden . . . dieselbigen doch / (wann sie noch einmahl abgeschrieben werden) *dupl*iret / und gleichsam in zwey Chor / als *Vocalem* und *Instrumentalem* vertheilet / und mit angeordnet werden können.'
50 'In obgesetzten wird *Coro Secondo* für eine *Capell* gebraucht / und dahero starck bestimmet / weil aber *Choro 1.* welches ist *Choro Fauorito* hingegen schwach / und nur von vier Sängern ist'.
51 'welches er leicht thun wird können / weñ alle Stimmen durch andere bestellet seyn'; Printz 1678, p. 8.
52 'Die Stimmen müssen so eingetheilt seyn, daß eine Proportion unter ihren ist, und keine Stimme die andre überschreyet, und also nicht zwey Discantisten oder Sopranisten, 1 Altist, 6 Tenoristen und 3 Bassisten. Wo aber ja dieser Fehler in einem Stadtchore ist, und man die Sänger nicht anders hat, so muß man die Stimme, die zu starck besetzt ist, gewöhnen schwach zu singen, oder man stellt die höchsten Tenoristen an zu tiefen Altisten oder der tiefsten Tenoristen zum Basse, denn die Baß darf nur ein weniges stärcker seyn, als die andern Stimen'; Petri 1767, pp. 50–1.
53 'Die meisten bringen es ja auch selbst in der Musik nicht gar zu weit, und wenn sie vom Sopranisten bis zur *Praefectus* im Chore gekommen sind, so singen sie wohl nach 8 und mehr Jahren noch ohne Zierlichkeit und ohne Affect, wenn sie nur als Ripienisten stets mit gesungen, und den guten Vortrag nicht studiret und geübt haben, und keine Theorie haben erlernen wollen.' Petri 1782, p. 196.

Notes to pages 113-18

54 However, according to Wolf 1787 the traditional definition of the 'Konzertist' – as someone who sang the solo sections but who was also responsible for the performance of the entire part – was still valid during the closing years of the century (see chapter 6, p. 171 below).
55 Two recent articles, Wagner 1986 and Schulze 1989, have challenged Rifkin's conclusions. Yet the very fact that both cite contemporaries of Bach, namely Mattheson and Scheibe, who speak out against performance of choruses with single singers, suggests that such economical forces were indeed still an option at that time. Both Wagner and Schulze privilege considerations of historical context and 'external' factors over the internal evidence of the original performing parts. Yet, as their studies and the present examination show, the external evidence can point both ways. Critics of Rifkin tend to discount his examination of the original parts without even attempting to address the very convincing arguments he has developed from their internal coherences.
56 'und ist nur der Unterschied / daß die andern mit dem Maul / sie mit der Hand und Fingern die Notten nennen müssen.'
57 'Also ist an die andern / bevorab aber die jenigen / welchen der rechtmässige Tact über vorgedachte heutige Music / und die schwartzen Noten / so wohl auch der stäte ausgedehnete musicalische Strich auff dem Violin / bey uns Deutschen / nicht bekand noch in übung ist ... mein freundliches bitten / sie wollen / ehe und zuvor sie sich unterstehen / eines oder das andere dieser Stücken / offentlich zugebrauchen / sich nicht schämen / deswegen zuvor eines Unterrichts / bey solcher Manier Erfahrnen zu erholen / auch an der Privat übung keinen Verdruß zu schöpffen'.
58 'die *Coloratur*en und geschwinde Läufflein vornen / wo der Bogen leicht ist / machen und streichen.'
59 'Ich an meinem Ort will keinem seine Meinung verwerffen / wann nur die *Composition* nicht *deform*irt / sondern deß *Componisten Scopus* erreicht wird. Jedoch stehets gar wol und fein / wann die Striche hübsch mit einander überein kommen.'
60 'Etliche ziehen einmahl herunter / und zweymahl hinauf / jedoch wird dardurch der Strich in etwas verzwiket / indem der Aufzug *ordinari* kürtzer / als der Niderzug ist; Die erste Art ist besser.' Merck 1695, p. 10.
61 'Dieses ist *Incipient*en höchst nöthig zu wissen / und Anfangs gleich anzugewehnen; und zwar I. in der rechten Hand setzt man den Mittel-Finger auf einen gewiesen *clavem*, so dann den Gold-Finger auf den andern *clavem*, ferner schrencket man den Mittel-Finger wieder über den Gold-Finger auf den dritten *clavem*, da dann der Gold-Finger auf den vierdten *clavem* kommt'; Speer 1697, p. 33.
62 'Nach diesem soll man ihnen mit beyder Hände Gebrauch / eine leichte / völlige und kurtze Anstimmung auß jedem Thon zeigen / wovon einige bequeme Exempel beysetzen wollen / auch gleich zu *Moderant*en und Triller zu machen anhalten.' Speer 1697, p. 34.

63 'Ein Violinist hat sich übrigens wie alle andere Instrumentisten, stets zu befleissen die Singstimme vollkommen nachzuahmen.' Kürzinger 1763, p. 70.
64 'Um ein Musikus zu werden und Einsicht vom Ganzen der Musik zu bekommen, lerne er ein Hauptinstrument, als das Clavier oder die große Harfe und studiere den Generalbaß, und endlich dadurch die Composition, besonders lese und studiere er fleißig Partituren von großen Meistern.' Petri 1767, pp. 62–3.

5 Ornamentation and the relation between performer and composer

1 This chapter is a revised and much expanded version of an earlier article, Butt 1991.
2 For a comprehensive survey of Italian practices in the sixteenth century, see Brown 1976; for a general survey of diminution in composition and practice, see Ferand 1956 and Horsley 1963.
3 '*Instructio pro Symphoniacis* Wie die Knaben / so vor andern sonderbare Lust und Liebe zum singen tragen / uff jetzige Italianische Manier zu informiren / und zu unterrichten seyn.' Praetorius 1619, pp. 229–40.
4 Mylius relies heavily on Praetorius's study of *intonatio* in his description of 1685; to the latter's account of singers beginning up to a fourth below the first note, Mylius adds that some also begin from above; but all of these are undesirable if the text is to be pronounced more gently. His own advice is to begin a semitone under the first note in a half-muted manner: 'Etliche derselben fangen solchen . . . von oben / als auch von unten auf / welche beyde letztere im *Texte* (wenn er mehr gelinde angesprochen wird) einen unanständigen *Raptum* oder Riß verursachen / daher ich davor halte / daß man einen Gesang mit einem halb gedämpften *manierlichen* / im *Semitonio* unter dem ersten Thone anfange / und also ferner fortfahre'; Mylius 1685, ch. 5.
5 'Wenn die Noten folgender Gestalt im Halse gezogen werden.' *Ibid.*, p. 232.
6 'und müssen scherffer alß die *Tremoli* angeschlagen werden.' *Ibid.*, p. 236.
7 'Je geschwinder und schärffer nun diese Läufflein gemacht werden / doch also das man eine jede *Noten* recht rein hören und fast vernemen kan: Je besser und anmütiger es sein wird.' *Ibid.*
8 'wie ein Vogel vom andern *observiren* lerne.' *Ibid.*, p. 237.
9 'Sind geschwinde Läuffe / welche beydes *Gradatim* und auch *Saltuatim* durch alle *Intervalla*, so wol *ascendendo* alß *descendendo*, uber den *Noten* so etwas gelten / gesetzet und gemacht werden.' *Ibid.*, p. 240.
10 Italian sources likewise give little indication of the connection between diminution and text sense; see Gallo, Groth, Palisca and Rempp 1989, pp. 288–90.
11 For a thorough survey of Herbst's extensions of Praetorius's definitions, see Allerup 1931, pp. 14–18.
12 Falck 1688, p. 108; Herbst also specified this exercise as a preparation to the *trillo* and *tremolo*; Allerup 1931, p. 14.
13 Allerup 1931, pp. 9–10.

210 Notes to pages 129–34

14 For extensive but dated overviews, see Goldschmidt 1890/1978; Kuhn 1902/1969; Allerup 1931.
15 'Wenn ein Knabe / in denen *Clavibus, Intervallen* und Tact *perfect* ist / so ist rathsam daß man ihn den Text singen lasse / da man ihn zugleich mit allgemach die Figuren kan lehren.' Printz 1671, ch. 7.
16 'Dieweil aber solches auff Anordnung derer Herrn *Scholar*chen in unsere Stadtschul öffentlich zu *docir*en schon *Anno 1665 introducir*et; auch solches an andern Orten beliebet worden: Als bin ich gezwungen worden . . . zu rediviren'; Printz 1671, foreword.
17 'und wanns nicht gehn will / mit der Hand an die Gurgel klopffen und also gewohnen.'
18 e.g. Printz 1678, pp. 42–74. For a brief guide to Printz's figures, see Horsley 1963, pp. 138, 153, although this author confuses the *Compendium musicae* of 1668 with the different work of the same title of 1689.
19 'Wir kommen nun auf das achte *Requisitum* eines guten Sängers / welches ist die Wissenschafft / und zierliche *Form*irung der *Musical*ischen *Figuren* / welche gleichsam das Saltz der Melodeyen sind: Denn gleich wie eine ungesaltzene Speise; also ist eine Melodey ohne *Figur*en wenig annehmlich.' Printz 1678, p. 42.
20 '*Pausa* ist eine schweigende Figur / und ein sehr kurtzes Stilleschweigen zwischen geschwinden Noten.' Printz 1671, ch. 7/23.
21 '*Vitium Concordantiarum* ist / wenn der Sänger nicht wol auff das *Fundament* und Neben-Stimme acht hat / und also eine Figur formiret / welche verursacht / daß zwey *Unisoni* oder *Quint*en oder *Octav*en auff einander folgen.' Ibid., ch. 8/16.
22 Feyertag 1695, an extensive treatise which is constructed from a number of earlier accounts, adopts something of the spirit of Printz's terminology: *figura conjuncta* is a figure comprising several simple figures; figures can be divided into running (*cursoria/lauffende*), fluctuating (*agitata/schwebende*) and mixed figures (*mixta/vermischte*) (Feyertag 1695, p. 225).
23 'jedoch so / daß die Stimme nicht gar geschleiffet werde.' Printz 1678, p. 45.
24 That these figures are specifically important in late Baroque music is suggested by J. G. Walther's specification of the *corta* and *suspirans* as part of his definition of 'Figura' in his *Lexicon* of 1732, p. 244; the *messanza* has an entry to itself, its description as a 'vermengte Figur' taken directly from Printz; Ibid., p. 401.
25 'Wil aber jemand diese *Figur* recht lernen / so halt er den Athem in der Kehle in etwas zurück . . . zwinge die Stimme mit einem Beben und mittelmässiger *Vehemenz* heraus / und *imiti*re solche Sänger / die diese *Figur* recht und lieblich *form*iren können.' Printz 1678, p. 58.
26 Müller-Blattau 1926, pp. 31–9.
27 O. Gibel also makes a distinction between plain singing and that employing diminution; see p. 49 above.
28 Bernhard also includes three devices which do not belong specifically to what we now define as ornamentation: *fermo*, a firm, grounded voice, *forte*,

Notes to pages 138–44 211

piano and *ardire*, a sort of vibrato that is only to be sparingly applied. This points to the close, virtually indissoluble connection between expressive singing and ornamented singing at this time.

29 But Feyertag on the other hand still defines it, after Praetorius, as the fast trill or mordent used mainly by organists; Feyertag 1695, p. 221.

30 'ist ein hefliges jedoch mannirliches und liebliches Zittern und ganz geschwindes Wancken der Stimme / dessen Anschlag soll in etwas scharf seyn / und mit einem Accentu *intendente* geendigt werden.' Feyertag 1695, pp. 221–2.

31 Spener's famous tract was first published in 1675 and marked the beginning of the Lutheran Pietist movement.

32 'wenn einer aus denen Sängern sich sonderlich vornimt in einem völligen Stücke in einer Schluß-*Cadentz* zu *passaggi*ren / die andern Sänger so lange ihr *trillo* machen sollen / biß er zum Schluß komme / und ein ieder Raum und Platz habe / in einem guten Stücke seine Kunst hören zu lassen.'

33 'Allein man hat sich itzo wegen des *passaggi*rens und *diminui*rens nicht so sehr über die *Vocali*sten und *Instrumenti*sten zu beschwehren / als über die *Componi*sten selbst. Dän die wenigsten wissen die *Figuras Musicas* zu rechter Zeit / und an gehörigen Orten an zu wenden'; Ahle 1704, pp. 80 1.

34 It may have been from Ahle that Mattheson drew the same comment in 1739; Harriss, p. 481.

35 'Die lieben Alten haben zwar von solchen Figuren wenig gewust / nach deme aber die *Componi*sten schon vom vorigem *Seculo* an / haben angefangen / einige Arten solcher Figuren zu setzen / welches gleich *Judiciosen Musicali*schen Ohren wohl eingeleuchtet / dann solche Figuren sich so wohl der *Dissonanti*en / als *Consonanti*en bedienen. Auch nach und nach / von vortrefflichen Singern / und *Instrumenti*sten / ist immer höher gebracht worden / und endlich so hoch gestigen / daß die *Music* heutiges Tags / wegen Menge der Figuren / absonderlich in dem / da mahl noch unerfundenen *Stylo recitativo*, wohl kan einer *Rhetoric* verglichen werden.' Stierlein 1691, p. 18.

36 However, Stierlein's example seems merely to show the addition of various appoggiaturas and runs.

37 '*Vitium multiplicationis* ist / wenn ein *Super*-kluger *Musicus* immer noch einmal so viel *Noten* und *Manie*ren machet / als auffm Papier stehen / die sich zu dem darunter *General Bass* offt schicken / als eine Faust auffs Auge und ein Igell-Fell zum Nase-Futter.' Fuhrmann 1706, p. 77.

38 'Lieben Herren verspart eure Kunst anderswo / wir verlangen solche hier nicht zu hören; Streicht die *Noten* nur schlecht und recht / gerad und gleiches Strichs weg / so wie sie der *Autor* gesetzt / wenn der die *Noten* hätte wollen *variirt, diminuirt* und in kleine Stücken als Lümmel zerhackt haben / so hätte er sie eben so bund-krauß *componi*ren können'; Ibid.

39 Fuhrmann's instructions on ornamentation are directly copied in the Swiss treatise by Steiner 1728.

40 Mattheson 1739, p. 109.

41 'Was etwa von dergleichen Sachen noch rückständig seyn mögte, insonderheit wenn die Zier-Figuren sein groß und lang werden, als da sind die *Passagi*,

Bombi, Mistichanze u.s.w. solches ist eigentlich des Setzers, nicht des Sängers Werck'; *Ibid.*, p. 120.

42 One exception – if it can be viewed as relevant to the literature used in schools – is Herbst's *Arte prattica & poetica* 1653, the sections on improvised counterpoint being a translation of a Latin treatise by G. B. Chiodino.

43 In Italy it seems that singers in the more distinguished establishments were quite fluent in counterpoint; see Ulrich 1973, p. 13.

44 'sondern auch mit gutem Verstande / und vollkommener Wissenschafft der *Music*'; Praetorius 1619, p. 229.

45 Federhofer 1989, pp. 110–27.

46 G. M. Artusi, *L'Artusi, ovvero, Delle imperfezioni della moderna musica* (1600), trans. in Strunk 1981, vol. III, p. 33.

47 See also Horsley 1963, pp. 130–2.

48 Müller-Blattau 1926 pp. 8, 12; see also Federhofer 1964, pp. 76–90, esp. 86.

49 'es beydes einem Sänger / als auch einem *Componist*en sehr nützlich seyn könte'; Printz 1696, part 2, p. 44.

50 'Denn gleich wie eine ungesalzene Speise; also ist eine Melodey ohne *Figur*en wenig annehmlich.' *Ibid.*, p. 46.

51 'Ich will aber hier nicht handeln *de Variatione*, so geschicht *conjunctionibus & Dissonantiarum*, und dergleichen / davon du gnugsam berichtet bist aus der *Musicâ Poeticâ*, sonder *de Variatione*, aus welcher alle und iede Erfindungen eines *Componist*en fliessen.' *Ibid.*

52 'Daher ich derer Meynung nicht seyn kan / welche alles nur an eine Manier binden wollen / vielweniger derer / welchen durchaus nichts gefället / als was sie selber geschaffen unnd was ihres Gebackes ist'.

53 'Daß ich in meine *Compositon*en je bißweilen ein klein Leuff- oder Schleifflein zu *inseriren* pflege / geschicht nicht / wie etliche wol vielleicht ihnē einbilden mögen / ohne ursach / viel weniger aus Unverstand / als ob ich nicht wüste / daß einem *Compositor* / den Gesang zu *componiren* / einem *Cantor* aber denselben zierlich zu *passeggioniren*, eigentlich zustünde: Sondern zu deme ich anderer vornemer Autorn Exempel vor mir habe / weil die Italiänische jetzo gebräuchliche anmutige *manier* zu singen in gemein noch nicht sonderlich bekant / Als wil ich hiermit nur den einfeltigen (vornehmen *Capell-Musicis* hiermit nichts *praejudiciret*) eine kleine anleitung / den Sachen ferner nachzufragen / an die hand geben.'

54 'Verständige Komponisten wissen wohl / daß die *intrinsecè* kurzen *Dissonant*ien keinen fehler hindern / und auch keinen machen können.' Ahle 1699, p. 20.

55 'Nur dieses ist darbey noch zu beobachten, daß dergl. *Figuren* mit einer anständigen *moderation* angebracht werden müßen, damit diejenigen Noten, so die *Consecution* zweyer *Quinten* machen, gantz unvermerckt von unsern Ohren vorbey streichen.' Walther MS 1708, part 2, p. 182 (see Benary 1955, p. 121).

56 '*Figuram* nenne ich eine gewiße Art die *Dissonantzen* zu gebrauchen, daß dieselben nicht allein nicht wiederlich, sondern vielmehr annehmlich werden, und des *Componisten* Kunst an den Tag legen.' Bernhard, *Tractatus compositionis augmentatus* (MS), in Müller-Blattau 1926, p. 63.

57 'Bey gefundenen solchen *Variationen* muß ein *Componist* gute Acht haben, daß er nicht gar zu altväterische erwehle, welches einem geübten leicht zu wissen ist.' *Ibid.*, p. 74.

58 'Die Vermischung der Figuren und mancherley Verzierung der Melodey ist eines von den vornehmsten Stücken, welche die heutige Music von der alten unterscheiden . . . Die Reguln der Vollkommenheiten erfordern ja, daß mannigfaltige Sachen mit einander vereiniget seyn, und zu einem Zwecke mit einander vereiniget seyn, und zu einem Zweck mit einander übereinstimmen müssen.' Ruetz 1752, p. 54.

59 This is somewhat similar to Marpurg's distinction, see p. 145 above.

60 'Die *Figurae Musicae*, die sogenannte *Manierae, Coloraturae* & c. seynd die Zierd und Geschmuck der harmonischen *Composition*. Die erste, nemlich die *Figura Musicas* . . . setzet der *Compon*ist zu Papier. Die andere, s.c. die Manieren, *Coloraturen* & c überlasset man dem *Judicio* oder Beurtheilungs-Geist, und *Virtuosite* der Herren *Voca*listen und *Instrument*alisten.' R. P. M. Spiess 1745, p. 135; see also pp. 155ff. This division of figures into those for the composer and those for the performer is very popular with writers of the mid eighteenth century and is perhaps influenced in part by the French method of notating the performer's ornaments in symbols within the notation.

61 Maybe this practice of notating two versions of the music was influenced by the publication of B. Barbarino's *Secondo libro delli motetti* (Venice, 1614); see Horsley 1963, p. 127. In any case there is a famous precedent in the aria 'Possente spirto' from Monteverdi's *Orfeo*.

62 'Dieweil ich auch in etlichen / dieser und dergleichen Art *Concert*-Gesänge / den *Choral* in den *Vocal*-Stimmen auf die jetzige italiänische Manier in etwas nach meiner Wenigkeit *diminuiret* / und wie es sonsten gennenet wird / *coler*iret und zerbrochen habe'.

63 Newcomb 1980, vol. I, especially pp. 76–83.

64 '(denn wo er da nicht zu Hause ist / so mag er so gut und so *delicat* spielen oder singen / als er will / wird er doch nicht viel besser seyn / als etliche Vögel / welche ihre Lieder auch gar niedlich und wohl herpfeiffen) . . . Und ist ein *Musicus* ohne *Praxi* eben so was ungeräumtes als ein Redner / der aber stumm ist.' Kuhnau, *Der musicalische Quacksalber* (Dresden, 1700), p. 503; Werckmeister 1700, pp. 43–4.

6 The decline of the Lutheran cantorates during the eighteenth century

1 'Sie singen daher meistentheils ohne Licht und Schatten, in einerley Stärke des Tones. Die Nasen- und Gurgelfehler kennen sie kaum. Die Vereinigung der Bruststimme mit dem Falset ist ihnen eben so unbekannt, als den Franzosen . . . Den simpeln Gesang hengen sie nicht genug an einander, und verbinden denselben nicht durch vorhaltende Noten: weswegen ihr Vortrag sehr trocken und einfältig klingt. Es fehlet diesen deutschen Chorsängern zwar weder an natürlich guten Stimmen, noch an der Fähigkeit

etwas zu lernen: es fehlet ihnen vielmehr an der guten Unterweisung. Die Cantores sollen, wegen der mit ihrem Amte immer verknüpfeten Schularbeiten, zugleich halbe Gelehrte seyn. Deswegen wird öfters bey der Wahl mehr auf das letztere, als auf die Wissenschaft in der Musik gesehen. Die nach solchen Absichten erwähleten Cantores treiben deswegen die Musik, von der sie ohnedem sehr wenig wissen, nur als ein Nebenwerk.'

2 Charles Burney, *An eighteenth-century musical tour in central Europe and the Netherlands*, ed. P. Scholes (London, 1959), p. 154.

3 While Hiller affirms the importance of music to religion in the preface to his second treatise of 1780, he notes, with approval, that the Italians make a practice of employing famous virtuosos for special feasts. In other words the German schools were clearly not providing musical performances of the professional standards he desired. One solution Hiller proposes is to make use of the recent developments in musical life by setting up concert societies with weekly rehearsals which could take over the church music: 'Man errichte, nach Beschaffenheit des Orts, Concertgesellschaften, wöchentliche Uebungen, wobey man hauptsächlich sein Augenmerk auf die Verbesserung des Gesanges richtet.' Hiller 1780, Vorrede, p. xiv.

4 'Die Ursachen, warum es vor Alters nicht geschehen ist, passen nicht auf unsre Zeiten; und wenn wir nichts gut finden wollen, was nicht vor Alters auch so war, so sind wir gewiß von der Einrichtung dieser irdischen Welt, und von dem Endzweck unsers Aufenthalts in derselben schlecht unterrichtet. Ich dächte, wenn wir etwas besser zu machen wissen, daß es unsere Pflicht wäre, es besser zu machen, ohne erst die Alten darum zu fragen.' Hiller 1780, foreword p. xiii.

5 'Jedermann singt, und der größte Theil Singt – schlecht!' Hiller 1774, 'Vorrede'.

6 See, for instance, the remarkably traditional format of Weselius 1726.

7 See note 1 above.

8 See Quantz's comments, note 1 above. Certainly at the time of Bach's appointment as cantor of the Thomasschule, Leipzig in 1723, there was a conflict on the town council between those members who desired the more glamorous Kapellmeister-style cantor and those who supported a more academic cantor of the traditional type. On Bach's death the council was firm in recording that his tenure had been an exceptional situation and that it was now appropriate to appoint a cantor of the traditional type. See Siegele 1983, 1984 and 1986. Similar demands were made elsewhere: a 1788 directive from the *Magistrat* of the Rheine in Westphalia decreed that the principal purpose of the school was to teach Latin and not to fulfil the church service. See Salmen 1963, p. 189.

9 'Freylich könnte ich leicht etliche Bogen anfüllen, wenn ich alle Compendien der Musik, alle Anleitungen zum Singen die seit zwey hundert Jahren in Deutschland gedrukt worden, anführen wollte. Ich zweifle, daß ie in Italian, wo man doch gewiß besser singt, so viel Bücher darüber sind geschrieben worden.' Hiller 1774, 'Vorrede'.

10 'Auf öffentliche Singschulen, wie in Italien, dürfen wir uns in unsern deutschen Städten noch lange keine Rechnung machen, besonders in protestantischen Staaten, oder wenigstens werden diese Schulen sehr selten seyn. Daher wird unser Unterricht immer gut genug seyn, wenn wir gewissenhaft das unsrige thun, ob uns gleich in unsern verborgenen Winkeln kein Kenner in unsern Lehrstunden besucht, noch unsre Schüler durch Belohnung ermuntert.' Petri 1782, p. 195.

11 'Unsere Vorfahren trugen Sorge, die Kirchenmelodien in den Schulen lehren zu lassen; die Cantoren mußten dabey so viel nur immer möglich auf Reinigkeit der Intonationen sehen; durch das Singen der Schüler auf den Straßen wurden die Melodien auch andern Personen nach und nach bekannt und geläufig, so daß durch diese Sorgfalt der öffentliche Choralgesang der Gemeinde wenigstens denjenigen Grad der Reinigkeit und Sicherheit erhielt, der bey einer Vereinigung so verschiedener, mehr oder weniger geübter Stimmen möglich ist.' Forkel 1801, p. 15.

12 Die Unwissenheit der Lehrer selbst ist es, die den Schüler meistens mit solchen Dingen um Zeit, Mühe und Geld bringt, die kaum Musik genannt zu werden verdienen und ihn auf keine Weise zum Genuß und Urtheil wahrer Werke der Kunst führen können. Ein Tanz, ein Volksliedchen, eine Ariette aus einer komischen Operette, und wenn es recht hoch kommt, eine Sonate im Styl und Charakter jener erheblichen Kunstwerke, ist fast alles was unsere Meisten Lehrer der Musik vermögen, folglich auch fast alles, was sie ihre Schüler lehren können.' Forkel 1801, p. 21.

13 In his *Lexicon* of 1787, Wolf makes his use of the old terminology explicit: 'Konzertist . . . means those singers or players who both perform the sections and complete pieces which are to be sung or played alone, and must also be responsible for the performance of the entire part. The expression is particularly useful with the singing choirs.' ('Konzertist . . . bedeutet denjenigen Sänger oder Spieler welcher theils die Stellen und ganzen Stücke, welche allein gesungen oder gespielt werden, vorträgt, theils für die Ausführung der ganzen Stimme sorgen muß. Der Ausdruck ist besonders bey den Singechören gebräuchlich'; Wolf 1787, p. 110.)

14 'In Singestunden, wo von einer Tafel gesungen wird, lasse man einen Schüler mit einem Stocke auf die Noten zeigen, die eben gesungen werden, dies erregt die Aufmerksamkeit, und hülft zum schnellern Fortschreiten.' Wolf 1784, pp. 14–15.

15 'Die Erlernung eines andern Instruments, besonders des Claviers, neben dem Singen, ist nicht nur nützlich, sondern sogar nöthig. Ein Sänger kann sich damit, wenn er sich allein übt, in Falle der Noth, zurecht weisen; er lernt die Grundsätze der Musik immer besser einsehen; und wenn er, vermittelst des Clavierunterrichts, zu einer vollständigen Kenntniß der Harmonie gelangt, so wird ihm dieß in der Folge beym Gesang die wichtigsten Dienste leisten.' Hiller 1774, p. 29.

16 'Ubrigens sollen sie sich in der Stunde nach Tisch allezeit im Singen üben'; Leipzig *Ordnung* 1733, p. 14.

216   Notes to pages 175–81

17 See R. Strohm, 'Die Epochenkrise der deutschen Opernpflege', in *Johann Sebastian Bachs Spätwerk und dessen Umfeld*, 61. Bachfest der Neuen Bachgesellschaft, Duisburg 1986, ed. C. Wolff (Kassel, 1988), pp. 155–66.
18 'Alle Manieren, alle kleine Auszierungen, und alles, was man unter der Methode zu spielen verstehet, druckt er mit eigentlichen Noten aus'; Scheibe, critique of Bach, 14 May 1737, *Bach-Dokumente* II, p. 286; translation in David and Mendel, p. 238.
19 'so sind die doch nicht das Wesentliche des Gesanges, sondern nur willkührliche Auszierungen desselben, die aber, für unsern Geschmack, zur Nothwendigkeit geworden sind.' Hiller 1780, pp. 34–5.
20 'Es ist indeß kein Componist deßwegen zu tadeln, so lange nicht alle Sänger gleiche Fähigkeit und Einsicht haben.' *Ibid.*, p. 35.
21 'Die Kunst den Athem zu sparen, muß einem Schüler gleich anfangs bekannt gemacht, und mit ihm geübt werden. Man lasse zu dem Ende ihn einen einzigen Ton mäßig starck, oder schwach mit zunehmender Stärcke aushalten. Die Brust gewöhn sich dadurch nicht allein an das Zurückhalten des Athems, sondern die Stimme bekommt auch dadurch die gehörige Festigkeit.' Hiller 1792, p. 15.
22 'die nothwendigste Zierde des Gesanges', *Ibid.*, p. 19.
23 'In unsern Choralgesängen ist überall Gelegenheit das Trillo zu üben, und ein eifrige Singschüler wird nicht unterlassen, sich diese Gelegenheit zu nutze zu machen.' *Ibid.*, p. 20.
24 'Ein großer Vortheil nicht nur zur Deutlichkeit, sondern auch zu desto sicherer Beobachtung einer gleichen Bewegung des Tacts, ist es, wenn man von vier oder drey geschwinden Noten, allemal der ersten einen kleinen Nachdruck giebt'; Agricola 1757, p. 129.
25 The information he gives on the possibilities of articulation (likening the varieties of articulation to the varieties of string bowing) in his treatise of 1780 is perhaps the most detailed to be found in any treatise on singing to be found within this survey.
26 'The thorough-bass is the most complete foundation of music. It is played with both hands on a keyboard instrument in such a way that the left hand plays the prescribed notes, while the right hand strikes consonances and dissonances, so that this results in a well sounding *Harmonie* for the Honour of God and the permissible delight of the soul.' Niedt 1700, trans. Poulin and Taylor 1989, p. 28.
27 'Da es aber dennoch nicht möglich ist, allen Mißbrauch der lieben Musik gänzlich abzuschaffen, wie es wohl zu wünschen: so sind die Feinde der Kirchenmusik geschäftig, aus solchem Mißbrauch Waffen zu schmieden, um diejenigen damit zu bestreiten welche fest über ihr halten.' Steffani 1699, ed. Albrecht 1760, p. 45.
28 'Das Singen der *Italiaener* in unsern Kirchen / weil ihnen nichts böses zu singen verstattet wird / ist gut und bleibet gut / wann gleich die *Italiaener* und *Castrati* böß und gottloß sind.' Motz 1703, p. 20.
29 'Die *Musici* zuhacken / und zerstümlen die Texte nicht / sondern sie thun vielmehr das *contrarium* und *repetiren* gantze *Sentenz*, damit umb so viel mehr die Eigenschafft des *Textes* exprimiret werden möge.' Motz 1703, p. 76.

30 'die Prediger sollen in ihrem Eifer gegen die Musik nicht zu weit gehen.' Forkel 1801, p. 76.
31 'Es muß dieser Mißbrauch mit der eiteln *Instrumental-Music* in Koppenhagen auch groß gewesen seyn, weil der letzt-verstorbene König in Dennemarck im Jahr 1730 die Kirchen-*Music* gantz und gar durch ein scharffes *Edict* verboten und abgeschaffet hat, welches denen grossen *Musicis* sehr wehe thun wird.' Gerber 1732, p. 226; Gerber also notes what he takes to be a similar ban in Moscow, *Ibid.*, p. 283.
32 'So verehren wir also dadurch unsern Schöpfer; wir machen uns dadurch edler und tugendhafter; und endlich so versüßen wir auch damit die Last unserer Geschäffte.' Scheibe 1739, p. 286.
33 'Es ist bereits eine ausgemachte Sache, daß die Musik ein nöthiges und unentbehrliches Stück eines vernünftigen und wohlgeordneten Gottesdienstes ist.' *Ibid.*, p. 510.
34 For an illuminating analysis of the dispute, see P. S. Minear, 'J. S. Bach and J. A. Ernesti: A case study in exegetical and theological conflict', in *Our common history as Christians: Essays in honor of Albert C. Outler*, ed. J. Deschner, L. T. Howe, and K. Penzel (New York, 1975), pp. 131–55.
35 'Ja, es sind solche Klimperer da; ich wollte aber, es wären keine zugegen.' Mattheson 1749, p. 268.
36 'so schicke sich doch solches *epitheton* keinesweges zur vorhabenden Sache.' *Bach-Dokumente* II, p. 463. The additions can be inferred by comparing the printed pamphlet with Schröter's original text in *Bach-Dokumente* II, pp. 462–4.
37 'Und endlich (mit wenigen viel gesagt) laufft oben besagtes *Programma* wider hohe Landes-Fürstliche Kirchen-Ordnung, *Plaisirs* und *Interesse*; Denn wann niemand mehr (nach des *Autoris* Abmahnung) *Musicam studi*ren soll, wo bliebe die Kirchen-Musick? wo würde man *Operi*sten und *Cappelli*sten hernehmen? und was würde die Tranck-Steuer darzu sagen?'
38 'Hätte Satan schon damals seinen Willen bekommen, so würde es schon jetzt bey uns eingetroffen seyn, was der HErr durch seine Propheten drohet: Ich will heraus nehmen allen fröhlichen Gesang. Jerem 25, 10. Ich will mit dem Getöne deines Gesangs ein Ende machen, daß man den Klange deiner Harffe nicht mehr hören soll. Ezech. 26, 13'; Ruetz 1753, introduction.
39 'Daher es eine wichtige Regul der Redner Kunst: wer einen andern in einen Affeckt setzet will, der muß zuvor denselbigen Affeckt annehmen.' Ruetz 1753, p. 68.
40 'Wer es prächtig auf Saitenspielen machen soll, muß sich täglich darauf üben, kann also nicht auf andere Art sein Brot erwerben. Wer eine erbauliche feyerliche Kirchenmusik komponieren soll, muß freyen Geistes seyn, nicht mit Nahrungssorgen gequält, oder mit Arbeiten überhäuft seyn, die den dazu erforderlichen freyen Geist unterdrücken.' Forkel 1801, p. 27.
41 'Ueberall wird man unübersteigliche Schwierigkeiten finden, und nur zu bald gewahr werden, daß der gänzliche Verfall der Singechöre, der Verfall dieser in manchen Augen geringfügig scheinenden Anstalt, auch den Verfall

mancher andern nützlichen und fürs Ganze unentbehrlichen Anstalten nothwendig nach sich ziehen muß.' Forkel 1801, p. 34.

42 The Leipzig *Ordnung* of 1733 still advocates traditional singing practices as part of the curriculum: the singing lesson should take place directly after meals, and the pupils benefit from the cold and harshness of their various singing duties; pp. 14, 18.

43 'Aber die eigentliche Quelle aller solcher Beschuldigungen, die man den Chorschülern macht, liegt in einer gewissen Neigung der meisten Menschen, ärmern Kindern überhaupt weniger Nachsicht zu beweisen als den Kindern reicher Aeltern.' Forkel 1801, p. 40. That music was often associated with the upkeep of the poorest boys is suggested by the ordinance for Frankfurt am Main in 1765, in which music is only mentioned under 'Leges, die armen Schüler betreffend'. See Schipke 1913, p. 49.

44 'So ist noch vor kurzem an der Michaelisschule zu Lüneburg eine beträchtliche Anzahl von Freytischen für Chorschüler nebst andern Beneficien unter verschiedenen Namen, als Mettengelder eingezogen, und das Jahrhunderte lang an dieser Schule befindliche Starke und gute Chor völlig aufgehoben und alle Musik in der dazu gehörigen Kirche abgeschafft worden.' Forkel 1801, p. 63. See also Walter 1967, p. 84 for an account of the decline of the cantorates in Lüneburg during the last decades of the century.

45 e.g. Flensburg in 1797 (Detlefsen 1961, pp. 198, 249), where the music was taken over by the Stadtmusiker and organists; the choirs of Halberstadt were dissolved in 1774; the cantor at Lübeck was not replaced in 1801 and the connections between school and church music were steadily loosened (Stahl 1952, pp. 108–9); the cantorate at Württemberg was dissolved in 1807 (Schipke 1913, pp. 51–2).

46 'Welche Stadt in Deutschland, ausser Dresden, hat etwas, das unserm Alumnäe gleich käme?' *Berlinische Musik Zeitung* 8 (1793), p. 29. See Schipke 1913, p. 51.

47 'Unsere Tempel sollen Sitze des besten Geschmacks in Künsten und Wissenschaften seyn, so wie es bey den gebildetsten Völkern des Alterthums gewesen sind.' Forkel 1801, p. 49.

48 'Die Schullehrer hatten selbst in ihrer Jugend den allgemeinen Musik-Unterricht genossen, und die Erfahrung an sich gemacht, daß musikalische und andere Kenntnisse gar wohl neben einander bestehen können, und daß ein Kopf, der die Lehren der Harmonie zu fassen vermag, auch den Homer, Virgil, Cicero und Horaz nicht zu fürchten braucht.' Forkel 1801, pp. 61–2.

49 See *NG IV*, 'Chorus', p. 351.

Bibliography

Primary sources

Agricola, J. F. 1757, *Anleitung zur Singkunst* (Berlin); annotated German translation of Tosi 1723.
Agricola, M. 1528, *Ein kurtz deudsche Musica* (Wittenberg).
    1529, *Musica instrumentalis deudsch* (Wittenberg).
    1532, *Musica figuralis deudsch* (Wittenberg).
    1533, *Musica choralis deudsch* (Wittenberg).
    1539, *Rudimenta musices* (Wittenberg); trans. and ed. by B. Rainbow (Aberystwyth, 1991).
    1543, *Quaestiones vulgatiores in musicam* (Magdeburg).
    1560, *Deutsche Musica und Gesangbüchlin* (Nuremberg).
Ahle, J. G. 1695, *Musikalisches Frühlings-Gespräche* (Mühlhausen).
    1697, *Musikalisches Sommer-Gespräche* (Mühlhausen).
    1699, *Musikalisches Herbst Gespräche* (Mühlhausen).
    1701, *Musikalisches Winter-Gespräche* (Mühlhausen).
    1690/1704, *Kurze doch deutliche Anleitung zu der lieblich- und löblichen Singekunst* (Mühlhausen); new, enlarged editions of original text by J. R. Ahle 1673.
Anon. 1601, *Idea musicae, artificio plane novo canendi artem* (Frankfurt).
    1689–1753, *Kurtzer jedoch gründlicher Wegweiser* (Augsburg).
    1750, *Rechtmässige Vertheidigung wider die groben Lästerungen, welche Herr M. Johann Gottlieb Biedermann . . .* ('Deutschland').
    1752, *Kurze Anweisung zu den ersten Anfangs-Gründen der Musik* (Langensalz).
    1793, *Kurzer und leichter auch für die Jugend . . . Unterricht* (Ulm).
Anton, J. E. 1743, *Principia musices, oder ersten Anfänge der Music* (Bremen).
Anwander, G. 1606, *Christliche Predigt von der vocal und instrumentalischen Music* (Tübingen).
Auriemma, D. 1622, *Breve compendio di musica* (Naples).
Avella, G. d' 1657, *Regole di musica* (Rome).
Bähr (Beer), J. 1697, *Ursus murmurat, das ist: klar und deutlicher Beweiss* (Weimar).
Banchieri, A. 1614, *Cartella musicale nel canto figurato fermo, et contrapunto* (Venice); trans. C. A. Cranna (Ph.D. dissertation, Stanford University, 1981).

Bibliography

Baron, E. G. 1727, *Historisch-theoretisch und practische Untersuchung des Instruments der Lauten* (Weimar); trans. D. A. Smith (Redondo Beach, 1976).
Beer, J., see Bähr, above
Bendeler, J. P. 1706, *Directorium musicum, oder gründliche Erörterung dererjenigen Streitfragen* (Quedlinburg).
Beringer, M. 1610, *Musicae, das ist der freyen lieblichen Singkunst* (Nuremberg).
Bernhard, C., Three manuscript treatises, in Müller-Blattau (Kassel, 1926/1963); trans. W. Hilse in *The Music Forum* 3 (1973), pp. 1–196.
Beurhaus, F. 1581, *Musicae rudimentae* (Dortmund).
Beyer, J. S. 1703, *Primae lineae musicae vocalis* (Freiberg); facsimile (Leipzig, 1977).
Bidermann, J. G. 1649, *De vita musica* (Freiberg).
  1750, *M. Johann Gottlieb Biedermanns Abgenöthigte Ehren-Rettung wider die unverschämten Lästerungen über seine Einladungsschrifft De Vita Musica* (Leipzig).
Boecklin, F. F. S. A. von 1790, *Beyträge zur Geschichte der Musik, besonders in Deutschland* (Freiberg).
Bona da Brescia, V. 1596, *Essempi delli passaggi delle consonanze et dissonanze* (Milan).
Bononcini, G. M. 1673, *Musico prattico* (Bologna); German version (Stuttgart, 1701).
Bovicelli, G. B. 1594, *Regole, passaggi di musica* (Venice).
Burmeister, J. 1601, *Musica autoschediastike* (Rostock).
  Musicae Practicae sive artis canendi ratio (Rostock; extract from *Musica autoschediastike*).
  1606, *Musica poetica* (Rostock); facsimile (Kassel, 1955).
Büttner, E. 1625, *Rudimenta musica, oder deutscher Unterricht* (Coburg).
Caccini, G. 1601, *Le nuove musiche* (Florence); trans. in Strunck 1981.
Calvisius, S. 1602, *Compendium musicae pro incipientibus* (Leipzig).
Carissimi, G. 1692, *Ars cantandi* (Augsburg) added to second edition of Anon., *Kurtzer jedoch gründlicher Wegweiser* (see p. 219 above).
Cerone, P. 1613, *El Melopeo y maestro* (Naples).
Coclico, A. P. 1552, *Compendium musices* (Nuremberg); facsimile (Kassel, 1954); trans. A. Seay (Colorado Springs, 1973).
Conforti, G. L. 1593, *Breve e facile maniera d'esercitarsi ad ogni scolaro* (Rome).
Conrad von Zabern 1474, *De modo bene cantandi choralem cantum* (Mainz).
Crappius, A. 1599/1608, *Musicae artis elementa* (Helmstedt).
Cretz, J. 1553, *Compendiosa introductio* (Augsburg).
Crüger, J. 1654, *Synopsis musica* (Berlin).
  1660, *Musicae practicae praecepta brevia* (Berlin).
Crusius, J. 1595, *Compendiolum musices* (Nuremberg).
dalla Casa, G. 1584, *Il vero modo di diminuir con tutti le sorti di stromenti* (Venice).
Daubenrock, G. 1613, *Epitome musices pro tyronibus* (Nuremberg).
Dedekind, H. 1589, *Eine Kinder Music* (Erfurt).
Demantius, J. C. 1592, *Forma musices. Gründlicher und kurtzer Bericht der Singekunst* (Bautzen).
  1607/1632, *Isagoge artis musicae ad incipientium captum maxime accommodata* (Nuremberg/Freiberg); for other editions see *RISM*.
Dieterich, M. 1631, *Musica signatoria oder Singekunst* (Leipzig).

Bibliography 221

Doles, J. F. c.1760, *Anfangsgründe zum Singen* (MS); reprinted in *Beiträge zur Bach-Forschung* vol. VII (Schneiderheinze, 1989).
Doni, G. B. 1640, *Annotazioni sopra il compendio de' generi e de' modi della musica* (Rome).
Dressler, G. 1571, *Musicae practice elementa* (Magdeburg).
Durante, O. 1608, *Arie devote le quali contengono in se la maniera di cantar con gratia l'imitation delle parole* (Rome).
Eichmann, P. 1604, *Praecepta musicae practicae* (Stettin).
Eisel, J. P. 1738, *Der sich selbst informirende Musicus* (Erfurt).
Eisenhut, T. 1682, *Musicalisches Fundament* (Kempten).
Erhardi, L. 1660, *Compendium musices latino-germanicum* (Frankfurt).
Faber, H. 1548, *Compendiolum musicae* (Brunswick); see *RISM* for subsequent editions.
Falck, G. 1688, *Idea boni cantoris* (Nuremberg); trans. with commentary by R. M. Taylor (DMA dissertation, Louisiana State University, 1971).
Fesser, J. 1572, *Kindtliche Anlaytung* (Augsburg).
Feyertag, M. 1695, *I.N.I. Syntaxis minor zur Sing-Kunst* (Duderstadt).
Finck, H. 1556, *Practica musica* (Wittenberg).
Fokkerodt, J. A. 1698, 1718, *Gründlichen musikalischen Unterrichts* vols. 1, 3 (Mühlhausen, Bielefeld).
Forkel, J. N. 1801, *Allgemeine Geschichte der Musik* vol. 2 (Leipzig).
Friccius (Frick), C. 1631, *Music-Büchlein oder nützlicher Bericht von dem Uhrsprunge, Gebrauche und Erhaltung christlicher Music* (Lüneburg).
Friderici, D. 1618/1624, *Musica figuralis* (Rostock).
Friedrich, M. 1610, *Encomium musicae* (Jena).
Fuhrmann, M. H. 1706, *Musicalischer-Trichter* (Frankfurt an der Spree).
  1715, *Musica vocalis* (Berlin).
  1729, *Die an der Kirchen Gottes gebauete Satans-Capelle* (Cologne).
  (undated), *Musicalische Strigel* (Leipzig).
Gengenbach, N. 1626, *Musica nova, newe Singekunst* (Leipzig); facsimile (Leipzig, 1980).
Gerber, C. 1732, *Historie der Kirchen-Ceremonien in Sachsen* (Dresden/Leipzig).
Gibel, O. 1645, *Seminarium modulatoriae vocalis* (Zelle).
  1659, *Kurtzer, jedoch gründlicher Bericht von den Vocibus musicalibus* (Bremen).
Gradenthaller, H. 1676/1687, *Horologium musicum* (Regensburg).
Gruber, E. 1673, *Synopsis musica* (Regensburg).
Gumpelzhaimer, A. 1591/1600, *Compendium musicae* (Augsburg).
Hack, J. C. 1677, *Der Christliche Capellmeister* (Gotha).
Harnisch, O. S. 1608, *Artis musicae delineatio* (Frankfurt).
Hase, W. 1657, *Gründliche Einführung in die edle Music* (Goslar).
Herbst, J. A. 1642/1653, *Musica practica* (Nuremberg, enlarged edition: *Musica moderna prattica*, Frankfurt).
  1643, *Musica Poëtica* (Nuremberg).
  1653, *Arte Prattica & Poëtica* (Frankfurt).
Hiller, J. A. 1774, *Anweisung zum musikalisch-richtigen Gesange*, 2 vols. (Leipzig).
  1780, *Anweisung zum musikalisch-zierlichen Gesange* (Leipzig); facsimile (Leipzig, 1976); trans. S. J. Beicken (DMA dissertation Stanford University, 1980).
  1792, *Kurze und erleichterte Anweisung zum Singen* (Leipzig).

222 Bibliography

Hizler, D. 1623/1628, *Newe Musica oder Singkunst* (Tübingen).
Hoffmann, C. 1693, *Musica synoptica* (Zittau).
Hofmann, E. 1572, *Musicae practicae praecepta* (Wittenberg).
Holtheuser, J. 1586, *Eine kleine deutsche Musica für die Schulerlein* (Nuremberg).
Kirnberger, J. P. 1782, *Anleitung zur Singekomposition* (Berlin).
Kraft, H. 1607, *Musicae practicae rudimenta* (Kopenhagen).
Kretzschmar, J. 1605, *Musica latino-germanica* (Leipzig).
Kuhnau, J. 1696, *Frische Clavier-Früchte* (Leipzig).
    1700, *Der musicalische Quacksalber* (Leipzig); reprint (Berlin, 1900).
    1700, *Musicalische Vorstellung Einiger biblischer Historien*; foreword (Leipzig).
    Introduction to cantata texts, in *MfMG* (1902), pp. 147–54.
Kürzinger, I. F. X. 1763, *Getreuer Unterricht zum Singen mit Manieren* (Augsburg).
La Marche, F. de 1656, *Synopsis musica* (Munich).
Lange, J. C. 1688, *Methodus nova et perspicua in artem musicam* (Hildesheim).
Lasser, J. B. 1798, *Vollständige Anleitung zur Singkunst* (Munich).
Leipzig, *Ordnungen und Gesetze der Schola Thomana* 1634, 1723, 1733; facsimile (Leipzig, 1987).
Leisring, V. 1615, *Breviarium artis musices* (Jena).
Lippius, J. 1612, *Synopsis musicae* (Strasbourg); trans. B. V. Rivera. Colorado Springs, 1977.
Listenius, N. 1533/1537, *Rudimenta musicae* (Wittenberg); for later editions see *RISM*.
Lorber, J. C. 1696, *Lob der edlen Music* (Weimar).
    1697, *Verteidigung der edlen Music* (Weimar).
Lossius, L. 1563, *Erotemata musicae practicae* (Nuremberg).
Maffei, G. C. 1562, . . . *un discorso della voce e del modo d'apparare di cantar di garganta* (Naples).
Magirus, J. 1596, *Artis musicae methodice legibus* (Frankfurt).
Maier, J. F. B. C. 1732/1741, *Neu-eröffneter theoretisch- und pracktischer Music-Saal* (Nuremberg).
Marbach, C. 1726, *Evangelische Singe-Schule* (Breslau/Leipzig).
Marpurg, F. W. 1763, *Anleitung zur Musik überhaupt, und zur Singkunst besonders* (Berlin); facsimile (Leipzig, 1975).
Martius, C. E. 1762, *Dass eine wohleingerichtete Kirchenmusik Gott wohlgefällig* (Weida).
Mattheson, J. 1739, *Der vollkommene Capellmeister* (Hamburg); trans. by E. C. Harriss (Ann Arbor, 1981).
    1749, *Matthesons-Mithridat wider den Gift einer welschen Satyr* (Hamburg).
Megerle, A. (and Abraham à Sancta Clara) 1711, *Etwas für alle* vol. 2 (Würzburg).
Merck, D. 1695, *Compendium musicae* (Augsbug).
Metzel, H. 1660, *Compendium musices* (Hamburg).
Meyer, J. 1726, *Unvorgreiffliche Gedancken über die neulich eingerissene theatralische Kirchen-Music* (Göttingen).
Michael, T. 1637, *Musicalische Seelen-Lust* part 2, preface to *Quinta vox* (Leipzig).
Mithobius, H. 1665, *Psalmodia Christiana. Ihr Christen, singet und spielet dem Herrn* (Jena).

Bibliography 223

Motz, G. 1703/1708, *Die vertheidigte Kirchen-Music* (Tilse).
Muller, C. 1630, *Nucleus musicae practicae* (Erfurt).
Münster, J. J. B. 1748, *Musices instructio in brevissimo regulari compendio* (Augsburg).
Murschhauser, F. X. A. 1721, *Academia musico-poetica bipartita. Oder: hohe Schul der musicalischen Composition* (Nuremberg).
Muscovius, J. 1694, *Bestraffter Mißbrauch der Kirchen-Music* (Lauben).
Mylius, W. M. 1685, *Rudimenta musices, das ist: eine kurtze und grundrichtige Anweisung zur Singe-Kunst* (Mühlhausen).
Niedt, F. E. 1700, *Musicalische Handleitung oder gründlicher Unterricht* (Hamburg); trans. P. L. Poulin and I. C. Taylor (Oxford, 1989).
Nopitsch, C. F. W. 1784, *Versuch eines Elementarbuchs der Singkunst* (Nördlingen).
Orgosinus, H. 1603, *Musica nova qua tam facilis ostenditur canendi scientia* (Leipzig).
Oridryus, J. 1557, *Practicae musicae utriusque praecepta brevia* (Düsseldorf).
Ornithoparchus, A. 1517, *Musice active micrologus* (Leipzig; trans. J. Dowland, London, 1609).
Peetsch, P. 1672, *Synopsis musica . . . ein kurtzer und fertiger Unterricht* (Stettin).
Petri, J. S. 1767/1782, *Anleitung zur practischen Musik* (Lauban, Leipzig); facsimile of 1782 (Prien am Chiemsee, 1969).
Poland, N. 1605, *Musica instrumentalis* (Leipzig).
Portmann, J. G. 1785, *Musikalischer Unterricht* (Darmstadt).
Praetorius, C. 1574, *Erotemata musices in usum scholae lunaeburgensis* (Wittenberg).
Praetorius, J. 1629, *Musicae practicae et arithmeticae* (Stettin).
Praetorius, M. 1614–15, *Syntagma musicum* vol. I (Wolfenbüttel); facsimile (Kassel, 1959).
  1619, *Syntagma musicum* vol. III (Wolfenbüttel); facsimile (Kassel, 1954).
  1619, *Polyhymnia caduceatrix et panegyrica* (Wolfenbüttel).
Printz, W. C. 1671, *Anweisung zur Singe-Kunst* (Guben).
  1676–7/1696, *Phryis Mytilenaeus oder Satyrischer Componist* vol. II (Quedlinburg; reprinted Dresden/Leipzig).
  1678, *Musica modulatoria vocalis* (Schweidnitz).
  1687–9, *Exercitationes musicae theoretico-practicae* (Dresden).
  1689, *Compendium musicae signatoriae et modulatoriae vocalis* (Dresden).
  1690, *Historische Beschreibung der edelen Sing- und Kling-Kunst* (Dresden).
Profe, A. 1641, *Compendium musicum, das ist: kurtze Anleitung* (Leipzig).
Quantz, J. J. 1752, *Versuch einer Anweisung, die Flöte traversiere zu spielen* (Berlin; trans. E. Reilly, London and Boston, 1966).
Quehl, J. 1682, *Engel-Schall der Kirchen* (Gotha).
Quirsfeld, J. 1675, *Breviarum musicum* (Dresden).
Quitschreiber, G. 1598, *De canendi elegantia* (Jena).
  1607, *Musicbüchlein für die Jugend, in deutschen und lateinischen Schulen* (Jena).
Raselius, A. 1589, *Hexachordum seu quaestiones musicae practicae* (Nuremberg).
Reusch, J. 1553, *Elementa musicae, practicae pro incipientibus* (Leipzig).
Reyher, A. 1636, *Margarita philosophica in annulo* (Nuremberg).
Ribovius, L. 1638, *Enchiridion musicum, oder kurtzer Begriff der Singekunst* (Königsberg).
Rist, J. 1666, *Die aller edelste Belustigung Kunst- und Tugendliebender Gemühter* (Hamburg).

224 Bibliography

Roggius, N. 1566, *Musicae practicae* (Nuremberg).
Rosinus, P. 1615, *Cantorey-Predigt . . . nützliche Erinnerung . . . Figurel Gesang* (Freiberg).
Ruetz, C. 1750, *Widerlegte Vorurtheile vom Ursprunge der Kirchenmusic* (Lübeck).
    1752, *Widerlegte Vorurtheile von der Beschaffenheit der heutigen Kirchenmusic* (Lübeck).
    1753, *Widerlegte Vorurtheile von der Wirkung der Kirchenmusic* (Rostock/Wismar).
Samber, J. B. 1707, *Continuatio ad Manuductionem organicam* (Salzburg).
Sartorius, E. 1635, *Institutionum musicarum tractatio* (Hamburg).
Scheibe, J. A. 1738–40, *Der Critische Musicus*, 2 vols. (Hamburg); facsimile (Hildesheim/New York, 1970).
    1754, *Abhandlung vom Ursprunge und Alter der Musik* (Altona/Flensburg).
Scheibel, G. E. 1721, *Zufällige Gedancken von der Kirchen-Music* (Frankfurt/Leipzig).
Schein, J. H. 1624, *Diletti pastorali, Hirten Lust* (Leipzig).
Schleusingk, J. V. 1657, *Musices choralis practicae medulla* (Cologne).
Schmelz, R. P. S. 1752, *Fundamenta musica cantus artificialis* (Irsee).
Schmidt, J. M. 1754, *Musico-theologia, oder erbauliche Anwendung* (Bayreuth).
Schmiedeknecht, J. M. 1699, *Tyrocinium musices, das ist: Erster Anfang zur Sing-Kunst* (Gotha).
Schneegass, C. 1591, *Isagoges musicae libri duo* (Erfurt).
    1592, *Deutsche Musica, für die Kinder und andere* (Erfurt).
Schornburg, H. 1582, *Elementa musica* (Cologne).
Schröder, L. 1639, *Ein nützliches Tractätlein vom Lobe Gottes* (Kopenhagen).
Schröter, C. G. 1749, *Christliche Beurtheilung des von Herrn M. Bidermann. . .*
Schubert, J. F. 1804, *Neue Sing-Schule oder gründliche und vollständige Anweisung zur Singkunst* (Leipzig).
Schütz, H., prefaces to music editions:
    1619, *Psalmen Davids* (Dresden).
    1623, *Historia Der frölichen und Siegreichen Aufferstehung unsers einigen Erlösers* (Dresden).
    1636, *Kleine geistliche Concerten*, part 1 (Leipzig).
    1636, *Musicalische Exequien* (Dresden).
    1647, *Symphoniae sacrae*, part 2 (Dresden).
    1648, *Geistliche Chor-Music* (Dresden).
    1650, *Symphoniae sacrae*, part 3 (Dresden).
    1664, *Historia, der Freuden- und Gnadenreichen Geburth Gottes und Marien Sohnes, Jesu Christi* (Dresden).
Singer, J. 1531, *Ein kurtzer Ausszug der Music* (Nuremberg).
Sorge, G. A. 1745, *Vorgemach der musicalischen Composition* (Lobenstein).
Speer, D. 1687/1697, *Grund-richtiger, kurtz, leicht und nöthiger Unterricht* (Ulm); facsimile (Leipzig, 1974).
Sperling, J. P. 1705, *Principia Musicae, das ist: Gründliche Anweisung zur Music* (Bautzen).
    1708, *Porta musica, das ist: Eingang zur Music* (Görlitz/Leipzig).
Spiess, J. M. 1745, *Kurtzer, doch hinlänglicher Unterricht* (Heidelberg).
Spiess, R. P. M. 1745, *Tractatus musicus compositorio-practicus* (Augsburg).
Staden, S. T. 1648, *Rudimentum musicum, das ist: Kurtze Unterweisung dess Singens* (Nuremberg).

Bibliography 225

Steffani, D. A. 1699, *Send-Schreiben,* ed. and annotated A. Werckmeister (Quedlinburg/Aschersleben); further ed. J. L. Albrecht (Mühlhausen,1760).

Steiner, J. L. 1728, *Kurz-leicht- und grundtliches Noten-Büchlein: oder Anleitung zur edlen Sing- und Kling-Kunst* (Zurich).

Stenger, N. 1635/1659, *Manuductio ad musicam theoreticam, das ist: Kurtze Anleitung zur Singe-Kunst* (Erfurt).

Stierlein, J. C. 1691, *Trifolium musicale consistens in musica theorica, practica et poetica* (Stuttgart).

Stiphelius, L. 1614, *Compendium musicum Latino-Germanicum* (Jena).

Tilesius von Tilenau, N 1599., *Christliche und gründliche Erweisung, dass die Musica und Singekunst Gott wolgefellig* (Stroppen).

Tosi, P. F. 1723, *Opinioni de' cantori antichi, e moderni* (Bologna); trans. into English by Galliard (London, 1742); for German translation, see Agricola 1757.

Trautmann, H. 1618, *Musicae compendium Latino-Germani* (Lindau).

Trümper, M. 1668, *Epitome oder kurtze Ausszug der Musik* (Gotha).

Ulich, J. 1682, *Kurtze Anleitung zur Singe-Kunst* (Wittenberg).

Vockerodt, G. 1697, *Missbrauch der freyen Künste* (Frankfurt).

1698, *Wiederholetes Zeugnüs der Wahrheit gegen die verderbte Musik* (Frankfurt/Leipzig).

Vogelsang, J. 1542, *Musicae rudimenta* (Augsburg).

Vulpius, M. 1608, *Musicae compendium latino germanicum M. Heinrici Fabri* (Jena).

Walder, J. J. 1788, *Anleitung zur Singkunst* (Zurich).

Walliser, C. T. 1611, *Musicae figuralis praecepta brevia* (Strasbourg).

Walter, J. G. 1708, *Praecepta der musicalischen Composition* (MS); first published in an edition by P. Benary (Leipzig, 1955).

1732, *Musicalisches Lexicon; oder, musicalische Bibliothec* (Leipzig); facsimile (Kassel, 1953).

Weide, M. 1627, *Kurtzer discursus musicus* (Danzig).

Weimar, G. P. 1795, *Versuch kurzer praktischer Uebungs-Exempel allerley Art für Schüler* (Leipzig).

Werckmeister, A. 1698, *Die nothwendigsten Anmerckungen und Regeln, wie der Bassus continuus oder General-Bass wol könne tractiret werden* (Aschersleben).

1700, *Cribum musicum oder musicalisches Sieb* (Quedlinburg/Leipzig); facsimile (Hildesheim/New York, 1970).

See also Steffani 1699.

Wesselius, F. 1726, *Principia musica, oder gründlicher Unterricht zur musicalischen Wissenschaft* (Nuremberg).

Wilflingseder, A. 1561, *Musica teutsch* (Nuremberg).

1563, *Erotemata musices practicae* (Nuremberg).

Wolf, G. F. 1784, *Unterricht in der Singekunst* (Halle).

1787, *Kurzgefasstes musikalisches Lexicon* (Halle).

Zarlino, G. 1558, *Le istitutioni harmoniche* (Venice).

Zedler, J. H. 1732–50, *Grosses vollständiges Universal Lexicon aller Wissenschaften und Künste,* 64 vols. (Halle, Leipzig).

Zerleder, N. 1658, *Musica figuralis* (Bern).

Bibliography

Secondary literature

Adrio, A. 1961, 'Tobias Michaels Musicalische Seelenlust', in *Festschrift Helmuth Osthoff*, ed. L. Hoffmann-Erbrecht and H. Hucke (Tutzing), pp. 115-28.

Allerup, A. 1931, *Die 'Musica Practica' des Johann Andreas Herbst und ihre entwicklungsgeschichtliche Bedeutung* (Emsdetten).

Bach-Dokumente, ed. W. Neumann and H.-J. Schulze, 3 vols. (Leipzig and Kassel, 1963, 1969, 1972).

Banning, H. 1939, *Johann Friedrich Doles: Leben und Werke* (Leipzig).

Bartels, U. 1989, *Vokale und instrumentale Aspekte im musiktheoretischen Schrifttum der 1. Hälfte des 17. Jahrhunderts*. Kölner Beiträge zur Musikforschung vol. CLX (Regensburg).

Benary, P. 1961, *Die deutsche Kompositionslehre des 18. Jahrhunderts. Im Anhang: Johann Adolph Scheibe: Compendium musices*. Jenaer Beiträge zur Musikforschung vol. III (Leipzig).

Beyschlag, A. 1908/1953, *Die Ornamentik der Musik* (Leipzig).

Bösken, F. 1937, *Beiträge zur Geschichte der Musik in Hochstift Osnabrück* (Regensburg).

Bremer, H. 1976, *Musikunterricht und Musikpflege an den niederrheinischen Lateinschulen im Späthumanismus (1570-1700)*. Beiträge zu Rheinischen Musikgeschichte vol. CX (Cologne).

Brown, H. M. 1976, *Embellishing sixteenth-century music* (Oxford).

Butt, J. A. 1990, *Bach Interpretation* (Cambridge).

1991, 'Improvised vocal ornamentation and German Baroque compositional theory – An approach to "Historical" performance practice', *JRMA* 116, pp. 41-62.

Carter, T. 1984, 'On the composition and performance of Caccini's *Le nuove musiche*', *EM* 12/2, pp. 208-17.

Dahlhaus, C. 1986, 'Seconda pratica und musikalische Figurenlehre', in *Claudio Monteverdi: Festschrift Reinhold Hammerstein zum 70. Geburtstag*, ed. L. Finscher (Laaber), pp. 141-50.

Dammann, R. 1967/1984, *Der Musikbegriff im deutschen Barock* (Cologne).

David, H. T., and Mendel, A., eds. 1945/1972, *The Bach Reader* (New York/London).

Detlefsen, H. P. 1961, *Musikgeschichte der Stadt Flensburg bis zum Jahre 1850* (Kassel).

Eggebrecht, H. H. 1959, 'Zum Figur-Begriff der Musica poetica', *AMw* 16, pp. 57-69.

Federhofer, H. 1964, 'Marco Scacchis "Cribrum musicum" (1643) und die Kompositionslehre von Christoph Bernhard', *Festschrift Hans Engel zum 70. Geburtstag*, ed. H. Heussner (Kassel), pp. 76-90.

1989, 'Christoph Bernhards Figurenlehre und die Dissonanz', *Mf* 42, pp. 110-27.

Ferand, E. T. 1938, *Die Improvisation in der Musik; eine entwicklungsgeschichtliche und psychologische Untersuchung* (Zurich).

1956, 'Improvised vocal counterpoint in the late Renaissance and early Baroque', *Annales Musicologiques* 4, pp. 129-74.

1961, *Improvisation in nine centuries of western music: an anthology with a historical introduction* (Cologne).

1966, 'Didactic embellishment literature in the late Renaissance: a survey of the sources', in *Aspects of Medieval and Renaissance Music – A birthday offering to Gustave Reese*, ed. J. LaRue (New York), pp. 154–72.

Finkel, K. 1973, *Musikerziehung und Musikpflege an den gelehrten Schulen in Speyer* (Tutzing).

1976, *Pädagogik und Musikunterricht im Schulwesen des ehemaligen Herzogtums Pfalz-Zweibrücken* (Tutzing).

1978, *Musik in Unterricht und Erziehung an den gelehreten Schulen im pfälzischen Teil der Kurpfalz* (Tutzing).

Forchert, A. 1985–6, 'Musik und Rhetorik im Barock', *Schütz-Jahrbuch* 7/8, pp. 5–21.

Foreman, E. V. 1969, *A comparison of selected Italian vocal tutors of the period c.1550–1800* (DMA dissertation, University of Illinois).

Fortune, N. 1954, 'Italian 17th-century singing', *ML* 35, pp. 206–19.

Fröde, C. 1984, 'Zu einer Kritik des Thomanerchores von 1749', *BJb* 70, pp. 53–8.

Gallo, F. A., R. Groth, C. V. Palisca, and F. Rempp, 1989, *Italienische Musiktheorie im 16. und 17. Jahrhundert*. Geschichte der Musiktheorie vol. VII, ed. F. Zaminer (Darmstadt).

Goldschmidt, H. 1890/1978, *Die italienische Gesangsmethode des XVII. Jahrhunderts* (Breslau).

1907, *Die Lehre von der vokalen Ornamentik* (Charlottenburg).

Greenlee, R. 1987, '*Dispositione di voce*: passage to florid singing', *EM* 15, pp. 47–55.

Hitchcock, H. W. 1970, 'Vocal ornamentation in Caccini's *Nuove Musiche*', *MQ* 56, pp. 389–404.

Horsley, I. 1951, 'Improvised embellishment in the performance of Renaissance polyphonic music', *JAMS* 4, pp. 3–19.

1960, 'The sixteenth-century variation and Baroque counterpoint', *MD* 14, pp. 159–65.

1963, 'The diminutions in composition and theory of composition', *AcM* 35, pp. 124–53.

Kalb, F. 1965, *Theology of worship in 17th century Lutheranism*, trans. H. P. A. Hamann (St Louis).

Krickeberg, D. 1965, *Das protestantische Kantorate im 17. Jahrhundert*. Berliner Studien zur Musikwissenschaft vol. VI (Berlin).

Krüger, L. 1933, *Die hamburgische Musikorganisation im XVII Jahrhundert* (Strassburg).

1956, '"Verzeichnis der Adjuvanten, welche zur Music der Cantor zu Hamburg alle gemeine Sontage höchst von nöthen hat"', in *Beiträge zur Hamburgischen Musik-Geschichte*. Schriftenreihe des Musikwissenschaftlichen Instituts der Universität Hamburg vol. I, ed. H. Husmann (Hamburg), pp. 15–21.

Kuhn, M. 1902/1969, *Die Verzierungs-Kunst in der Gesangs-Musik des 16.–17. Jahrhunderts* (Leipzig).

Leaver, R. 1991, 'Bach and Pietism: similarities today', *Concordia Theological Quarterly* 55/1, pp. 5–22.
Moyer, A. E. 1992, *Musica Scientia* (Ithaca/London).
Müller-Blattau, J. 1926/1963, *Die Kompositionslehre Heinrich Schützens in der Fassung seines Schülers Christoph Bernhard* (Kassel).
Newcomb, A. 1980, *The madrigal at Ferrara 1579–1597*, 2 vols. (Princeton).
Niemöller, K. W. 1969, *Untersuchungen zu Musikpflege und Musikunterricht an den deutschen Lateinschulen*. Kölner Beiträge zur Musikforschung vol. LIV (Regensburg).
  1986, 'Von der Ars musica zur "Singekunst"', in *Festschrift Martin Ruhnke*, (Neuhausen-Stuttgart), pp. 255–64.
  1987, 'Musik als Lehrgegenstand an den deutschen Universitäten des 16. Jahrhunderts', *Mf* 40, pp. 313–20.
Petzoldt, M. 1983, 'Zur Frage nach den Funktionen des Kantors Johann Sebastian Bach in Leipzig', *MuK* 53, pp. 167–73.
  1985, '"Ut probus & doctus reddar". Zum Anteil der Theologie bei der Schulausbildung Johann Sebastian Bachs', *BJb* 71, pp. 7–42.
Preussner, E. 1924, 'Die Methodik im Schulgesang der evangelischen Latinschulen des 17. Jahrhunderts', *AMw* 6, pp. 407–49.
Rainbow, B. 1989, *Music in educational thought and practice* (Aberystwyth).
Rautenstrauch, J. 1906, *Luther und die Pflege der kirchlichen Musik in Sachsen* (Leipzig).
Rifkin, J. 1972, 'Schütz and musical logic', *MT* 113, pp. 1,067–70.
  1982, 'Bach's chorus: a preliminary report', *MT* 123, pp. 747–54.
  1985, ' ". . . Wobey aber die Singstimmen hinlänglich besetzt seyn müssen . . .": zum Credo der h-moll-Messe in der Aufführung Carl Philipp Emanuel Bachs', *Basler Jahrbuch für Musikpraxis* 9, pp. 157–72.
Rivera, B. V. 1980, *German music theory in the early 17th century: the treatises of Johannes Lippius*. UMI Studies in Musicology vol. XVII (Ann Arbor).
Ruhnke, M. 1955, *Joachim Burmeister; ein Beitrag zur Musiklehre um 1600*. Schriften des Landesinstituts für Musikforschung, Kiel vol. V (Kassel).
Salmen, W. 1963, *Geschichte der Musik in Westfalen bis 1800* (Kassel).
Sanford, S. A. 1979, *Seventeenth and eighteenth century vocal style and technique* (DMA dissertation Stanford University).
Sannemann, F. 1903, *Die Musik als Unterrichtsgegenstand in den evangelischen Lateinschulen des 16. Jahrhunderts* (Berlin).
Schering, A. 1926, 1941, *Musikgeschichte Leipzigs* vol. II, 1650–1723 (Leipzig); vol. III, 1723–1800 (Leipzig).
Schipke, M. 1913, *Der deutsche Schulgesang von Johann Adam Hiller bis zu den Falkschen Allgemeinen Bestimmungen* (Berlin).
Schmitz, A. 1952, 'Die Figurenlehre in den theoretischen Werken Johann Gottfried Walthers', *AMw* 9, pp. 79–100.
Schneiderheinze, A. 1989, 'J. F. Doles "Anfangsgründe zum Singen"', *Beiträge zur Bach-Forschung* vol. VII (Leipzig).

Schulze, H.-J. 1977, ' "... da man nun die besten nicht bekommen könne..." Kontroversen und Kompromisse vor Bachs Leipziger Amtsantritt', in *Bach-Konferenz Leipzig 1975 – Bericht über die Wissenschaftliche Konferenz zum III. Internationalen Bach-Fest der DDR*, ed. W. Felix, W. Hoffmann and A. Schneiderheinze (Leipzig), pp. 71–7.
  1989, 'Johann Sebastian Bach's orchestra: some unanswered questions', *EM* 17, pp. 3–15.
Schünemann, G. 1928, *Geschichte der deutschen Schulmusik*, 2 vols. (Leipzig).
Sevier, Z. V. D. 1974, *Theoretical works and music of Johann Georg Ahle* (Ph.D. dissertation, Chapel Hill).
Siegele, U. 1981, 'Bachs Ort in Orthodoxie und Aufklärung', *MuK* 51 (1981), pp. 3–14.
  1983, 1984 and 1986, 'Bachs Stellung in der Leipziger Kulturpolitik seiner Zeit', *BJb* 69, pp. 7–50; 70, pp. 7–43; 72, pp. 33–67.
Smiles, J. E. 1978, 'Directions for improvised ornamentation in Italian method books of the late eighteenth century', *JAMS* 31, pp. 495–509.
Stahl, W. 1952, *Musikgeschichte Lübecks* vol. II, *Geistliche Musik* (Kassel).
Stiller, G. 1970/1984, *Johann Sebastian Bach and liturgical life in Leipzig*, trans. H. J. A. Bouman, D. F. Poellot, H. C. Oswald; ed. R. A. Leaver (St Louis).
Stroux, C. 1976, *Die Musica poetica des Magisters Heinrich Faber* (Ph.D. dissertation Freiburg).
Strunck, O. 1952/1981, *Source readings in music history* vol. III (London).
Ubert, M. 1981, 'Vocal techniques in Italy in the second half of the 16th century', *EM* 9, pp. 486–95.
Ulrich, B. 1910/1973, *Concerning the principles of voice training during the a capella period and until the beginning of opera (1474–1640)*, trans. J. W. Seale, ed. E. Foreman (Minneapolis).
Wagner, G. 1986, 'Die Chorbesetzung bei J. S. Bach und ihre Vorgeschichte', *AMw* 43, pp. 278–304.
Walter, H. 1967, *Musikgeschichte der Stadt Lüneburg* (Lüneburg).
Wolff, H. C. 1972, *Original vocal improvisations from the 16th-18th centuries*, trans. A. C. Howie. Anthology of music vol. XLI, ed. K. G. Fellerer (Cologne).
Wustman, R. 1909, *Musikgeschichte Leipzigs* (Leipzig).

Index

Abendmusik (Lübeck), 19
Abraham à Sancta Clara, 29, 222
abruptio, 142
accento/accentus, 125, 128-9, 133, 134, 135, 136, 141, 144, 145, 154, 159, 174-5
acciaccatura, 144
acoustics, 79
addressees of primers, 53
Adrio, A., 203, 226
affective power of music, 26, 41-6, 64, 155, 181, 186, 187, 189
Agricola, J. F., 83, 88, 90, 91, 93, 144, 146, 166, 171, 174, 175, 176, 177, 179, 216, 219
Agricola, M., 6-7, 8-9, 53, 194, 219
Agricola, M. G. L., Kapellmeister in Gotha, 50
Ahle, J. G., 15, 29, 37, 38, 39, 44, 57-8, 59, 64, 101, 138-9, 140-1, 143, 153-6, 159, 160, 198, 199, 211, 212, 219
Ahle, J. R., 37, 39, 57-8, 59, 64, 155, 198, 219
Albrecht, J. L., 180-1, 216, 225
Allerup, A., 195, 203, 209, 210, 226
Alumni, 5
amateur attitudes and market, 64, 188
anticipatione della syllaba/nota, 134, 135
Anton, J. E., 60, 102, 198, 201, 205, 219
Anwander, G., 15-16, 195, 196, 199, 219
applicatio textus, 59, 136, 140
appoggiatura, 144, 171, 175, 176, 179
ardire, 70, 135, 211
aria, 191
Aristotle
  music and morals, 27
  substance and form, 38
articulation, 79, 90-2, 175, 216
  of figures, 133, 178-9
Artusi, G. M., 148, 212
attitudes of singers, criticism of, 29

Augsburg, 201
Augustine, 35, 198
Auriemma, D., 219
Avella, G. d', 203, 219

Bach, C. P. E., xiv, 19, 113, 190
Bach, J. S., xi, xii, xiv, 13, 17, 19, 23, 29, 33, 166, 179, 181, 190, 196, 200, 208, 214
  Bidermann controversy, 185-6, 187
  dispute with Ernesti, 33, 184, 217
  'Entwurff' (1730), 23, 44, 63
  Scheibe controversy, 36, 39, 46, 113, 149, 163, 164, 175
  Symbolum Nicenum from B Minor Mass, 113
balance, 106
Banchieri, A., 47, 128, 134, 200, 203, 219
Banning, H., 184-5, 186, 226
Barbarino, B., 213
Baron, E. G., 63, 220
Bartels, U., xv, 95, 99, 100, 106, 203, 226
bass as musical fundament, 39, 60, 106-7, 133, 206
bass line, holding of at cadences, 100
basse de violon, 119
bassoon, 119
Bebisation, 59
Bebung, 177
Beer (Bähr), J., 27-8, 186, 197, 219
behaviour of boys in church, 28
Beicken, S. J., 221
Belicius, 65
Benary, P., 212, 225, 226
Bendeler, J. P., 31-3, 184, 197-8, 220
Beringer, M., 60, 198, 200, 220
Bern, 204
Bernhard, C., xv, 30, 42, 49, 50, 53, 54, 69-70, 74, 77, 82, 121-2, 134-8, 141, 142, 144, 145, 147, 148-51, 156-7, 157-60, 163, 175, 177, 198, 200, 210, 212, 220

230

Index

Beurhaus, F., 220
Beyer, J. S., 36, 58, 59, 82–3, 142, 145, 220
Beyschlag, A., 226
Biber, H. I. F. von, 117
bicinia, 65
Bidermann, J. G., 33, 184–6, 220
Birnbaum, J. A., 33
Bobisation, 59
Boecklin, F. F. S. A. von, 178, 220
Boethius, xiii
Bolli, D., 134
bombi, 144
Bona da Brescia, V., 220
Bononcini, G. M., 220
Book of Wisdom (apocryphal), 38
Bösken, F., 113, 226
Bovicelli, G. B., 72, 73, 125, 220
breathing, 71, 73, 75, 79, 84, 87, 89, 91, 112, 133, 167–8, 171, 175, 178, 179
Breig school ordinance, 20
Bremen, 201
Bremer, H., 193, 194, 226
Brown, H. M., 209, 226
Brunswick school ordinance, 2
Bugenhagen, J., 2
Burmeister, J., 47, 49, 55, 59, 71–2, 95–6, 103, 122–3, 200, 201, 220
Burney, C., 166, 214
Butt, J. A., xii, 200, 209, 226
Büttner, E., 14, 24, 65, 195, 196, 220
Buxtehude, D., 19, 111, 129, 164

Caccini, G., 13, 47, 49, 72, 73, 83, 84, 125, 127, 204, 229
Caligula, 27–8, 185
Calvinism, 15, 182
Calvisius, S., 30, 34, 53, 59 71, 72 74, 81, 103, 105, 106, 190, 198, 200, 201, 203, 206, 220
canon, 7–8, 65, 172, 177, 179, 202
cantar d'affetto, 49, 69
cantar passagiato, 49, 69, 134
cantar sodo, 49, 69, 134
cantata, 182, 192
cantor, 3–4, 5, 13, 17, 18, 19, 22, 25, 30, 31–2, 62, 103, 163–4, 169, 189, 190, 214
Cantorei, 4, 5, 9, 14, 16, 22, 23, 30
capella, 108, 109–10, 112
Carissimi, G., 220
Carter, T., 226
Cartesian view of affects, 101
castrati, Italian, 112
castration, 80
Catholicism and Catholic practices, xii, xv, 15, 19, 189
cercar della nota, 134, 135, 159

Cerone, P., 80, 220
chamber music, 107
Charlemagne, 25
choir director's role, 99–103
chorale(s), xiii, 19, 65, 111, 118, 170, 177, 179, 193
   singing and improvisation, 146, 178
   intonations to, 118
Choro favorito, 109–10
chorus, 171
Chorus musicus, 4
Chorus symphoniacus, 4, 5, 9, 111
Christmann, J. F., 173
Cicero, 47
circolo mez/z/o, 133, 144
city musicians, 17
Claudius, 27–28
clavichord, 65, 65
clefs, 56
Coclico, A. P., 10–11, 122, 220
Collegium musicum, 21–2
coloratura, *see* diminution
Comenius, J. A., 66, 176, 202
composition, 83
concert style/tradition, 88, 167, 169, 177
concerted style, 103, 108
concertists, 18, 22, 23, 32, 171
concerto
   textures, 13
   church, 110
conciseness in presentation of material, 6, 65
conducting patterns, 100, 102
Conforti, G. L., 220
Conrad von Zabern, 70, 203, 220
consonance, rules of, 10
cornetto, 119
counterpoint, 164
court establishments, 17, 42
court musicians, 20, 62
Cranna, C. A., 47, 203, 219
Crappius, A., 55, 198, 220
Cretz, J., 220
Crüger, J., 57, 115, 117, 128–9, 147, 151, 164, 175, 200, 201, 220
Crusius, J., 220
Currende, 4, 9, 23, 190

da capo form, 44
Dahlhaus, C., 148, 226
dalla Casa, G., 220
Dammann, R., 16, 33, 38, 40, 205, 226
dance-movements, 119
Daubenrock, G., 220
David, H. T., and Mendel, A., 23, 29, 33, 216, 226
Dedekind, H., 54, 55, 220
definitions of music, 35–9

Demantius, J. C., 22, 42, 131, 198, 200, 201, 202, 204
Demelius, 195
Denmark, 182
Detlefsen, H. P., 17, 23, 182, 218, 226
Dieterich, M., 61, 65, 129, 147, 202, 220
digestion, music as an aid to, 3
diminution, *see* ornamentation
Director Musices, 5, 17, 18, 30, 33, 189
Diruta, G., 150
dissonance, 92
Dodart, 86
Doles, J. F., 57, 59, 89, 90, 91, 92–3, 102, 144, 175, 184, 205, 206, 221
Doni, G. B., 80, 221
Doppelschlag, 144
doppelter Accent, 138
dotted rhythm, 133, 176
Dresden, 16, 24, 25, 69, 175, 190, 200
Dressler, G., 9, 221
Durante, O., 221
dynamics, 69, 78, 82, 83, 84, 89, 90, 103

Eggebrecht, H. H., xii, 226
Eichmann, P., 65, 198, 221
Einicke, G., 185
Eisel, J. P., 67, 202, 221
Eisenhut, T., 201, 221
ellipsis, 141–2
employment of outside singers, 23
Enlightenment, 26, 32, 167, 173, 177, 184, 190, 192
Erfurt, 21
Erhardi, L., 41, 57, 66, 105, 109–10, 111, 203, 206, 221
Ernest the Pious, 17
Ernesti, J. A., 33, 184
Ewers, cantor at Flensburg, 17
exclamatio, 48, 73–4, 81, 88, 124–5
exercise, bodily, 80
exercises, vocal, 75, 86, 93

Faber, H., 6, 8, 35, 37, 53, 55, 59, 65, 69, 70, 82, 89, 168, 198, 221
Falck, G., xv, 20, 25, 36, 53, 57, 81–2, 115–17, 128, 129, 198, 205, 207, 209, 221
falsetto, 73, 85, 174, 203
faults of singing, 79
Federhofer, H., 157, 212, 226
Ferand, E. T., 209, 226
Ferdinand III, 25
fermo, 69, 135, 210
Ferrara, 148
Fesser, J., 8, 221
Feyertag, M., 136, 36, 42, 82, 102, 138, 199, 200, 201, 210, 211, 221

figurae (signs used in music), 56
figural music, 16, 17, 22
figures, 132–4, 147, 157–60, 210
 articulation of, 132–3, 178–9
 ornamental, 145, 151–3
figura corta, 133, 143
figura suspirans, 133, 142, 143
messanza, 133, 143
Finck, H., 8, 9, 70, 71, 87, 122, 123, 144, 221
Finkel, K., 53, 173, 194, 227
flageolet, 119
Flensburg, 17, 23, 218
flute, 119
Fokkerodt, J. A., 33–4, 35, 221
Folie d'Espagne, 43
Forchert, A., 50, 227
Foreman, E. V., 92, 204, 227
Forkel, J. N., 170, 187–91, 192, 215, 217, 218, 221
forte, 135, 210
Fortune, N., 227
Frankfurt am Main, 18, 218
Freiberg, 21, 22, 25, 33, 182, 184–5
Friccius (Frick), C., 14–15, 16, 39, 40, 42–3, 110, 199, 206, 221
Friderici, D., 35, 42, 56, 57, 74–7, 81, 97–8, 99, 100, 104, 107–8, 111, 130–1, 133, 147, 200, 201, 203, 204, 205, 221
Friedrich, M., 14, 15, 24, 221
Friedrich Wilhelm, King of Prussia, 182
Fröde, C., 166, 227
Frye, N., 200
'Fuga', 65
fugal passages, 71, 106, 119
Fuhrmann, M. H., 17–18, 19, 25, 36–7, 58, 67, 83, 112, 113, 142–3, 145, 195, 211, 221
funerals, 4

Gaffurio, F., xii, xiv, 64
galant style, 91, 93, 103, 171
Galilei, V., 148
Gallo, F. A. (with R. Groth, C. V. Palisca and F. Rempp), 150, 209, 226
Gengenbach, N., 35, 56, 57, 59, 66, 69, 70, 109, 201, 204, 221
Gerber, C., 181, 182, 217, 221
Gerber, E. L., 89
Gerstenbüttel, J., 29–30
gesture, 71, 74
Gibel, O., 49, 53, 59, 210, 221
Giganti, Herr Gottfried, 78
Goldschmidt, H., 210, 227
good and bad notes, 92, 175
Görlitz, 21
Gotha, 21, 27, 50
 ordinance issued by Ernest the Pious, 17

Index 233

Göttingen, 201
Gottsched, J. C., 46, 200
Gradenthaller, H., 21, 25, 61, 65, 105, 196, 202, 206, 221
Graun, C. H., 59, 171, 174, 177
Greenlee, R., 204, 227
Gregorian chant, 59, 193
groppo, 125, 128, 133, 136, 138, 144
Gruber, E., 15, 20, 64, 138, 221
Gumpelzhaimer, A., 8, 55-6, 198, 200, 221
Gymnasium pupils, 23

Hack, J. C., 40, 50, 199, 221
Halberstadt, 218
Halle, 17, 18, 30, 32
Hamburg, 14, 19, 16, 20, 21, 23, 29, 175, 197
Handel, G. F.
    Messiah, 192
harmony, 10, 60-1, 106, 172
Harnisch, O. S., 60, 198, 200, 221
Harriss, E. C., 84, 143, 211
Hase, W., 59, 198, 201, 221
Heinichen, J. D., 159, 164
Helmstedt, 32
Herbst, J. A., 18, 64, 82, 114-15, 116, 127, 128, 133, 134, 147, 164, 199, 200, 209, 212, 221
heterolepsis, 142
high notes, 71
Hiller, J. A., 167-9, 171, 173-9, 184, 190, 191-2, 214, 215, 216, 221
Hilse, W., 200, 220
history of music (ancient), 64
Hitchcock, H. W., 227
Hizler, D., 36, 53, 59, 61, 66, 69, 114, 198, 200, 202, 222
Hoffmann, G., 56, 58, 82, 102, 205, 222
Hofmann, E., 9, 36, 222
Hogarth, W., 88
Holtheuser, J., 8, 95, 222
Horsley, I., 209, 210, 212, 213, 227
humanism, xiii, 2-3, 36

instrumental music, 21, 26, 40, 173, 182
instrumental performance modelled on vocal, 119
instrumental technique, 118
instrument(s), 10, 15, 16, 18, 20, 21, 61-3, 67, 83, 113-20
    analogy with animals, 16
    criticism of, 27
    human voice as, 85
    posture and position of, 115
    tuning of, 105
intervals, 56, 66, 79, 174
intonatio, 124-125, 209
Isaac, H., 9

Italian musical examples, xv, 128
Italian style, new, 13, 15, 17, 25, 39, 41, 42, 47, 50, 51, 68, 70, 71, 74, 76, 81, 88, 97, 113, 115, ?-7, 153, 192
Italian terms, 61
Italy
    performers and conservatories, xii, 167, 169, 174, 175, 176, 190, 212, 214

Josquin Desprez, 1, 4, 9, 10, 141, 143
    In exitu Israel, 9
    Missa Hercules (canonic Agnus Dei), 9

Kalb, F., 1, 25, 195, 196, 227
Kapellmeister, 17, 18, 19, 20, 214
Keiser, T., 55, 59
keys, 57-8, 172
key signatures, 58
keyboard
    fingering, 118
    instruments, 83, 173
    technique, 118
Kircher, A., 37, 43, 49
Kirnberger, J. P., 164, 222
Kittel, K., 128
Kraft, H., 59, 65, 198, 222
Kretzschmar, J., 59, 198, 222
Krickeberg, D., 16, 17, 18, 19, 20, 21, 22, 25, 182, 195, 196, 227
Krüger, L., 16, 21, 22, 23, 30, 110, 111, 194, 227
Kuhn, M., 210, 227
Kuhnau, J., 17, 21, 22, 23, 29, 53, 149, 152-3, 156, 190, 200, 222
    Biblische Historien, 40, 45-6
    ClavierÜbung, 136
    Frische Clavier Früchte, 149-50
    Der musicalische Quacksalber, 29, 163, 213
Kürzinger, I. F. X., 36, 45, 89, 92, 94, 119, 144, 209, 222

La Marche, F. de, 5, 19, 87, 114, 131, 222
Lange, J. C., 195, 222
Lasser, J. B., 179, 222
Lasso, O. de, 9
Latin, xv, 2, 27, 193, 195, 214
Lauben, 26, 138
Leaver, R., 196, 228
Leipzig, 17, 20, 22, 23, 30, 32, 33, 89, 113, 167, 185, 190, 195, 196, 200
    instrumentalists, 21
    Thomasschule and its ordinances
        (*Ordnungen*), 12, 19, 20, 21, 22, 23, 24, 31, 53, 54, 57, 59, 66, 89, 153, 156, 166, 167, 173, 174, 178, 184, 195, 196, 197, 201, 202, 214, 215, 218, 222
Leisring, V., 21, 53, 61, 64, 201, 206, 222

234 Index

Leopold I, 25
lifestyle of singer, 79, 171, 174
  and diet, 78, 80, 82, 87, 174
ligatures, 56, 57
Lindau, 201
Lippius, J., 34, 37, 47, 51, 59, 150–151, 222
Listenius, N., xiii, 6, 7–8, 35, 53, 55, 65, 69, 70, 82, 89, 222
Löban school ordinance, 22
Lorber, J. C., 27, 222
Lossius, L., 53, 222
Lübeck, 19, 187, 218
Lüneburg, 190, 200, 218
lute, 10, 65
Luther, M., xiii, 1–2, 3, 6, 8, 12, 14, 25, 27, 36, 39, 40, 64, 183, 193

madrigal, 13, 96, 148
Maffei, G. C., 79, 204, 222
Magdeburg, 9
Magirus, J., 60, 198, 222
Maier, J. F. B. C., 164, 202, 222
Mancini, G., 176
Marbach, C., 222
Marpurg, F. W., 59–60, 89, 90, 91–2, 93, 94, 102, 112–13, 144, 159, 169, 171, 172–3, 174, 175, 177, 213, 222
Martius, C. E., 222
Mattheson, J., 20, 30, 83, 84–7, 88, 143–44, 149, 159, 182, 185, 203, 204, 205, 208, 211, 217, 222
mechanistic view of universe, 38, 50
Mediaeval theocentric thinking, xii, 36, 38
Megerle, A., 18, 29, 222
Meissen, 15
Melanchthon, P., 2, 4
memory, 78, 172, 173
mensural system and tempo, 96
  mensuration signs and proportions in, 56
Merck, D., 61, 62, 63, 117, 208, 222
messa di voce, 73, 88, 90, 175
metre and text, 101
Metzel, H., 222
Meyer, J., 182, 222
mezza di voce, see *messa di voce*
Michael, T., 24, 69, 107, 153, 154, 160, 163, 196, 206, 222
Minear, P. S., 217
mistichanze, 144
Mithobius, H., 14, 222
Mizler, L., 185, 186
moderanten, 125
moderiren, 82
modes, 56, 57
modulatoria, 143
monochord, 40, 79
monody, 13, 110, 128

monophony, 25
Monteverdi, C., 13, 134, 148, 213
mordant / mordent, 144, 171, 211
mordanten, 125
mordantiae, 123
Moscow, 217
motet, 16, 65, 96, 102, 109, 111, 112, 177
Motz, E., 181, 216, 223
Moyer, A. E., xiii, 202, 228
Mozart, W. A., xii
Muffat, G., 116–117
Mühlhausen, 29, 44
Muller, C., 223
Müller-Blattau, J., 54, 69, 159, 210, 212, 228
Münster, J. J. B., 201, 223
Murschhauser, F. X. A., 164, 223
Muscovius, J., 26, 28, 29, 32, 138, 197, 223
music
  and dogma, xiii, 15
  and nature, 38
  and science/mathematics, xiv, 37, 43, 198, 199
  and rhetoric, xii, 13, 46–50, 64, 70, 72, 74, 88, 126, 132, 141, 145, 155, 159–60, 165, 200
  as mirror of heaven and God, xii, 40, 50, 61, 180–1, 183
  as mnemonic, 20
  as refreshment from academic subjects, 20
  in the liturgy, xiii, 14, 183
music profession, low status of, 24, 184
Musicant, 33, 41
Musicus, 33–4, 35, 41
music theory, 2, 3
musica choralis, xvi, 2, 6, 7, 17, 56, 60, 193
musica figuralis, xvi, 2, 7, 17, 56, 50, 193
musica figuralis ornata, 82
musica modulatoria, 141, 164
musica poetica, xii, xiii, 8, 19, 35, 38, 47, 141, 146, 148, 164, 198
musica practica, xii, xiii, xiv, 8, 10, 19, 34–5, 38, 51, 61, 68, 113, 122, 141, 146, 164, 176, 198
musica reservata, 10
musica theorica, xiii, 8, 19, 35, 38, 198
speculative, 37
musical grammar, 155
Mylius, W. M., 22, 54, 81–2, 101, 105, 134–7, 149–50, 141, 175, 204, 209, 223

Nachschlag, 144, 145, 176
Nero, 27–8, 185
Neumeister, E., 44
Newcomb, A., 148, 213, 228
Niedt, F. E., 39, 163, 164, 181, 216, 223

Niemöller, K. W., 2, 3, 4, 5, 53, 55, 193, 194, 228
Nopitsch, C. F. W., 170-1, 223
Nordhausen, 185
   ordinance, 5, 16

ode, 3
opera/theatrical practice, 20, 22, 30, 44, 84, 88, 164, 177, 182, 200
opera buffa, 190
organ, 16, 112, 119
   dedications, 14, 15, 24, 39
organist, 19, 103, 127, 163-4
Orgosinus, H., 53, 59, 198, 223
Oridryus, J., 8, 223
ornamentation, 45, 48, 49, 72, 75-6, 78, 82, 83, 87, 88-9, 93, 94, 114, 121-65, 169, 172, 176, 177
   criticism of, 27, 28, 49, 140-1
   diminution/passages (*passaggi*)/coloratura, 10, 71, 73, 75-7, 79, 115, 125-6, 130-1, 136, 141, 144, 146, 148, 159, 174-5, 178-9, 182, 200
   instrumental, 116
   optional and essential, 145
   simultaneous application of, 112, 127, 140
   vocal and instrumental differences, 86
Ornithoparchus, A., 223
Orthodox Lutheran attitudes, 44, 180-1, 184, 196
Osnabrück, 113
Osteroda, 201

pagan tradition, 64
Palatinate, 53, 173
Paris Académie, 88
pausa, 132
pedagogic approach, 64-7
pedagogic reforms, 78, 172-8
Peetsch, P., 223
Petri, J. S., 55, 89, 90, 91, 93, 102, 103, 105, 113, 119-20, 144, 146, 169-70, 175, 177, 205, 206, 207, 209, 215, 223
Petzoldt, M., 19, 202, 228
philanthropic movement, 173
physiology of singing, 70
   awareness of, 84
piano, 135, 211
Pietism, 25-9, 32-3, 43, 44, 181-2, 186, 196, 211
pitch, 56, 71, 87, 167, 206
   setting of, 103-5
placement of singers, 74
Poland, N., 15, 223
polychoral music, 13, 106
port de voix, 144
Portmann, J. G., 223

posture, 71, 82, 84, 89, 115
Poulin, P. L., and Taylor, I. C., 163, 216, 223
Praetorius, C., 9, 71, 106, 122, 123, 200, 203, 223
Praetorius, J., 204, 223
Praetorius, M., xi, 13, 17, 24, 41, 42, 43, 47, 49, 57, 61, 68, 72-4, 76, 81, 82, 84, 85, 88, 94, 96-7, 98, 99-100, 101, 105, 106, 107, 108-9, 114, 115, 123-7, 128, 129, 130, 131, 132, 133, 134, 140, 144, 146-7, 150, 151, 160-3, 200, 204, 205, 206, 207, 209, 211, 212, 223
preludes, 105, 119
Preussner, E., 21, 25, 195, 228
prima prattica, 49, 148, 157
Printz, W. C., 22, 56, 64, 70, 77-81, 82, 83, 86, 89, 100, 101, 105, 111, 112, 113, 129-30, 132-4, 142, 143, 144, 147, 151-3, 156, 160, 163, 164, 171, 174, 178, 179, 196, 199, 200, 201, 204, 205, 207, 210, 212, 223
private instruction, 22, 32
Profe, A., 59, 66, 223
pronunciatio affectuosa, 71, 123
pronunciation, 78, 93-5, 147, 167-8, 170, 171, 174, 177
proportion, 56-7
Pythagorean view of music, xiii, 33, 40, 180

quadrivium, xiii, 3, 12
Quantz, J. J., 166, 168, 214, 223
Quasi transitus, 142
Quedlinburg, 31-2
Quehl, J., 223
question-and-answer style (*erotemata*), 8, 9, 54, 67
Quintilian, 47, 62, 71-2
Quintilianus, 64
Quirsfeld, J., 60, 81, 100, 101, 102, 200, 204, 223
Quitschreiber, G., 53, 56, 58, 60, 61, 64, 66, 71, 73, 95, 98, 100, 103, 104-5, 106, 194, 198, 201, 202, 206, 223

Rainbow, B., 202, 228
range, vocal, 73, 89
Raselius, A., 223
Ratsinstrumentisten, 23
Rautenstrauch, J., 228
recitative, 110, 191
rector, 3-4, 12, 30, 31-2
Reddemer, 65
Redivivus, H., 41
Reformation, 1
registers, 92-3, 174, 203
   blending of, 84
   shift in male voice, 84-5, 204

236 Index

Reichardt, J. F., 177
Renaissance
  conventions of, 159
  polyphony (see also *prima prattica*), 13, 25, 49, 150
retardatio, 142
Reusch, J., 3, 223
Reyher, A., 223
ribatutta di gola, 128, 144
Ribovius, L., 14, 38, 64, 66–7, 199, 203, 223
ricercar, 43
Rifkin, J., 113, 157, 208, 228
ripieno, ripienists, 108, 109, 113, 171
Rist, J., 14, 194, 223
Ritterakademien, xv
Rivera, B. V., 33, 35, 37, 47, 222, 228
Roggius, N., 224
Rognoni, F., 128, 134
Rosa, S., 185
Rosinus, P., 15, 16, 195, 224
Rostock, 201
Rousseau, J. J., 173
Rovetta, G., 134
Ruetz, C., 44, 159, 186–7, 199, 213, 217, 224
Ruhnke, M., xiv, 33, 47, 59, 70, 71, 96, 103, 123, 228

Sadler, J. E., 202
Salmen, W., 53, 214, 228
Samber, J. B., 149, 159, 224
Sances, G. F., 128
Sanford, S. A., 228
Sannemann, F., 228
sarabande, 43
Sartorius, E., 64, 201, 224
Saxon ordinances, 2, 4, 9, 20, 53, 184
scale, 66
Scheibe, J. A., 33, 175, 183–4, 208, 217, 224
Scheibel, G. E., 43–4, 112, 113, 182, 224
Scheidt, S., 18, 30, 197
Schein, J. H.
  Diletti pastorali, Hirten Lust, 153, 224
Schelle, J., 156, 160, 163
Schering, A., 21, 22, 29, 184, 228
Schipke, M., 173, 218, 228
Schleifer, 145
Schleiz, 20
Schleswig-Holstein, 181–2
Schleusingk, J. V., 224
Schmelz, R. P. S., 36, 201, 224
Schmiedeknecht, J. M., 57, 224
Schmitz, A., 228
Schneegass, C., 9, 56, 60, 71, 95, 98, 100, 106, 201, 224
Schneiderheinze, A., 57, 89, 93, 95, 96, 205, 206, 221, 228

Schornberg, H., 40, 224
Schröder, L., 224
Schröter, C. G., 185–6, 187, 217, 224
Schubert, J. F., 179, 224
Schulze, H-J., 20, 208, 229
Schünemann, G., 2, 3, 4, 5, 6, 20, 21, 173, 184, 193, 194, 229
Schütz, H., xi, 13, 24, 83, 129, 156, 157, 224
  Geistliche Chor-Music, 157
  Historia Der . . . Aufferstehung unsers einigen Erlösers, 99, 107
  Historia, der Freuden- und Gnadenreichen Geburth Gottes und Marien Sohnes, 42
  Kleine geistliche Concerten, 25
  Musicalische Exequien, 107, 110
  Psalmen Davids, 107, 110
  Symphoniae sacrae part 2, 25, 42, 115
  Symphoniae sacrae part 3, 110
Seay, A., 220
seconda prattica, 13, 148
Selle, T., 23, 110, 197
Sevier, Z. V. D., 29, 229
Siegele, U., 17, 214, 229
Singer, J., 10, 194, 224
singer as orator, 126
singing as specialist discipline, 169, 174
Singspiel, 185
Smiles, J. E., 229
Smith, D. A., 220
Snyder, K., 19, 111, 197
solmisation, 6, 8, 56, 58–60, 66, 172
  hexachords, 56, 58
  mutation, 56
sonata, 43
Sorau, 78
Sorge, G. A., 224
Speer, D., 36, 62–3, 83, 102, 118, 119, 208, 224
Spener, P. J., 138–9, 211
Sperling, J. P., 63, 81, 83, 119, 224
Speyer ordinance, 14
Spiess, J. M., 229
Spiess, R. P. M., 159, 213, 224
Staden, S. T., 205, 224
Stadtpfeiffer, 5, 21, 28, 62
Stahl, W., 210, 229
Staucha, 16
Steffani, D. A., 180, 216, 225
Steiner, J. L. 36, 211, 225
Steinfurt, 53
Stenger, N., 53, 54–5, 66, 198, 202, 225
Sternstorff, cantor of Flensburg, 23
Stierlein, J. C., 35, 58, 60, 81–2, 118, 136–8, 141, 149, 159, 198, 211, 225
Stiller, G., 182, 195, 229
Stiphelius, L., 225
street-singing, 22

string instruments, 15
  bowing, 114–15, 116, 117
  tuning, 115
Strohm, R., 216
Stroux, C., 229
Strunk, O., 204, 212, 229
stylus phantasticus, 43
stylus recitativus, 44
sustained singing style, 91, 175

tactus, beating of, 55, 95, 99, 100
taste, 44–5, 88, 172
Taylor, R. M., 25, 53, 163, 221
teaching as vocation, 172
Telemann, G. P., 19, 20, 22, 164, 190
tempo, 71, 56, 99, 101
  and mensural system, 96
  variation of, 95, 97–99
text setting, xii, 155
  comprehensibility of, 26, 27, 181
  underlay, 71, 92
  textual expression, 83, 171
theatrical practice/style, *see* opera
Thirty Years War, 17, 24, 39
Thomasius, rector in Leipzig, 20
thoroughbass, 39, 83, 118–19, 164
Tilesius von Tilenau, N., 225
timpani, 119
tirata, 125, 136, 144
  meza, 133
toccata, 43, 119
tone, 71
Tosi, P. F., 83–4, 88, 89, 98, 144, 146, 166, 171, 174, 175, 176, 177, 179, 225
transitus, 144
transposition, 58, 103, 104–5
Trautmann, H., 201, 225
tremolo/tremulo, 69, 92, 125, 134, 136, 138, 144, 176
triad, 39, 57
trill/*Triller*, 79, 144, 145, 171, 174–5, 176, 178, 179, 204, 211
trilletti, 79, 204
trillo, 48, 79, 125, 128, 133, 134, 135, 136, 138, 144, 175
Tristram Shandy, 167
Trivialschulen, 170
trivium, 2, 46–7, 70
trombone, 119
Trümper, M., 225
trumpet, 103, 119

Ubert, M., 229
Ulich, J., 198, 225
Ulrich, B., 80, 203, 204, 212, 229
university pupils as singers, 23

variatio, 159
variatio notae, 136, 139–50
vernacular, 6, 8, 65
Viadana, L., 99–100, 109
vibrato, 70, 138, 144
viola, 115, 119
viola da gamba, 115, 119
violin, 10, 66, 115, 119
vocal forces
  placement/positioning, 107
  size and distribution, 106–13
vocal production, 71, 81, 84, 87
vocal registers, 88
vocal scoring, 107–13, 207, 208, 215
voces concertatae, 108
Vockerodt, G., 21, 27–8, 30, 31–2, 43, 182, 185, 186, 225
Vogelsang, J., 225
voice teachers, 85
Vormbaum, R., 193
Vorschlag, 144, 145, 174–5
vowels, 70, 74, 84, 87
Vulpius, M., 200, 225

Wagner, G., 208, 229
Walder, J. J., 225
Walliser, C. T., 57, 198, 204, 225
Walter, H., 20, 218, 229
Walther, J. G., 117, 149, 159, 164, 210, 212, 225
Weckmann, M., 22
weddings, 4
Weide, M., 40–1, 60, 64, 225
Weimar, G. P., 179, 225
Weimar school ordinance, 21
Weissenburg, 201
Werckmeister, A., 30, 34, 35, 39, 51, 156–7, 163, 180–1, 213, 225
Wesselius, F., 37, 58, 84, 201, 214, 225
Westhoff, J. P. von, 117
Westphalia, 53, 214
  Peace of, 185
Wilflingseder, A., 8, 9, 225
Wolf, G. F., 171, 177, 208, 215, 225
Wolff, H. C., 229
women, education of, 53, 167
Württemberg, 218
Wustmann, R., 20, 21, 229

Zacconi, L., 150
Zahn, organist at Halle, 17
Zarlino, G., xiii, 71, 203, 225
Zedler, J. H., 19, 30, 34–5, 36, 45, 183, 225
Zerleder, N., 64, 198, 204, 225
Zwingli, U., 44

Printed in the United Kingdom
by Lightning Source UK Ltd.
126619UK00001B/100/A